GOD BE KNOWIN'

Dr. Lori Alyse Croom

I would like to dedicate this book to the Holy Spirit.

IN MEMORY OF

Mr. Ronald E. Croom (my dad)

Mr. Jessie Simon (my godfather/mentor/person)

Ellease Croom (my grandmother/best friend)

Sam Jones & Ruth M. Jones (my grandparents)

ACKNOWLEDGMENTS

I am grateful for the following people/places/things:

Mr. Brenton Bush (the love of my life)

Charity & Christen Jasper (my daughters)

Gloria Croom (my mother)

Rev. Dr. J.W. Croom, Jr. (my grandfather and first pastor)

Adrienne M. Nixon

Randall, Brandon, Elliot, Alexandria, Renita, & Rollin (my siblings)

Dr. Kelvin M. Bryant (my pastor) & Faith Walkers Church

First Baptist Church of Graymont

Tacos…always tacos.

The Croom, Jones, McHenry, and Simon Families

Spelman College & Hillman College

All Sorors of Delta Sigma Theta Sorority, Inc. & P.R.E.S.T.I.G.E.

All Patients of NowVision Eye Care

Bishop L. Spenser Smith, Dr. Jeronn C. Williams

INTRODUCTION

I already know what you're going to say. Al Green didn't invent the internet...it was Al Gore. Well, the truth is...neither one of them did! So the only Al I'm going to acknowledge right now is Green. Now that that's out of the way, let's get into the book!

Do you know what's crazy? I've been on Facebook for 15 years. A baby born when I created my FB account is now learning to drive! I personally have a love/hate relationship with social media, and I suspect that some of you do too. On one hand, it's amazing because it connects you with some beautiful people that you would have undoubtedly lost touch with otherwise. It also helps people grow their businesses and sell their products. Social media is also a great place for laughs that serve as a distraction from life's harsh realities. Everything (and I mean everything) is a joke to us. We use the internet to rally for social justice. It kept us going during the pandemic. The internet is undefeated. On the other hand, social media can be turrrrrible. Comment sections are brutal. Some people use social media as an outlet to spew their bigotry and hatred. Others use it to create the illusion of a lifestyle that they don't actually live. Still others use it to stalk people!

In summary, the internet is what you make of it. After 15 years, this book is what I have decided to make of it. Anyone who has spent time online knows that we have a completely different lingo that often only makes sense on the internet. It's like being fluent in another language. So I have taken 365 words and phrases that you may (or may not) recognize, and have used them to extract a daily word from the Lord. If you're deep in the game, you should recognize all of these. If you're newer to social media or only browse it on occasion, there may be some terms that you are unfamiliar with. In order to level the playing field, I have included definitions for each one.

It's wild how all things really do work together for good to those who love the Lord. There have been many times where I had no idea why things in life were happening in the ways that they were. Sometimes it wouldn't be until much later that I realized just how strategic God had been the whole time. God be knowin' man. I came up with the idea to write this book only a few months ago, yet I was able to draw on 15+ years of social media "experience." It blows my mind that God was knowin' this whole time that all my scrolling wasn't in vain! I bet you can look around in your own life too and see that God been knowin'. I pray that this book will be a blessing. -Lori

JUDGE YA MAMA

Judge Ya Mama – a phrase commonly used when a person expresses an idea or performs an action that they do not feel will be widely accepted. Generally speaking, a person who employs this phrase knows that while what they are doing may not be popular in the eyes of others, it is working for them. Anyone who has a problem with it is invited to take their judgmental energy and apply it to their own mother instead.

Example: I like my bacon wrapped in bacon…judge ya mama!

As you begin this 365-day spiritual journey, I think it is important to note that this way of learning is not for everyone. That's ok. Sometimes you must "get it how you live." Well many of us live on Al Green's internet, and social media-speak has become almost like an additional language for us. The objective here is to take something that we are already familiar with and use it to point us back to God. Some will think that we're crazy, and others will judge us for it, but by the end of the journey we will have grown spiritually. We will also establish for ourselves a daily routine of spending time with God and searching the scriptures. Lastly, when we are busy navigating the crazy world of social media, key words and phrases will now remind us of His word and of the promises that He has made to us. It sounds crazy to have a social media-themed devotional, but it works. Judge ya mama! Pray today that God allows you to be delivered from the opinions of others and free to do what you know is working for you.

READ TODAY: 1 CORINTHIANS 9:19-23

STIFF WHERE?

Stiff where? – a phrase popularized by a little girl who was really feeling herself in her mother's wig. She flipped her hair back and forth several times while repeatedly asking, "Stiff where?" She wanted viewers to see that "her" hair was moving freely and neither stiff nor constricted from movement in any way.

Example: My stylist did her thing on this silk press y'all! *shakes head* Stiff where? Stiff where?

Do you know the importance of being flexible? Sometimes believers can inadvertently become stiff and stuck in our ways. Sometimes this lack of flexibility prevents us from flowing with God as He is moving in our lives and attempting to do a new thing. We see this in churches and religious institutions all the time. It dates back to the Bible days. Once we experience God in one way, we like to put Him in this box that makes us feel safe and secure in understanding exactly how God works. It makes us feel that we can now predict how He will always work. Anything outside of that confinement, we reject. There is this really cool passage in the Bible that talks about the dangers of attempting to put "new wine" into "old wineskins." Apparently, if you make new wine but put it in an old container, that container will burst, and the new wine will be completely wasted. This is because the old wineskin is rigid and no longer flexible enough to meet the needs of the fermenting process, which causes expansion. New wine must be placed in new wineskins. In summary, let's do our best to remain flexible and not stiff when it comes to God. We never want to be so stiff and stuck in our ways that God cannot bring expansion into our lives. Let's pray today that we never become arrogant enough to believe that we know everything there is to know about God. This book is new wine. My prayer is that you are not too stiff to receive it.

READ TODAY: LUKE 5:36-39

GOD BE KNOWIN'

God Be Knowin'- a conclusion that is drawn following a series of unexpectedly favorable events. Often used to conclude a "testimony post."

Example: …and it turns out that the homeless man that I gave the dollar to, was really the CEO of the company in disguise. He offered me the job on the spot, y'all. God be knowin'!

The longer you live and the more you experience, the more you will understand that God really do be knowin'. Nothing catches Him off guard. The Bible tells us that He knows the end from the beginning. Sometimes when you find yourself in the midst of a difficult situation, it's hard to imagine that God is actually using it to bless you. We spend time worrying and wondering how we will make it through hard times, but how many times have we had to come to the conclusion **after-the-fact** that whatever we went through actually helped us? Here's an idea. What if we don't wait until afterwards to remember that God be knowin'? What if we **don't** freak out about the unknown because we are confident that it's not unknown to God? What if we remember that God knows exactly what we have need of before we even need it? What if we have faith enough to believe that God will take care of us today? In your prayer time today, let's ask God to forgive us for the times that we acted like we really didn't believe that He knew.

READ TODAY: MATTHEW 6:30-34

DIS TEW MURCH

Dis tew murch – an expression one might use to let others know that they have become overwhelmed by either an information or sensory overload. English Translation: *This is too much.*

Example: So you mean to tell me I'm supposed to work full-time from home, but my 3-year-old's daycare is shut down because of COVID? Dis tew murch.

What do you do when you feel overwhelmed? What happens when life seems to be too much to handle? The answer is simple. We must **ask for help.** Sadly, many of us have been trained to do the opposite. Are you one of those people (like myself) who have been conditioned not to ask for help unless somebody is literally dying? Even then, it's only once your own arms have fallen off from the CPR compressions! Whether it's pride, your inability to relinquish control, your disdain for inconveniencing others, or a bad experience with asking for help in the past, you need to understand that your refusal to **ask** for what you need can be damaging and unhealthy. The crazy part is that we do this with God as well. We will run around like chickens with our heads cut off wanting and needing help with something, yet we fail to **stop** and ask God. The coolest thing that I've learned about prayer is that we can use it for literally anything. Nothing is too small or too big. You can ask for help physically, spiritually, emotionally, or just practically. As a matter of fact, you can literally pray today and ask God for help with finding and receiving help! You can even pray and ask God to help your helper to do a better job of helping when it's time to be helpful! Okay, I think you get my point now. Hopefully this helped.

READ TODAY: PSALM 61:1-3

IYKYK

IYKYK – an abbreviation for the phrase "If you know, you know." It is often used when a post is referencing something that only a select group of people will understand because they are privy to certain background information that was not fully disclosed in the actual post.

Example: I had to get that #8 combo with extra lemon pepper sprinkles…IYKYK!

Okay, so the really interesting thing about God (not religion) is that He often reveals more and more about Himself to us as we journey farther into a One-on-one relationship with Him. Maybe a better way to say this is that there are certain things about God that you won't know until you **experience** them with Him. You might not fully grasp how gracious and merciful He can be until you find yourself in need of some grace and mercy, and He supplies it. You might not fully grasp the concept of His forgiveness until you have messed up and realized that He didn't hold it over your head. Sometimes we waste so much time trying to explain and even justify to others why we love God the way that we do. Sadly, some will never understand why we choose to remain faithful to Him because they haven't established their own personal relationship where they can experience His love for themselves. The person who ordered the #8 combo only knew that it would be good because they had already tasted it for themselves. Pray today for that person in your life who doesn't know because they don't know…even if that person is you. Pray that they will have an encounter with God that leads to a whole relationship.

READ TODAY: PSALM 34:8

YOU CAN CATCH THESE HANDS.

You can catch these hands – a warning issued to a person whose behavior is offensive or out of line. This serves as notification that the disagreement is eligible for escalation from verbal to physical interaction.

Example: ...and if you disrespect my mama one more time, please believe you can catch these hands!

Normally, the catching of hands is something that we'd much rather avoid. If someone offers you hands in this manner, it is not a proposal that you should accept. The hands in this scenario are generally going to come in the form of balled up fists coming towards your face at a high rate of speed and lots of momentum. These kinds of hands will leave you battered, bruised, confused, and unconscious. When it comes to God's hands, however, they are the total opposite. Sometimes the hands of life seem to beat us down so low that we feel out of reach. Sometimes sin drives us so far away that we feel as if we are too far gone. Sin can cause us to fall into feelings of isolation and loneliness. The awesome thing about God is that His hands stretch so far and wide, that you can still catch them no matter where you find yourself in life. Catching someone's hands can be dangerous and life threatening, but when you catch God's hands, you find safety, salvation, and consistency. When the hands of life deal you a harsh blow, you can count on God's hands to pick you back up, heal, and restore you. When you pray today, don't forget to thank God for His hands that can reach you no matter where you are.

READ TODAY ISAIAH: 59:1

I'VE GOT TIME TODAY.

I've got time today. – usually used to explain why a person who would otherwise be too busy or too important to engage in hostile online arguments, has chosen to do so at this particular juncture.

Example: So you're saying that peacefully kneeling during the national anthem is disrespectful to our troops, but committing treason and violently storming the Capitol building because your candidate lost an election is patriotism? I'll wait for you to explain this ridiculous logic…I've got time today.

Today we are going to think about procrastination. Procrastination is the devil. It's the wild assumption that you will always have more time to do a thing that you should and could be doing right now. Far too often, we procrastinate and then justify it by saying, "I just work better under pressure." While this may be true, why have we normalized it the way that we have? Why is it that we only feel the pressure to be productive when there is some potential for failure? Why can't we harness that same pressure and apply it to our desire to do God's will? Shouldn't that be a strong desire for us? Shouldn't failing on our God-given assignments be just as upsetting as failing to turn a paper in on time? When it comes to our obedience, let's not put it off any longer. We do have time today. I will always stand by the idea that people make time for the things that are truly important to them. If you don't feel that you have time to do what God has called you to do, it is clearly time to pray and ask God to help you re-prioritize.

READ TODAY: JOHN 9:4

LET'S BE VERY CLEAR.

Let's be very clear. – used by a person who is getting ready to set some sort of record straight by introducing the facts. A person who uses this phrase is usually about to drop a "truth bomb" that would be difficult to refute.

Example: Let's be very clear…I told her from the day she moved in that she had exactly six months to find a job and somewhere else to live.

Clarity is extremely important. As an optometrist, I help people with it every day. The world is full of things that can cloud our vision, our judgement, our hearts, or our minds. As believers, we have to guard ourselves from things that seek to rob us of our God-given clarity. We've all known someone who could not, for the life of them, see what everybody else saw as plain as day. That person has usually allowed something unhealthy into their heart that disables their otherwise good sensibilities. Bitterness, guilt, shame, lust, greed, grief, pride, envy, ignorance, and fear are just a few of the things that can prevent us from seeing things clearly. These things are just like cataracts to our vision, and if we want to be very clear, we must seek to remove them from our lives. Do not make any important decisions until you have searched your heart for things that might negatively alter your viewpoint. Pray today and ask God to remove anything that would keep you from seeing matters more clearly. God is the very best cataract surgeon you could ever find.

READ TODAY: MATTHEW 6:22-23

CHECK YOUR INBOX.

Check your inbox. – a phrase frequently seen in the comment section of a post. It is used to alert the poster that there is a message waiting for them in their inbox that they may have accidentally overlooked. (It's usually not accidental.)

Example: Person A: *posts picture of plate* I get down in the kitchen!
Person B: *comments* Hey! Check your inbox.
Person A: (never replies)

We need to talk about what we are allowing **in**. Some inboxes (like e-mail inboxes) have filters that determine which messages actually come through. You must be very careful about which messages are pertinent to your life and which ones are just there to scam or spam. Sadly, every person who speaks into your life does not do so with good intentions. What messages have you accepted into your heart or mind that did more harm to you than good? Did someone's words leave you with fear and/or insecurity? If the message is coming from God, it will be the opposite of that. He does not use fear or manipulation to move you. Here are the filters that you should run every message through: power, love, and a sound mind. Check your inbox (aka your mind). What messages have you accepted about yourself that need to be moved to the trash? In your prayer time today, ask God to help you clean up your inbox. Let's also ask Him to help us guard and filter it much better moving forward.

READ TODAY: 2 TIMOTHY 1:7

#QTNA

QTNA – abbreviation for "Questions That Need Answers." It is used to emphasize that a particular issue is confusing and lacks a clear-cut answer and/or solution.

Example: How come every time I decide to go on a diet, free food just magically appears in the breakroom? #QTNA

Do you have questions that need answers? Sure you do! As human beings, we often have questions, problems, issues, dilemmas, etc. As believers, however, we do have access to answers. For some strange reason though, we forget that. No, seriously! We will go hours, days, or months, (God forbid we go years!) struggling through an issue alone or with our friends before we realize that maybe we could just ask God for the answer. What is the point of being a follower of Christ if we don't take advantage of the fringe benefits? In His word, God tells us that when we have questions we can ask, seek, and/or knock. The word also tells us that there are things that we don't have simply because we never asked. Maybe we hesitate to ask questions to God because we are scared that the answer may not be what we were hoping for. Let me reassure you that His answer is what's in your best interest. He wants us to live a life of abundance, but also expects us to acknowledge Him and ask for help with everything that we come up against. In your prayer time today, don't be afraid to ask the hard questions that need truthful answers.

READ TODAY: MATTHEW 7:7

ON SIGHT

On sight – a phrase commonly used to warn another individual that you will physically fight them as soon as you see them, and that there will be no further discussion on the matter at that time. (Note: There is some general confusion amongst the culture as to whether the actual saying is *on sight* or *on site.)*

Example: Oh no, we done talkin' bout it! It's on sight whenever I see her raggedy a**!

Let's talk about faith today. Faith is the ability to **know** a thing even though you have not yet **seen** that thing. Faith is basically the opposite of sight. It's easy to believe the things that our natural eyes can see, but sometimes it's challenging to believe spiritual things, not because we can touch, taste, smell, hear, or see them…but simply because we believe **that strongly** in the God who spoke them to us. Too often, we are guided by the things in the natural world, not realizing that they aren't nearly as concrete as they may seem. It's God's word that is the sure thing. We are far too dependent on sight…and maybe even bound by it. Take that job, for example. We see the direct deposit hitting every two weeks, and that's why we trust it. But God said that He is Jehovah Jireh, our actual provider. If something were to suddenly happen to your job, would you freak out, or would your faith in God keep you calm? Use your faith to look into the spirit realm so that you can stop worrying about everything that you see going on around you. That's the only way to rise above it all. In your prayer time today, ask God to increase your faith and decrease your dependency *on sight.*

READ TODAY: 2 CORINTHIANS 5:7

ON SITE

On Site – a phrase, meaning "on location," that is commonly used to warn another individual that you will physically fight them as soon as you see them. Unlike the phrase "on sight," this phrase further specifies that the fighting event will take place no matter the location or venue of discovery. (Note: There is some general confusion amongst the culture as to whether the actual saying is *on sight* or *on site*.)

Example: I don't care if I see Rodney's triflin' a** in the grocery store on aisle six…hands will be thrown on site!

One amazing thing about God is that He is always on site. It doesn't matter where you may find yourself, God is always there. Some like to use the term "omnipresent" to describe Him. This means that He is everywhere at all times. Does knowing this make you feel uncomfortable, or does it make you feel comforted? I suppose the answer lies in your life choices, but that's neither here nor there (because God is both here **and** there). He's there when you're at church crying and snotty at the altar, and He's still there when you're at the club twerking on a complete stranger. He's there when you're lying in your own bed, and He's there when you sneak into someone else's. No matter the location, God is always on site. He's always ready, willing, able, and **present** for you. Let's pray today that God would help us to be more consciously aware of His presence in our lives.

READ TODAY: PSALM 139:1-14

FOCUS ON YOURSELF, KING.

Focus on yourself, king. – advice given to a man whose romantic pursuit of a woman is showing signs of complete futility. It is advised that rather than focusing on said woman, he should begin focusing on himself again. Also, referring to him as "king," is meant to soften the blow of reality.

Example: If she can't text you back all day on Sunday because she's at work, but she works at Chick-fil-A…focus on yourself, king.

Have you ever met a person who seems to have all the right answers for everyone else's problems, but they can't seem to fix their own? It's interesting how we can so easily focus our eyes to see other people's issues, but when it comes to our own, everything seems fuzzy. The sad part is that you could be as right as rain, but if your own life looks janky, people won't want to listen to what you have to say. The Bible tells us that we must first focus on ourselves, kings and queens, by getting the 2x4 wooden beam out of our own eye before we go trying to remove the tiny splinter from someone else's eye. Let us pray today that God would grant us focus and clarity on how to clean up our own mess first. When we do this, it's not only for ourselves. It allows us to be more effective in helping those around us who can now see us as a more credible source of wisdom.

READ TODAY: LUKE 6:42

HAVE A SEAT.

Have a seat. – a phrase used to let someone know that their input is neither wanted nor needed. This phrase is usually applied after someone has said or done something ignorant. It is very common to see the words "sir" or "ma'am" added to the phrase in order to give it just the right amount of nice-nastiness.

Example: Why are you always trying to tell women what to do to keep a man, yet you have never had a successful relationship yourself? Please have a seat, sir.

There was this one time in the Bible where Jesus was visiting two sisters, Mary and Martha. Martha got a little salty because she was serving and doing all the work in the kitchen while Mary decided to have a seat at the feet of Jesus to listen to Him speak. Today, I want you to think about what it would look like for you to sit at Jesus's feet. We weren't born during the time period that Jesus was here physically, but we can still sit as His feet and learn from Him. A great way to do this is by reading the Bible. Sometimes, like Martha, we get so encumbered with life's responsibilities that we don't make time to do this. There are so many dope lessons and principles that you can learn from the life of Jesus if you would just have a seat and pay attention. I remember when I first started reading the gospels. I was shocked to find out how petty Jesus had been at times! He was lowkey in there reading the overly religious people for filth, but it was because He wanted God's love to reign supreme. Anyway, my point is that you should have a seat and get to know Jesus for yourself like Mary did. You may be surprised with what you find. Pray today that God would grant you a clearer picture of who Jesus is and what He came here to do.

READ TODAY: LUKE 10:38-42

HAVE SEVERAL SEATS.

Have several seats. – a variation of the original phrase, "have a seat" (see yesterday) that includes a quantitative modifier for further emphasis.

Example: Before you get smart with me, I'm going to need you to learn how to spell. Have several seats ma'am. You can have all the seats in the Superdome.

When I think about having several seats, I think about sitting in a waiting room. Waiting rooms will sho'nuff test your patience! Say amen, somebody! It's like you work so hard to get yourself together and show up to the right place at the right time, only to be told that you must have several seats. I'm not going to lie, sometimes it feels that way with God. It feels like you have done the work, been obedient, and shown up to the right location only to be told to have several seats and wait some more. Not only do you have to wait, but you have to wait…patiently. It's not easy, but sometimes God will make us wait because we aren't quite ready for the next step. Sometimes He will make us wait while He sets up the circumstances just right to work in our favor. And sometimes He will make us wait simply to teach us a lesson about patience, which is really all about trust. If you trust that God has your best interest in mind at all times and that He will always come through for you, having several seats isn't all that bad. Stretch out, watch the movie, read the magazine, get comfy, and trust God's timing for your life. Let us pray today that God would help us to trust Him more so that we can wait with patience.

READ TODAY: ROMANS 8:25

DELETE YOUR ACCOUNT.

Delete your account. – a phrase that can be used either jokingly or seriously to let someone know that they have said or done something so utterly crazy that they no longer deserve to have said social media account.

Example: Ma'am…did you just go live on Facebook instead of helping the people in the accident or calling 9-1-1? Go ahead and delete your account.

The word "account" can also be defined as one person's report or description of an event or experience[1]. Sometimes we go through things in life that we are not particularly proud of. Do you know what the devil would love for you to do? He wants you to delete your account of what happened. If you delete your own report or description of what you have experienced and how you made it through, you delete your testimony. One of Satan's strategies is to riddle you with so much guilt, shame, and embarrassment over your experience, that you keep your testimony hidden and basically deleted. The Bible tells us, however, that our testimony is an important factor in helping others overcome the difficult things happening in their lives as well. Whatever you do, don't delete your account. I know that you may prefer to forget about the hard time, but don't let what you went through be in vain. Your account is one of the most powerful tools that we have to advance the kingdom of God. Instead of deleting it, pray and ask God for instructions on how to use your account for His glory.

READ TODAY: REVELATION 12:11

1.   Account. (2020) In *Oxford Advanced Learner's Dictionary (10th ed.)* Oxford University Press.

LOOKING LIKE A SNACK

Looking Like A Snack – a compliment given to a person (male or female) who looks particularly attractive physically. This phrase was frequently found in comment sections between 2016 and 2019 and indicates that the subject looks good enough to eat.

Example: Okay sis! Them squats got you looking like a snack out here!

Looking like a snack has been my endeavor for several years now. Who wouldn't want to be all fine and stuff? But what happens when you start looking like a snack to the wrong person? What happens when you start looking like a snack to the devil? The thing about Satan is that he literally spends his time trying to seize the opportunities of our vulnerability in hopes of being able to devour us. A common acronym used in counseling (and by one of my favorite preachers, Dr. Charles Stanley) is HALT, which stands for Hungry, Angry, Lonely, or Tired. Whenever you are either one of these things, you begin to look like a snack to Satan. He wants to take your time of weakness and use it to swallow you up. The Bible tells us that we need to remain sober-minded and watchful for this very reason. When you find yourself feeling Hungry, Angry, Lonely, or Tired, you must HALT, or stop. Because you feel this way, you must pause whatever you're doing, pray about it, and be very intentional about how you proceed. Pray today that God would grant you the ability to discern when you just need to go somewhere and "saddown." You don't want to be out here looking like the wrong kind of snack.

READ TODAY: 1 PETER 5:8

#SNACKLIFE

#snacklife – a hashtag used by a poster to indicate that they consider themselves to be a snack (see yesterday's definition) and are therefore living a lifestyle commensurate with said snack status. The lifestyle usually includes looking good, going places while looking good, taking and posting photos while looking good, and ignoring 95-100% of all romantic advances.

Example: *posts swimsuit photo* In Miami for the weekend with my bestie! #snacklife

What do you do when you feel stressed out? Many of us turn to food. Maybe it's because after dealing with the disappointments of life, we feel the need to turn to something that we know won't disappoint. We say things like, "KeKe may have let me down, but these donuts never do!" or "I may not be able to count on Rodney, but I know I can count on this tub of ice cream!" Americans spend an astronomical amount of money buying snacks each year, but what if I told you that there is something much better that you could be snacking on for free? Taking time to read or listen to God's word is literally like feeding yourself a snack. You don't even act like yourself when your body is hungry, so of course you won't act like yourself when your spirit man is starving. Next time you are experiencing stress or disappointment in life, don't forget to grab a snack from the vending machine that is God's word. This is the real #snacklife. Today, find at least one thing that God promised you in His word, and mention it to Him in your prayers.

READ TODAY: MATTHEW 4:3-4

...BUT GO AWF THO

...but go awf tho – meaning "...but go off, though." usually used to let a person know that they are loud and wrong. It is preceded by a statement of factual correction.

Example: **Person A**: I'm sick of all these Puerto Rican immigrants coming to the United States! Stay in your own country! **Person B**: Puerto Rico is a part of the United States and Puerto Ricans are U.S. citizens, but go awf tho.

If you've ever had to deal with a person who is loud, strong, and wrong, you know how annoying it can be. Sadly, we as believers can be some of the worst when it comes to this. How often have you seen a supposed follower of Christ spouting some completely non-biblical opinion as if it is a fact? I scroll on social media and see Christians saying crazy stuff all the time, and I think to myself, "The Bible never even said that, but go awf tho." It is so important to get into God's word and study it for yourself. If you depend solely on what someone else told you, there is a big possibility for error. While parents, pastors, and teachers are very valuable resources, nothing can replace time spent reading God's word and allowing the Holy Spirit to instruct you one-on-one. Let's pray and ask God to help us understand His word better, so that we won't be loud but ignorant.

READ TODAY: 2 TIMOTHY 2:15

MAKE IT MAKE SENSE.

Make it make sense. – used to request clarification regarding a confusing statement or scenario. Usually, the poster has tried on their own to make sense of what is being said or done but has come up short and is now seeking assistance.

Example: Why is Karen putting raisins in the cornbread dressing? Make it make sense!

Life has a way of throwing things at us that we can't seem to fully understand. Like...children die sometimes. How do you really explain that to a grieving parent? Sometimes we will try to use our intelligence to rationalize why certain things are happening the way that they are. No matter how smart we are though, it doesn't really mean much without a little something called wisdom. Wisdom is a God-given gift that allows us to "make it make sense." It also allows us to make sensible decisions concerning whatever situation we may find ourselves in. If a parent has lost a child, for example, wisdom might tell you to simply be there for them in a supportive capacity or as a shoulder to cry on instead of trying to fumble around for some spiritual explanation that you aren't really sure about in the moment. The cool thing about wisdom is that it is a gift that God gives to us quite liberally if we simply desire and ask for it. Let's pray and ask God to give us more wisdom so that we may be able to approach every situation with His help.

READ TODAY: JAMES 1:5

BOFFUM

Boffum – an abbreviation for the phrase "both of them." This term has been a part of the black southern vernacular dating back to…well I don't know…but I'm just saying it's not new.

Example: Person A: So his wife *and* his girlfriend are both pregnant?
Person B: Yup…boffum.

There are some things in this life that you can have in conjunction with each other, and there are other things that you cannot. For example, you can have cake *and* ice cream, but you cannot have (keep) your cake *and* eat it too. When it comes to God, His word tells us that we cannot serve two masters. More specifically, the Bible says that we cannot serve both God *and* money (mammon). Far too many of us are slaves to money, but this is not the way that God has designed it. Ask yourself if you are quicker to do something required by your job than you are to do something required by God. Ask yourself if you are more afraid to lose your check than you are to lose your connection to the Father. It's pretty ironic seeing how God is the one who gives us the power to get wealth anyway…just food for thought. In our prayer time today, let's repent for anything we have tried to place on the same level as God, not just money. There's no "boffum" when it comes to Him. He stands alone.

READ TODAY: MATTHEW 6:24

ONE GOTTA GO.

One Gotta Go. – this phrase is seen on top of pictographic memes in which the viewer is presented with (usually) four different things or people and asked to pick which one they would eliminate from history if one had to be eliminated. It is usually a difficult choice to make, causing people's brains to explode.

Example: *photo collage of Whitney Houston, Prince, Luther Vandross, & Michael Jackson* One Gotta Go.

If you had to look at your life and determine one thing that needs to go, what would it be? I know that's a loaded question, but I feel like you already know the answer in your heart. I want to call your attention to something Jesus said. He said every branch of His vine that doesn't bear fruit, God cuts away. He also says that even the ones that do bear fruit, God still prunes (cuts away excess) so that the branch can thrive and make even more fruit. If God is in the business of cutting away anything that inhibits life and growth, we should be too. We are made in His image, so it makes sense to copy His good practices. Are there things in your life that keep you from being as fruitful or as productive as you could be? Are there things that stunt your growth? These could be bad habits or even friends who serve as bad influences. Yes, even adults can be influenced negatively by the company they keep. So let's see…life, growth, productivity, or that dead weight…one gotta go. Pray and ask God for guidance and for the strength to eliminate whatever might be holding you back.

READ TODAY: JOHN 15:1-2

#CURRENTSITUATION

#CurrentSituation – a hashtag used as a caption to an accompanying photo that lets people know what you have going on at this very moment.

Example: *posts photo of a plate full of crab legs* #CurrentSituation

Sometimes it is easy to forget that whatever situation we find ourselves in is not permanent. When we are knee-deep into a situation, it can be easy forget that trouble doesn't last always. Our current situation is just that...current. Today's message is simply to remind you not to give up or throw in the towel based on something that is temporary. To that struggling single parent, one day that baby will be able to bathe themselves and buckle themselves into the car. To that person struggling to get out of debt, one day that car will be paid off. To that student staying up all night to study and complete assignments, one day you will be done with school. The Bible tells us not to give up on doing the right thing and not to faint in the process. The most important thing is to have faith and remain consistent with your hard work. If you continue to sow good seeds, your #CurrentSituation will eventually be a picture of a harvest. Pray and ask God for renewed strength to make it through your current situation.

READ TODAY: GALATIANS 6:9

…WAS MARKED SAFE.

…was marked safe. – used to indicate that a person has checked in on social media to let others know that they are safe in the midst of some kind of natural disaster or emergency situation that has taken place in their area. And because we turn everything into a joke, the designation is also used comedically.

Example: Monica "was marked safe" from The Great Pregnancy Wave of Quarantine 2020.

Sin was an emergency situation. I say that because sin, much like a natural disaster, can lead to death. As a matter of fact, sin *is* a natural disaster. Our human nature, if left to its devices, can lead us into some pretty disastrous situations. Because of Christ's work at Calvary, however, we can be marked safe. In the Old Testament of the Bible, the Israelites were marked safe from the plague of death by smearing the blood of a sacrificed lamb on the doorposts of their homes. This is known as "The Passover." In the New Testament, Jesus offered His life and became the sacrificial lamb for all of humanity. Because His perfect blood was shed on that cross, the plague of sin and death can now pass over us. Because of Jesus, we can be marked safe. All you have to do is accept Him into your heart if you have not done so already. Have you been marked safe? If so, take some time today thanking God and praying that others might accept the same beautiful gift.

READ TODAY: JOHN 3:16

#COYF

#COYF – an abbreviation meaning "Check on your folks." I'm not sure how widely this abbreviation is used, but in Birmingham, Alabama (where I live), it is used quite frequently by "street reporters" who are alerting social media about car accidents, fires, shootings, robberies, police checkpoints, etc.

Example: 8 cop cars and an ambulance outside the likka sto' on 5th! #COYF

Have you ever had to go through something alone? People knew you were struggling, but instead of checking on you, they just talked about you. That is the worst. You were the hot topic of conversation, but none of your so-called folks took the time out to check on you and make sure you were okay. Well since you know how that feels, wouldn't it be a good idea **not** to be one of those people? The Bible tells us that we shouldn't just be concerned about our own affairs, but that we should also check on our folks. Our love of Christ should compel us to show more love towards others. If someone you know is struggling, and you are aware of it, how is it that you have enough time and energy to gossip, but not enough to send a "hey, you good?" text message? Make it make sense. You might have some serious soul searching to do if this is you. So next time when you are tempted to talk about somebody's struggles, ask yourself if you've even checked on them. Let's pray and ask God to equip us to be vessels that can be used to pour into others. As with everything, allow the Holy Spirit to guide you and show you who to check on and how.

READ TODAY: PHILIPPIANS 2:4

IMMA HEAD OUT...

Imma head out... – literally meaning "I am going to head out." This phrase is used by one who wishes to announce their decision to leave either a situation, conversation, or location. It is typically accompanied by a picture of SpongeBob rising from his chair.

Example: Wait, did they just run out of chicken wings at this cookout? Aight, Imma head out.

Here in the African American culture, we are very good at "heading out" or leaving a place when it no longer seems to be serving us well. Take church, for instance. When the preacher says, "as I get ready to close..." for the 3rd time, if you look towards the rear of the sanctuary, you will see people heading out. Even in the club, when those drunk people get to arguing and it looks like it could escalate to shots fired, you will see people heading right on out. Don't forget horror movies. As soon as something doesn't feel quite right in the abandoned farmhouse, the black folks are going to head out instead of going further to investigate. Why then, are we so terrible at "heading out" of sketchy situations in our personal lives? Why do we let dysfunction drag on for so long? Why are we afraid to walk away from ungodly things and people who drag us down and cause us to be a lesser version of ourselves? I think you know that there are some things, people, and places that bring out the worst in you, even if they seem familiar and comfortable. We should be so determined to fulfill our God-given purpose, that we are willing to walk away from anything that goes against it. In today's prayer time, let's ask God to show us the best way to head out of foolishness so that we can head into purpose.

READ TODAY: PROVERBS 14:7

WAYMENT

Wayment – a word literally meaning "wait a minute."

Example: Wayment! Is that the baby girl going to prom?! Seems like
she was just born yesterday!

It has been said that when you pray and ask God for
something, the answer will either be yes, no, or wait. How do you
handle situations in which you are forced to wait? Do you wait with
patience, or do you wait with frustration, anxiety, and depression? I
just want you to know that if God is making you wait a minute for a
particular thing to manifest, you'd be smart to trust Him. He knows
the perfect timing for every scenario, and although it may not feel
comfortable in the moment, you will be able to look back on your
waiting season and see how it worked in your favor. Not only does
God's timing work the situation out in your favor, but it also helps to
grow you up. If you haven't learned how to wait with patience, are you
really ready for the blessing? This is just food for thought. Pray today
that God would increase your faith to the level where you can wait for
Him with patience and maturity.

READ TODAY: ROMANS 8:25

I'M CRIIIINE.

I'm criiiine. – a phrase literally meaning, "I am crying." It is usually in response to something funny and indicates that the person has laughed so hard that they are now crying.

Example: Did that dog just speak in tongues?! Haaa! I'm criiiine!

If you were blessed enough to have parents who took you to church or taught you the Bible, one of the first verses that you may have learned was John 11:35. It says, "Jesus wept." This is known as the shortest verse in the English translation of the Bible, and it is easy to recite. But do you know exactly *why* Jesus was criiiine? Jesus had just learned that his friend Lazarus had died, and his friends Mary and Martha were trippin' out. They blamed Jesus, saying that if he had gotten there sooner, Lazarus wouldn't have died. There are a few different theories as to why Jesus wept. The one that makes the most sense to me is that Jesus was saddened, not because Lazarus was dead (He knew He was about to raise Lazarus up in a few minutes), but because of how His friends acted. Even though they had been around Jesus and were privy to who He was and how powerful He was, they acted as if they had forgotten. Sometimes we do this to Jesus as well. He has a well-established history of working in our lives, but when trouble arises, we act like we have forgotten all about it. Let us pray today that the Holy Spirit would help us to remember how powerful Jesus is and how powerful He has always been. His name alone makes people mad, uncomfortable, and nervous. Think about it.

READ TODAY: REVELATION 2:4

FIND THE LIE.

Find The Lie. – this phrase is usually used when an unpopular, yet true sentiment is shared. It challenges others to identify what has been said that was not true.

Example: A girl will text you "goodnight," and then turn around and text another guy "I can't sleep." Find the lie.

Let's talk about fear today. Do you know where fear comes from? All fear is based in some sort of lie. Do you know where lies come from? All lies come from Satan, who is also known as the Father of Lies. Let's recap the chain of events: Satan -> Lies ->Fear -> Worry ->Anxiety -> Desperation -> Regret -> Depression ->Defeat...okay, I think you get the point, but maybe you need an example. One of my homegirls had gotten it in her head that she would not be okay without a man. She was walking around in fear of what would "happen" to her if she never got married again, and it was causing her to accept things that were honestly unacceptable. The lie was that she would not be okay without a man. The truth was that God has already promised to supply all of our needs, period. Once she realized this, she got rid of the fear and was free to operate as her highest self. A huge part of Satan's strategy to defeat you is to get you to believe a lie. If you find yourself living in fear of something, I challenge you to get to the root of the fear by finding the lie that you have believed about yourself, about your situation, or about God. God does not use fear as a tool, it is always one of Satan's tactics. Once you find the lie, you can dismantle it using the truth of God's word over your life. Let's pray today for God's help in identifying lies and replacing them with the truth.

READ TODAY: 2 TIMOTHY 1:7

NO LIES DETECTED.

No Lies Detected. – a fancy, new-age way of saying, "Amen." It means that a statement has been scanned for inaccuracies and none were found.

Example: Person A: Kids going to prom these days really got us beat.
Person B: No Lies Detected.

God is dope. That's it. That's the devotion. Have a good day. Okay, wait…maybe I should explain a little further what's on my mind today. God is dope because He's not like man. He doesn't lie. Everything that He's ever said is true. When it comes to God, there are no lies detected. Sometimes the truth can be painful, but God loves us so much that He refuses to lie to us simply to cater to our feelings. He wants to see us grow and prosper. He wants us to be free. Lies cause us to be bound, but truth makes us free. Sometimes we are afraid to go to God with our problems, because we are afraid to hear the truth. A lie, however, will cause much more pain and destruction in the end. When you pray today, ask God the question that maybe you've been afraid to ask Him, and take some time to listen for the real answer.

READ TODAY: NUMBERS 23:19

AHT! AHT!

Aht! Aht! – a rebuke. This phrase originated from a sound effect that parents often make to communicate warnings to a toddler who is on the verge of getting in trouble. It is now used frequently on the internet by adults who are warning other adults that they are on the verge of getting in trouble.

Example: Aht! Aht! Get out of my inbox sir (ma'am) before I screenshot this and send it to your wife (husband).

If you have the Holy Spirit living inside of you, you may be very well acquainted with "Aht! Aht!" Some people liken the Holy Spirit to having a conscience. Although it's not exactly the same thing, the Holy Spirit acts like a guide and will often hit you with a warning to let you know when you are headed towards trouble. The question becomes, what do you do when you know the Holy Spirit is telling you to chill out? Do you ignore it and continue, or do you go somewhere and saddown? As inconvenient as it may feel to not to get your way all the time, think of the Holy Spirit as that loving parent who doesn't want their child touching a hot stove. We would be wise to listen and obey. Pray today that God would help you to better discern the Holy Spirit's guidance in your life.

READ TODAY: 1 PETER 5:10-11

I WAS TODAY YEARS OLD…

I was today years old – a phrase used to indicate that a particular tidbit of (usually common) knowledge has just been acquired within the past 24 hours.

Example: I was today years old when I discovered that the drawer at the bottom of my oven is a food-warmer and not extra storage for the big pots and pans!

One of the most beautiful aspects of life is the ability to continue learning, growing, and moving forward every single day. Every day that we wake up is another opportunity to get stronger, better, faster, or wiser. In nature, things only stop growing when they are dead. When learning to ride a bicycle without training wheels, you will certainly fall flat if you fail to keep moving forward. In optometry school, we had to take a course in geriatrics (the study of elderly people). On the first day, our professor said, "The first rule of geriatrics…you sit, you die." Basically, if you stop moving forward, death will be right around the corner. Even the Apostle Paul said that he needed to press on towards better. As spiritually advanced as he was, he never got to a place where he felt that he was perfect and didn't need to reach higher. Let us learn from Paul's example. Let's not be ashamed to learn and grow, even if we are "today years old" when we do it. Let's pray that God would help us to take full advantage of each learning opportunity that we encounter today.

READ TODAY: PHILIPPIANS 3:12-14

PLATE PIC

Plate pic – literally a picture of your plate. Plate pics are taken year 'round but are most popular on Thanksgiving and Christmas when everyone wants to show off their holiday food.

Example: Happy Thanksgiving everyone! I know everybody's eating the same stuff, but I'm posting my plate pic anyway!

Let's talk about your plate today. If you were to take a picture of your plate, would it be pretty like the ones on the cooking shows, or would it be a hot mess like the ones from those people who think Kraft Singles go on top of mac and cheese? Oh wait. You think we're talking about food. My bad. I was talking about your life. What is on your plate? Is everything on your plate supposed to be there? Are you overwhelmed by things on your plate that God never even told you to add? Are you stressed out because you feel as if you have bitten off more than you can chew? When you are feeling lost and overwhelmed, you **must** find your way back to God. What are the things that **He** is requiring of you? What was arbitrarily placed on you by others? What is simply a result of your inability to say no? Are certain things happening because you are living above your means? I think it's time to take a good look at your plate pic. Add and/or subtract based on God's will for your life. Pray today for the strength and courage to do what must be done.

READ TODAY: PSALM 61:2

THOUGHTS AND PRAYERS

Thoughts and Prayers – what people say whenever they feel sorry for you but aren't planning to actually take any action.

Example: Person A: I was laid off last month, and my kids are hungry.
Person B: You all are in my thoughts and prayers!
fans self with money and chomps on biscuit

When something unfortunate happens, many people will claim that you are in their thoughts and prayers, although a large percentage of those people will continue to scroll down their timelines without ever thinking about it again. Even fewer will actually stop to pray. It has become synonymous with saying, "Aww, that's too bad." I'm writing this page after a long day of work, so let's just cut to the chase. Your thoughts…**should lead to prayers**. All day long we have these thoughts running around in our heads. Some of our thoughts are brilliant and beautiful while others may be low-level and toxic. Honestly, we should pray about **all** of them. If something seems like a great idea, don't fool yourself. It still needs to be taken to God just like the thoughts that may seem wrong or bad. In prayer, you can ask God to show you which thoughts you should continue to meditate on, and which thoughts need to be switched out for better ones. If you read today's scripture, you will find a bit of a cheat code for this. When you pray today, try to be intentional about turning all those things that you think about into things that you pray about.

READ TODAY: PHILIPPIANS 4:8

LOOKING FOR RECOMMENDATIONS

Looking For Recommendations – an automated designation given (usually on Facebook) to a person who is asking his or her social media acquaintances for help finding a quality product or service.

Example: I want some knotless box braids, but I'm not trying to be in there for 12 hours. – Looking for Recommendations.

There will be plenty of times when you don't know where to go or what to do in a particular situation. One of the major tools that God has given us is prayer, which you will see me talking about repeatedly. But God can also use the people in our lives to help us see things more clearly. When you are looking for recommendations, it is very important to consider the source. Far too often, we will accept advice from people who are not qualified to give it. Have you ever been given relationship advice, for example, from someone who was clearly bitter about their past experiences? "Don't post anybody on your social media page until after y'all are married!" So basically, you're saying that yoooouuuuu posted somebody on yooooouuuurr social media, and it messed up yooooouuuurrr weak relationship? See that? Now they are making up arbitrary rules for other people's completely different situations. Now they are injecting doubt and fear of embarrassment into another person's psyche. Stuff like this happens all the time. If you are not careful, their tainted viewpoint can infiltrate your heart and mind as well. A good practice would be to compare any advice or recommendation to God's word. If it goes against that, you already know it's wrong. Does it play on your fears or cause confusion? God does not operate that way. In your prayer time today, pray and ask God to help you discern wise from foolish counsel.

READ TODAY: JAMES 3:17

WHEW CHILE!

Whew chile! – an expression one might use when they are experiencing sensory overload and having trouble putting their thoughts or feelings into words. Literally meaning "whew child," this phrase can be used to express any overwhelming emotion, including (but not limited to): joy, sadness, frustration, confusion, love, or anger.

Example: Whew chile! Let me tell you what went down after you left, cuz baby these folks done cut a fool in the middle of the restaurant!

Whew chile. Do you remember being a child? You probably remember it as being much easier than being an adult. Sadly, we didn't fully appreciate what we had when we had it. Let's admit that we got tricked. We thought adulthood just meant freedom to do whatever we wanted. Now we long for the days when we had our bills paid for us, a built-in chauffeur, and long midday naps devoid of guilt or shame. Now I know adulthood can be challenging, but there's not much worse than a grown man or woman who still acts like a child. Adulthood comes with more freedom, but it also comes with more responsibility. We have a responsibility as adults to examine ourselves and determine if we have any childish ways still operating within us. As much as I love children, they can be self-centered, greedy, impatient, uninformed, dramatic, manipulative, reckless, spoiled, dishonest, and immature individuals with poor communication skills. Whew chile! Carrying any of these traits over into adulthood can have a very negative effect on the quality of your life and your relationships with others. Let's pray and ask God to help us grow into the grown men and women that He designed us to be.

READ TODAY: 1 CORINTHIANS 13:11

THE GHETTO (1)

The Ghetto – an expression often used to describe persons, places, or things that are operating below an acceptable standard. This expression is often preceded by the phrase "whew chile."

Example: *watching people storm the Capitol building and embarrass the nation on January 6th, 2021* "Whew chile…the ghetto."

We could get into a very long and "woke" conversation about the ghetto. We could spend hours discussing how and why ghettos were created in America. We could argue about the problems that plague them, the systems of oppression that keep them in existence, the mental bondage that keeps generations of families from ever leaving them, and the industries that make millions off of them. Today, however, we are simply going to say that the ghetto is a place that often operates below an acceptable standard. Before we judge the ghetto so harshly, however, let's consider ourselves. Are there things in your life or even in your mind that are operating below the level that God created you to operate on? Are there certain dysfunctions that you have become comfortable in accepting? Are there certain areas where you no longer strive for improvement or advancement? Are there certain thought processes or actions that you don't even care to put in check? If we were to take a peek into your private thoughts, would they be ghetto? The Bible tells us that we shouldn't use our knowledge of God's grace as an excuse to continue being a hot mess. Pray today for God to give you a renewed sense of excitement about simply doing better and being the best version of yourself.

READ TODAY: ROMANS 6:1-2

PLAY STUPID GAMES, WIN STUPID PRIZES.

Play stupid games, win stupid prizes. – an expression signifying that a person who has sown bad seeds, has reaped the corresponding bad harvest.

Example: Y'all! Federal agents just removed a lady from the airplane saying she is charged with treason for storming the Capitol. Welp…play stupid games, win stupid prizes. Bwaaahaha!

Storytime! Once upon a time, I could eat whatever I wanted without gaining weight. That time is long gone, but it gave me a false sense of security in thinking that my actions weren't directly tied to any consequences. Later, I got fat. The end. The story that I have just described to you is an example of Satan's strategy to defeat us. If our actions in life don't seem to have any immediate consequences, we may get lulled into thinking that there aren't any. The truth, however, is that when we continue to sow bad seeds, we will eventually reap bad harvests. That triple bacon cheeseburger wrapped in a bacon cheeseburger may seem harmless today, but when your cholesterol is through the roof and that heart attack hits "all of a sudden," it's really not cute. On the flipside, the good news is that if we continue to sow good seeds, we will reap good harvests. Let's pray smart games and when dope prizes. Pray today and ask God to help you identify whether you are sowing seeds that may result in a harvest that you don't want.

READ TODAY: ROMANS 6:23

#YACHTLIFE

#YachtLife – a hashtag used when posting pictures or videos from an actual yacht. The pictures usually show the poster and his or her friends looking much cooler and richer than the rest of us.

Example: *posts picture in bathing suit on deck of yacht* Cruising to Miami for lunch. #YachtLife

#YachtLife is basically synonymous with easy living. Usually when you're cruising on a yacht, you're not in a rush to get anywhere. You're not working, and you're not pressed about much of anything. Your biggest worry is running out of your favorite champagne and being forced to open a bottle of your second favorite champagne. Well there was a man in the Bible named Jonah who tried to live his best yacht life, but failed. He got on a boat trying to chill when he was supposed to be on his God-given assignment somewhere else. Long story short, he ended up facing turmoil and lack of peace even on the boat. He couldn't escape the calling on his life. There is nothing wrong with enjoying life and the blessings that God grants us. It's important, however, not to get so caught up that we forget about the assignments that we've been given. Are you unsure about the things that God has sent you here to do? When you pray today, ask God to remind you of your purpose and to show you a clear vision on how to move forward in it.

READ TODAY: JONAH 1:1-4

#WAITFORIT

#WaitForIt – used to alert viewers that a particular video is worth watching until the end, and although it may not grab your attention right away, your patience will eventually be rewarded.

Example: OMG! Y'all this giraffe is hilarious! #WaitForIt

Let's talk about your harvest. A harvest is what you get back after you have sown your seeds and put in the required work. Here are some interesting things to note about your harvest. 1) You will reap **what** you sow. You're not going to sow a kernel of corn and get fried chicken. You will get corn. 2) You will reap **more** than you sow. You're not going to sow one kernel of corn only to get one kernel of corn back. You will get a whole corn stalk with several ears. 3) You will reap **later** than you sow. You don't sow a kernel of corn and reap a stalk of corn on the same day. You must #WaitForIt. So if you have sown good seeds, I'm simply here to encourage you. Sometimes we get frustrated because it seems like the good that we do goes unnoticed. At times, it seems like all of the hard work amounts to nothing. But you can rest assured that even if no one else acknowledges it, God saw. Don't give up or throw in the towel before the reward comes. With God's help you will reap a beautiful and bountiful harvest of goodness that makes all of your hard work and sacrifice look very small in comparison. If you were thinking about giving up...don't. Just #WaitForIt. Pray today for the strength to continue what you started.

READ TODAY: GALATIANS 6:9

FLEWED OUT

Flewed out – to have been flown out of town by someone who desires your presence and subsequently pays for your flight as well as all other expenses incurred. This is usually in reference to a romantic interest, but it is also possible to be "flewed out" for business purposes.

Example: Person A: Where are you?
Person B: Girl! I got flewed out to Miami for the weekend!

I don't know if you've ever been "flewed out" before, but it is a nice feeling to know that someone desires your presence so much that they are willing to pay the cost to transport you to the destination. It reminds me of the time when the world was lost in sin, but Jesus came along and flewed us out of it. He paid the cost to transport us away from a life of sin and misery and into a life of victory and abundance. Jesus paid that airfare with His own life. I don't know about you, but I'm grateful that sin and death have no more authority in my life. If you don't know about Jesus and the price that He paid for you, it's not too late to learn. Begin by reading the gospels (Matthew, Mark, Luke, & John). This will give you a better idea of what was done on your behalf. I am grateful that God flewed Jesus out of heaven (temporarily) so that He could come and flew us out of sin. In our prayer time today, let's give thanks and praise to God for sacrificing His very own son.

READ TODAY: 1 CORINTHIANS 6:20

#SHOTSFIRED

#ShotsFired – used to notify either onlookers or the parties involved that someone has gone on the offensive. Although this is used figuratively in the social media world, the phrase was lifted from police, who usually shout it out loud whenever actual gunshots are being fired in their vicinity.

Example: We could probably get to church on time if soooomebody didn't spend five hours in the mirror every morning. #ShotsFired

It's crazy how we can just be minding our own business and not bothering anybody, yet all of a sudden, shots are fired in our direction. I know we don't like to think of it this way, but the truth is that we do have an enemy combatant who is always seeking to come in and find ways to occupy our territory. Satan is always trying to fire his little shots. The Bible refers to these shots as "fiery darts of the wicked," and teaches us how to shield ourselves from them. Surprisingly, the best way to shield yourself is with **faith**. I'd like to think that's because the shots are taken at your heart. If the devil can just get you to stop believing God for better, then he can be more productive in occupying territory in your life. This is why we must continue to build up our faith and work every day to strengthen our relationship with the Lord. You are doing a great job simply by reading your word, praying, meditating, and dedicating time to spiritual matters such as this. Let's thank God today that even though shots are constantly fired, because of our faith, we don't have to absorb every hit.

READ TODAY: EPHESIANS 6:16

SHADE

Shade – a passive-aggressive expression of disdain or resentment towards another person, place, or thing.

Example: I voted for him because he kept his campaign focused on the issues and wasn't out here throwing shade at other candidates.

Shade, similar to the shade you may experience from a tree, represents a noticeable shift in the atmosphere, but is slightly more subtle in nature than "night vs day." Shade can be thrown, somewhat like a ball, and those who throw shade on a regular basis are known as "shady" individuals. I know we are talking about shade, but did you know that you are a light? No really, when Jesus was preaching one time, He said it. He said that we are the light of the world and that we should let that light shine for the world to see. He even went on to say that nobody turns on a light only to hide it somewhere. I said all that to say, please do not let anyone or anything throw shade on you to dim your light. Don't let anyone make you feel as if you are too much or too bright for their liking. Please never forget that the light was given to you by God so that you could impact the world in a positive way. In a world full of shade and darkness, never let anyone make you ashamed to be dope. Your dopeness and your light encourages the others. It actually brightens the world so that the people around you may be able to see themselves and their own paths more clearly. Don't dim it. Let us pray and ask God to give us the boldness and strength to continue shining brightly.

READ TODAY: MATTHEW 5:13-16

NO SHADE

No shade – used to notify others that a statement was not intended to be malicious. It is usually used as a clarification for a statement that has the potential to be interpreted as shady.

Example: I just don't like to wear all that weave in my head. No shade to anybody who does, though. It just makes my head itch.

Have you ever tried to tell someone something, but it came out all wrong? Perhaps the person got offended, even though you were simply trying to help. Many relationships have been strained due to offense. This is why we have to be very careful with not only what we are saying, but also **how** we are saying it. We have to remember that other people are not mind-readers, and that our words are not likely to be effective if they are shady or even just interpreted as shade. Of course there are those who are offended at any and everything, but I'm not talking about those people right now. I'm talking about us. The Bible tells us that we should always speak the truth in **love** and that our words should be seasoned with **grace**. That's because you can be right all day long, but if you speak the truth in a shady and passively aggressive way, people won't want to receive it. Let's pray and ask God for help in becoming more intentional and loving with our communication.

READ TODAY: COLOSSIANS 4:6

I LOVE IT HERE.

I love it here. – a popular catchphrase used to signal that a particular location, atmosphere, or season of life is particularly enjoyable and satisfying.

Example: When you're in your 30s, you stop caring about dumb stuff, and you don't let unimportant things bother you. I love it here.

Today's talk will be about gratitude. In this crazy world of adulting, it is very easy to get caught up in the situations of life that make it hard to deal. As adults we have bills that want to be paid, kids that want to be fed, kitchens that want to be cleaned, jobs that want to be worked, and homes that want to be cleaned and maintained. It is very easy to slip into a life of constant complaining. We've all seen the people who get on social media and gripe all day, every day. I think grateful is something that we must consciously **decide** to be. Contentment is when you can learn to love your life, even though there are things that may feel imperfect to you. It's okay to be content, appreciative, and grateful with where you are in life, even as you strive for greater. Gratitude is so underrated. You don't want years of life to pass you by, only to look back and realize that you could have loved it there if only you had embraced gratitude sooner. In your prayer time today, try thanking God for as many things as you can think of, big or small.

READ TODAY: PHILIPPIANS 4:11-13

I HATE IT HERE. (1)

I hate it here. – a popular catchphrase used to signal that a particular location, atmosphere, or season of life is particularly unpleasant and dissatisfying.

Example: Every bill wants to be paid on time. Ugh, I hate it here.

One thing I find interesting about humans is our fear of change. Many of us will literally remain in terribly unhealthy situations or conditions for long periods of time, simply to avoid...change. How do you literally hate it where you are, yet feel comfortable there at the same time? Humans are weird that way. I admit that change can be difficult, but if you hate it where you are, it may be time to think about how to get moving up out of that place. The first place where change must take place is in your mind. The Bible tells us that your entire world can be transformed if you simply take on some new, Christ-centered thought processes in your mind. I can personally testify that this is true. Life is short, and tomorrow isn't promised to anyone. Don't waste time hating it where you are, when you have the God-given ability to move out, move on, or move on up like The Jeffersons did. Even if it's nothing more than moving from one mental outlook to another, change can work wonders. Let's pray and ask God to give us the courage to embrace the changes that He has **already** empowered us to make.

READ TODAY: ROMANS 12:2

IDK WHO NEEDS TO HEAR THIS, BUT…

Idk who needs to hear this, but… – a phrase used to introduce a helpful message with no specified recipient. The message is intended for anybody who may need to hear it.

Example: I don't know who needs to hear this, but stop trying to make everybody happy but yourself. That's why you're miserable.

I don't know who needs to hear this, but today's devotion is about faith. Maybe you know that faith is supposed to be this really powerful thing, but you don't know where it comes from or how to get it. The Bible tells us that faith comes by **hearing**. It goes on to say that hearing comes from the word of God. In more simple terms, to build on your faith, you must hear and listen to what God has to say. Thankfully, we have the Bible as our compass as well as teachers and preachers who have been put in place by God to help us gain further clarity. We also have the Holy Spirit who speaks to us as well. If you can understand this concept, then by now you must realize just how important it is to be careful about what and who you listen to. The things that you hear, can easily become the things that you believe and have faith in. If you are always hearing negativity, you will begin believing in and adopting a negative outlook on life. I don't know who needs to hear this, but it's okay to turn your ear away from things that do not build up your faith. Let's pray and ask God to speak to us today and allow us to hear Him clearly.

READ TODAY: ROMANS 10:17

MY WHOLE WORLD IN ONE PICTURE

My whole world in one picture – a photo caption often used by newly separated or divorced women. The photo usually includes a woman and her child/children. The woman's ex is noticeably missing from her "whole world." This is usually used to signal to the public that she has decided to move on without said ex.

Example: *woman posts new photos of herself and man-man*
            Caption: My whole world in one picture!

Do you ever feel like things in your life are out of control? Do you ever look at social media and the news and get to feeling like the whole world is out of control? It's easy to do. With a never-ending list of things to do, laundry, bills, dirty dishes that never stop, death, natural disasters, wars, global pandemics, and nonstop political foolery, it's easy to begin picturing your whole world as nothing but chaos. Trust me, I get it! But I want to challenge you today to put your focus back on God. The Bible tells us that the earth and everything in it still belongs to the Lord. Just as the woman in our example today has decided to focus on the beautiful things that **remain** in her world, we can also make that choice. No matter what you see going on in the world around you, I want you to remember that God is still good, the devil is still a liar, and you still have the victory. No matter who leaves your world and who stays, God will always take care of you and yours. When you pray today, be sure to let God know that you still trust Him with your whole world.

READ TODAY: PSALMS 24:1

I DO NOT OWN THE RIGHTS TO THIS MUSIC.

I do not own the rights to this music. – a disclaimer used when a person posts a video with background music that they do not have permission to use. It is a common misconception that by using this disclaimer, the poster is absolved of copyright infringement.

Example: *posts wedding slideshow w/Luffa Vandross in background*
       Caption: I do not own the rights to this music.

It has always amazed me that there are no two people on this earth who are exactly alike. Even identical twins have their differences. It stands to reason that God made us all differently on purpose. We often forget this. We see other people doing things that we like, and we try to copy them. There's nothing wrong with having positive examples to look up to, but never get so caught up in trying to be like someone else that you fail to be yourself. You don't own the rights to anybody else's "music," but what's stopping you from making your own? I am mostly talking about "making music" in a figurative way, but honestly it applies literally as well. God has blessed us with some amazing recording artists, but when was the last time you made up a new song and sang it to the Lord on your own? We don't ever have to hear it. It doesn't even have to rhyme, and it may be a little pitchy. But today, let's do an exercise. I challenge you to sing unto the Lord a new song that you **do** own the rights to. Just let it flow from your heart as a reflection of your personal relationship with Him and see what happens! Have fun!

READ TODAY: PSALMS 96:1

SMH

SMH – an acronym standing for "shaking my head." Usually used to signify disdain, disappointment, or disgust in the actions of another.

Example: Why do these girls insist on coming to the grocery store in their bonnets? SMH.

For some strange reason, human beings seem to find confusingly large amounts of enjoyment in judging others. This is just an observation! I'm not judging anyone. Okay, maybe I am a little bit. Many of you know that I wrote a devotional before this one. It was my first book and a huge learning experience, especially since I had never considered myself to be a writer. It was a great success, but some days I will read pages and cringe over the fact that maybe I said what I said in a judgmental way. My goal was simply to challenge myself as well as readers to elevate their lives in certain areas. How do you challenge people to win at life without making them feel like losers? If only people knew that the only reason that I could speak on certain topics was because I had been there myself. I wanted to show them a more excellent way than I had traveled. But when people feel judged, whether it's intentional or not, they are far less likely to be receptive. They are far more likely to go on the defensive, even if they are simply being told the truth. All I want to say is that sometimes it's better to do the other SMH. Instead of shaking my head, I should **share my healing**. Our testimonies are extremely powerful and sharing how God brought you from "a mighty long way," can help others to see that you aren't looking down upon them. Don't try to come off as perfect. It's okay to let people know that you have been where they are too. Let's pray and ask God to refresh our memories on what He has delivered **us** from.

READ TODAY: 1 TIMOTHY 1:15

NOT TODAY, SATAN.

Not today, Satan. – An affirmation used to remind one's own self that today can and will be awesome in spite of the devil's attempts to frustrate you.

Example: I couldn't even get in the building good and get my coffee before I got ambushed with problems. Not today, Satan!

The Bible tells us that life and death are in the power of the tongue. We must take better advantage of that. This means that we can and should speak positively over our day. As followers of Christ, we must look at the example that He set for us while He was on earth. One thing that Jesus did a few times in the Bible was rebuke or dismiss the devil away from Himself. We can put this into practice for ourselves as well. When you see Satan trying to disrupt your day from the moment you roll out of the bed, be careful not to agree with that verbally. When things go haywire, don't say things like, "Today is already trash." Instead, say things like, "Not today, Satan! This is still the day that the Lord has made, and I **choose** to rejoice and be glad in it!" It's a small thing but a big thing. Spend some time today using God's word to speak positively over yourself.

READ TODAY: PROVERBS 18:21

THROW THE WHOLE THING AWAY.

Throw the whole thing away. – a phrase used to signify that a certain thing is not worth the problems or issues that it creates.

Example: We found a snake in our house. I no longer want the house! Throw the whole thing away! Looking for realtors!

How do you decide when something is worth keeping vs when it's not? How do you know when something is simply broken and in need of repair vs when it should be bagged up and kicked to the curb? These are some of life's greatest questions. Knowing the difference is crucial. So many of us have held on to things that needed to be discarded while throwing away things that simply needed to be kept and given some extra TLC. This, my good friends, is where wisdom comes in to play. I don't have a magic answer for whether or not you should stay or go. I can't give you an easy and foolproof formula that tells you if you should discard or keep. The first thing you need to do is pray and ask God to give you wisdom and guidance for all of your decision-making. The second thing you must do is examine your situation and compare it to God's word. Does it match up? Is it causing you to sin? Is it unhealthy? Does it give peace or steal peace? It's important to remain completely dependent on God in all things that we do or don't do. This should be an ongoing process in your life that never stops. Never make assumptions without seeking God for wisdom, guidance, and direction. If you have a decision to make, pray and ask God to show you what's best.

READ TODAY: PROVERBS 3:6

#WFH

#WFH – a hashtag acronym that stands for "Work From Home." This hashtag saw increased popularity during the COVID-19 pandemic in which many found themselves working from home.

Example: I'm on a Zoom meeting with my boss and I currently have no pants or draws on. #WFH

I have always admired people who know how to take care of home. No really, I stare at them with heart eye emojis like a creep. It's so easy to get caught up in our careers and other obligations outside of the home, that we forget to put in the work that's needed **at** home. I'm not talking about cooking or cleaning. I'm talking about spending quality time with your family. I'm talking about listening to them. I'm talking about becoming a better person yourself so that you can be better to them. I'm talking about healing from past traumas so that you don't project that onto them. I'm talking about learning how to deal with stress so that you don't take it out on the people at home who love you and care for you the most. It's not fair to go to work at a job you don't even like, give those people the best of you, and then go home and give scraps. We should work from home as well. When we put in this work, we create a beautiful home environment where we can actually rest well. I've seen people who literally hate going home. Oh wait, I've *been* people who literally hate going home. It's tragic. Pray today for God to grant you the wisdom and understanding that's needed to build a beautiful home.

READ TODAY: PROVERBS 24:3-4

ZERO STARS. DO NOT RECOMMEND.

Zero Stars. Do not recommend. – used to alert others that you had a bad experience with a person, place, or thing, and would not recommend that they follow in your footsteps.

Example: "I dated a Virgo once. Zero Stars. Do not recommend."

Bad experiences…we've all had them. If you are an entrepreneur, you are well-aware that people are far more likely to share their bad experiences than they are to share good ones. Let's say you served 99 people well and messed up on one person. Would you care to guess who will be the one person to go write a review? I'm not exactly sure why this is the case, but I wonder what would happen if we were to keep that same sharing energy and apply it to ourselves? When we make mistakes, we often sweep them under the rug in hopes that people will continue to think that we are perfect. As believers, however, we have the awesome opportunity to transform our bad experiences into lessons that will help us as well as others in the future. I tried to do things on my own without seeking God first. Zero stars. Do not recommend. I held unforgiveness in my heart for too long. Zero stars. Do not recommend. I was bound by the opinions of others. Zero stars. Do not recommend. See how that works? If you don't get anything else out of the situation, get an understanding of it. Pray today and ask God to help you find the lesson in what you went through.

READ TODAY: PROVERBS 4:7

GET INTO THIS...

Get into this... – a phrase used to call a viewer's attention to something that is impressive.

Example: *zooms in* Y'all get into this detail on my wedding dress! Yes, that is 50,000 Swarovski crystals.

If you aren't careful, it's easy to overlook things that are actually quite impressive. When someone urges you to get into something, it is because they feel that it's especially dope or uncommon and that it deserves special attention. Do you know what is really impressive? I would like to call your attention to the Word of God. I know it's probably a cheesy way to say it, but get into this! Get into your Bible. There are many great Bible teachers out there, but there is nothing that can replace getting into it for yourself. When you study for yourself, you don't have to depend on the understanding of others who may be right, wrong, or biased. I think you are off to a good start by reading these devotions and looking up the scriptures. That gets you into the habit of being in the word at least once in the day. Many of us have Bibles on our phones, but I am going to challenge you to get yourself a printed Bible as well if you don't already have one. There's no special magic in a printed vs digital copy. I just noticed that sometimes when I use the actual book, I end up reading more than I thought I would. Pray today and ask God to speak to you through His written word.

READ TODAY: 2 TIMOTHY 3:16

#brb (1)

#brb – a hashtag acronym for the phrase, "be right back." This is usually used when a person is going to be away from their phone or computer but plans to return shortly.

Example: Getting ready to board my flight, so my phone will be on airplane mode for a few hours! #brb

Have you ever gone through a bout of depression? I'm not just talking about being diagnosed with a clinical form of depression. Maybe yours was just situational. Maybe you experienced the loss of a relationship or maybe you just made a mistake at work that continued to weigh on your psyche. Did you feel icky? Did you start overeating or drinking to feel comfort? Did you sleep all day? If you've ever experienced what it's like to feel depressed, you know it is not fun. We will all experience it if we live long enough, but how do we bounce back? How do you come right back from an event that has caused you despair? The Bible tells us that one way we can come back is to remember the times and ways that God has come through for us in the past. Once you remember, you can bounce back with a praise. You can literally use your own memory to give you hope. Do you remember the last time you were down, but God took care of you? With all that goes on, it's easy to forget. Maybe we can start keeping a journal and referring to it when we need to come back from a low place. We've all seen that person who never bounced back from a bad experience. It wreaks havoc on their entire life. We all have down times, but it's a slippery slope, so we must be careful not to stay down long. Pray and ask God to help you remember how He brought you through the last time, and then praise Him until you feel better.

READ TODAY: PSALMS 42:5-6

HOW SWAY?

How Sway? – a question fervently posed by Kanye West during an interview with a radio host named Sway. It is now used widely on social media to question how something is even possible.

Example: So you're saying you want us to donate money to bury all of your loved ones, yet we see you taking international pleasure trips every month while we are stuck at work? How Sway?

Have you ever reflected on a time period of your life and wondered exactly how you made it through? I have two daughters that are two years apart. It takes literally almost everything I have in me to make it some days. Yet my parents raised five children all two years apart, worked full time, had us in church every week, and sent us all to college. How Sway?! I am currently practicing optometry, running my clinic, managing my employees, raising two young children, cooking and cleaning, writing books on the side, and trying to be fine for the 'gram. How Sway?! Listen, it's not even about how at this point. It's about **who**. You have supernatural help from God. When you make righteous efforts, God puts His super on your natural and you will be able to do things that otherwise seem impossible. When you think about all of the tasks before you, do you find yourself feeling overwhelmed trying to figure out how it will all get done? Take a moment today to breathe and remember that God is a very present Help. Take pressure off of yourself by realizing that if God doesn't step in to do it…oh well, it just won't get done!

READ TODAY: PSALM 121

WHERE THEY DO THAT AT?

Where they do that at? – a question posed when observing something that seems to be particularly weird, crazy, or irrational. The question seeks to understand where people come from who do such things.

Example: This man is wearing some black Air Force 1 Low Tops with white socks. Where they do that at?

Some things are just extremely difficult to fathom. Some things will have people completely dumbfounded and asking, "where they do that at?" I will give you one good example. Have you ever prayed for your enemies? I knooowwwww! It sounds wild, but the Bible literally tells us we should do it. Jesus even prayed for the people who were crucifying Him. They beat Jesus and left Him hanging for dead, and He prayed, "Father, forgive them. For they know not what they do." Chiiilllleeee!!! Where they do that at? Here. Here is where. When people purposely do us dirty, it is easy to become consumed with anger and look for revenge. That is not the way. We are to forgive people, even when they may not be sorry, and pray for them. Think about it. God said that vengeance belongs to Him and that He would repay those who have done us wrong. Umm…that's a pretty scary thought. I wouldn't want to be on the other end of God's vengeance. Those people need your prayers! When an enemy tries to come at me, I wash my hands of it and pray this simple prayer. "Lord, go easy on 'em. They didn't know I belonged to You." Try it.

READ TODAY: MATTHEW 5:43-44

THIRST TRAP

Thirst Trap – an attention-seeking mechanism that involves posting sexy or suggestive photos in hopes that people will react by commenting and/or sliding in your DMs. Once a person has been attracted by the picture, the poster then begins acting like they didn't want the attention and that the person responding is the "thirsty" one.

Example: I wish these ladies would stop trying to set thirst traps if they don't want guys to fall in.

I know it sounds crazy, but one time Jesus set a thirst trap. Yup. It was one of the greatest thirst traps of all times. He came to a well and sat down. A woman then came to the well to draw some water, and Jesus asked her if she could give Him a drink. She gave Him a lil' smart reply, and then Jesus quickly flipped the script on her. He told her that if she knew who He was, she would have been the one asking Him for a drink because the water that He gives is so good that anyone who drinks it will never thirst again. He went on to tell her all of her own business that she thought no one knew. This is how she realized that Jesus was the real deal. She left there and told everybody she knew about Him. What a set up! Jesus is still offering us that same water today. When we drink H_2O, it is certain that we will eventually be thirsty again. Jesus offers us His love which is a never-ending well of living water that never runs dry. It's not really a trap though, it's more of a treasure. Once we drink of it, we should be like the woman at the well who went and shared it with others. Let's thank God today for sending His own Son to quench our thirst.

READ TODAY: JOHN 4:13-14

PERIODT

Periodt – a word used to emphasize that there are no ifs, ands, or buts about a particular matter. The "t" at the end is often added for the additional effect of a hard stop. It is interchangeable with the phrase "periodt pooh" as well as the phrase "…and that's on period."

Example: I am leaving work early today. At 3:00, I will be in
       my car driving away, periodt.

We all know that a period indicates the conclusion of a sentence, but I like how sometimes we say it aloud to further emphasize that there is nothing to be added or taken away from what was said. This is exactly how it is with God's love for us. He loves us, periodt! Over the years, people have attempted to add to that or take away from it, but once God showed us His love by giving us His only begotten Son, it was a wrap. People will make you feel as if God will love you less if you make a mistake. This is false. People will make you feel as if God will turn His back on you if you are less than perfect. This is also false. You can't make God stop loving you. The most you can do is turn your back on Him and deny that His love is there. But if and when you turn back around, His love will be standing there right where you left it. God's love for us is unconditional, also known as agape love. Agape love is simply love that is on periodt! Let's spend some time today thanking God for that.

READ TODAY: ROMANS 5:8

IMMA JUST LEAVE THIS RIGHT HERE.

Imma just leave this right here. – a phrase used to signify that a more descriptive caption is not needed for a post, but that the post should be self-explanatory.

Example: *A personal trainer posts a before and after picture of his client who has lost 100lbs* Imma just leave this right here.

There are some things in life that need to be dropped off and left where they are without explanation. You may have already guessed that I'm talking about sin today. The Bible tells us that we should "lay aside" things that can weigh us down on our journey. Some of us have been carrying things that make it very hard for us to get ahead in our own personal race. Do you feel as if your pace in life is slower than it should be? Consider that there may be some things that you need to leave right here. I don't think I have to name them out, but I want you to sit and think about anything that is clouding your heart, mind, or spirit from being pure. This could be anything from unforgiveness to chemical dependencies. It may be hard to drop certain things after you have carried them for so long, but think about how much better it will feel to reach your goals and walk more fully in your purpose and destiny while you're here. Pray today and ask God to help you let go of any sin in your life, and then leave it right here so that you may move forward.

READ TODAY: HEBREWS 12:1

MISS ME WITH ALL THAT.

Miss me with all that. – a phrase used to tell others that you prefer not to be bothered with certain trivial matters.

Example: I always see folks arguing back and forth with strangers in the comment sections. Y'all can miss me with all that, because you will get blocked!

Have you ever been in a situation where people tried to involve you in some drama? Maybe you thought it was a good idea to pop yourself some popcorn and grab a front row seat to the dramatic train wreck of someone else's issues. The thing about having a front row seat to a train wreck though, is that you will probably get burned in the explosion due to your proximity. Drama is fun when it's on TV, but in real life, we must be careful not to take pleasure or enjoyment in being messy. When people bring certain things to you, it's okay to tell them to miss you with all of that. It's okay to protect the "gates" of what you accept into your spirit. If you are an empath (a person who can literally feel what other people are going through), I hope you are listening. You will find yourself in turmoil over things that should have never included you in the first place. Life throws enough at us as it is. Don't adopt things that God did not ordain for you to take on. Let's pray and ask God for the discernment on when to duck, dodge, and let the foolishness miss us.

READ TODAY: 1 THESSALONIANS 4:11-12

BUT Y'ALL AREN'T READY FOR THAT CONVERSATION...

But y'all aren't ready for that conversation... – a phrase used to introduce a taboo topic that often goes unacknowledged.

Example: Just because your grandma let you borrow her car with the handicap tag, doesn't mean you should park in the handicap space when there's nothing wrong with you. But y'all aren't ready for that conversation...

At the time of this writing, Angela Bassett is 62 years old. By the time this book is published, Angela Bassett will be 63 years old. Both times, (Lord willin' and the creek don't rise) Angela Bassett's "bawdy" will be looking better than almost all of ours. So many women look at her and wish they could be as beautifully fit and healthy at 33 as she is at 63. What people don't want, however, is to do what she does. Angela Bassett doesn't look the way she does by coincidence, but y'all aren't ready for that conversation! That's the problem with looking at what people have in an envious manner. The Bible calls it "coveting." Coveting is apparently so problematic, that it was listed in the original Ten Commandments as one of the things that thou definitely shalt **not** do! Stop comparing yourself to others and wishing you had the things that they have. You have absolutely no idea what it took for them to acquire and then to maintain those things (go to YouTube and search for a video called "3 Things You Must Do to Look Like Angela Bassett," and you will see what I mean). You see people stunting for social media but have absolutely no idea if they are even happy. Take your eyes off of others and ask God to show you a clearer vision of your own personal greatness. That's the conversation you should be having.

READ TODAY: HEBREWS 13:5 (KJV)

GOOD MORNING TO EVERYBODY EXCEPT...

Good morning to everybody except... – a way to wish your friends good morning while simultaneously throwing shade or expressing disdain towards someone or something else.

Example: Good morning to everybody except the people at Sallie Mae who called my cousins house looking for me and asking when I was gonna pay back those student loans.

If your mornings are anything like mine, they are extremely busy. If I hit snooze one too many times, I find myself waking up in a rush. There are so many things to do before I can get out of the house with two young children. There are times when I have gotten all the way to work before realizing that I have said good morning to everything and everybody except the One who actually woke me up and started me on my way. That's not right. Hey, I'm working on it. Don't judge me! When we acknowledge God early in the morning, it centers our minds, allows us to express our gratitude, and gives us a chance to listen to God's directions for the day. It also allows us to prepare our spirits for whatever darts Satan may try to launch in our direction. Did I ever tell you that you can pray about any and everything? It may sound crazy, but let's start praying and asking God to give us a better strategy for how to seek Him early in the morning before we begin focusing on the other tasks.

READ TODAY: PSALM 63:1

FOLLOW FOR MORE
RELATIONSHIP ADVICE!

Follow for more relationship advice! – used when a social media personality uses "relationship advice" memes to attract more followers. Sometimes the relationship advice is valid, and sometimes it is completely bogus.

Example: Ladies, if he doesn't pick up the phone it's because he wants you to pull up at his house unannounced. Follow for more relationship advice!

When Jesus was down here in the ghetto…I'm sorry…I mean the earth…He had to gain some followers. Instagram wasn't a thing, so He literally just walked up to some people and asked them to follow. Jesus was anointed by God, so those guys followed Him because they could feel that there was something dope about Him. Over time, Jesus would teach them stuff not only with His words, but also with his example. The other awesome thing that Jesus did with His close followers (The 12 Disciples), was to build up real relationships with them. Let's look at what Jesus did and learn from that. Do you feel like you're smart, but no one ever listens to you? If we want people to listen to what we have to say or follow our advice, we have to use more than words. We have to use our actions as an example, and we also need to build up real relationships with those people we are seeking to affect. People are much more likely to accept guidance from someone whom they know truly cares about them as an individual. Hey…follow Jesus for more relationship advice! He told us that if we follow Him, He will show us how to connect with others. Let's pray and ask God to show us who He wants us to establish a better relationship with, so that we might be a positive influence in someone else's life.

READ TODAY: MATTHEW 4:18-20

"WHO GONE CHECK ME, BOO?"
-SHEREE WHITFIELD

"Who gone check me, boo?" – A question posed by Sheree Whitfield during a heated argument with an event planner on an episode of *Real Housewives of Atlanta*. It is now colloquially used to mean, "I'm going to do what I want to do, and no one can stop me."

Example: I'm eating fried chicken, mac & cheese, and sweet potato pie for breakfast. Who gone check me, boo?

Accountability is a dirty word these days. Accountability simply means having someone who is allowed to check you, boo. I think the cool thing now is just to do whatever you feel like doing, even if it is destructive, without people saying anything to you. I know it's a wild idea, but sometimes you just don't know any better, but other people do. I know this is mind-blowing, but sometimes there are people who have more wisdom than we do! When you find someone who cares about you and has proven wisdom, you have found someone who can check you, boo. This is what it means to have accountability. We must humble ourselves enough to know that if left to our own devices, we might unwittingly do some things that are detrimental to ourselves and others. Having someone who can check you when you are wrong, is an important tool in a successful person's life. Let's pray today that God will show us the people in life who should be a part of our circle of accountability.

READ TODAY: JAMES 5:16

THAT PART

That Part – a phrase used to respond to someone who has brought up a good point that others may not have considered.

Example: Person A: How am I supposed to get excited about Juneteenth becoming a federal holiday when states are steadily passing laws to make it harder for my people to vote? Person B: That Part!

Today, I want to talk about a specific part. There was this one time in the Bible where Bro. Moses was used by God to part the Red Sea. Yup. The children of Israel had gone as far as they could go naturally and now stood in need of a life-saving miracle. God came through in the clutch, and when Moses lifted his rod, God parted the sea and allowed the people to walk through on dry land. I am here to encourage someone today. You may feel as if you have gone as far as you can go, and you may feel like giving up or turning around. But there is still one part that maybe you haven't considered. God is yet able to turn the situation around in your favor. Don't forget that part. Don't let what you see in the natural world make you forget that we still serve a God of miracles, even today. Have faith. Let's take time today to thank God for His part in our lives.

READ TODAY: EXODUS 14:21-22

THIS THE ONE.

This the one. – a phrase used to describe something as being uniquely the best or something that stands out from others in the same category.

Example: Post: Announcing the Anita Baker-Jill Scott-Erykah Badu-Brandy-Kirk Franklin-Stevie Wonder-Earth Wind & Fire-OutKast World Tour!
Me: Oh, this the one!!!

Do you know something that's really powerful? Have you ever seen two or more people coming together with the same vision, the same goal, and the same drive to achieve the aforementioned? Now imagine if you had five people like that! This is unity. The Bible calls it being of "**one** accord." When two or more people can come together in unity, they are able to achieve much more than the person working alone. It seems, however, that true unity is really hard to come by. Think about all of the amazing singing groups who broke up simply because they couldn't get along. People are really out here giving up on millions of dollars simply because they can't work together in unity. Now think about your own household. You can't control what other people do, but how can you foster an environment for unity to thrive? You can certainly prioritize unity within yourself while praying for others to do the same. And although unity is all about coming together as **one**, sometimes it will require humility and the ability to let someone else take the lead. I think that's where most unity gets messed up. Everyone thinks that they are the top dawg for every single project. Recognize the value and validity in someone other than yourself, and you will be on the path towards becoming one. Let's pray today and ask God to help all of our egos to decrease so that unity might increase. This the one.

READ TODAY: PHILIPPIANS 2:2

IT'S THE _____ FOR ME.

It's the ___ for me – used by an individual to point out which element of a picture, video, or post has brought them the most satisfaction.

Example: Post: *video of woman twerking upside in her living room*
         Person: It's the cat silently judging in the background for me!

It's interesting how 10 people can view the exact same content but get 10 different things out of it. The same video can do one thing for me and do a totally different thing for you at the same time. It's the same way with God. He has this way of being the very thing you need whenever you need it while also being the thing that I need when I need it. Even in the Bible, there are several different names for God. They would call Him Jehovah _____ to describe whatever need He was filling in that moment. Jehovah Jireh, for example, means "The Lord Will Provide." Jehovah Rapha means "The Lord Who Heals." The list goes on. You can Google it. So what is it for you today? Fill in the blank and call on the name of the Lord that you need the most. It's the Jehovah <u>Shalom</u> for me today. The Lord is my peace. Let's take time today to thank God for being so beautifully multifaceted.

READ TODAY: PHILIPPIANS 4:19

"IT GOES DOWN IN THE DM."
-YO GOTTI

"It goes down in the DM" – a line used by rapper Yo Gotti in his hit song "Down In the DM." The phrase refers to DMs (Direct Messages) on social media. DMs are private conversations between individuals and are usually where the most excitement occurs.

Example: Girl, he's always posting up scriptures and acting all holy on social media, but it goes down in the DM boo. He's a freak.

I have to agree. It does go down in the DM for sure. In the DMs you will see people sharing things that they would never want to say or post publicly. The DMs are where you get to know someone on a level that is deeper than what you may have seen or heard elsewhere. It's actually the same way with God. Yup. He may not have a social media account, but we are able to get direct messages to Him through the direct line of communication known as prayer. In the life of a believer, this is where it **really** goes down. Spending time in prayer helps us to establish a personal relationship with God that is deeper than the surface. When you strengthen your own relationship with God through prayer, you don't have to rely solely on what you may have seen or heard about Him elsewhere. You can be yourself and speak candidly with God. You can tell things to God in private that you don't want to say publicly, and you can have complete confidence that He won't screenshot it and laugh at you behind your back. It goes down in the spiritual DMs when you go down on your knees in prayer. Try it today.

READ TODAY: MATTHEW 6:5-6

...UNDERSTOOD THE ASSIGNMENT

...understood the assignment – a compliment. Used to indicate that someone did what they were supposed to do, exactly how they were supposed to do it. There is usually no *actual* assignment, but rather a theoretical task that was completed in an impressive fashion.

Example: Whew! These children went to prom looking good enough for the Oscars! They understood the assignment!

Well today is my birthday. Thanks! I don't know what it is about birthdays, but many of us use them as a time of reflection and introspection. On my birthday, I always ask myself whether or not I am doing what God sent me here to do. What is my purpose? Do I understand the assignment? Many of us know that we are meant to do something greater, but if we're honest, we can admit that we don't fully understand the assignment. Jesus once told a story about a master who gave differing amounts of money (talents) to three of his servants. They were to take care of his money while he was gone. He returned to find out that only two of them understood the assignment. Those two took his money and grew it, while the third man buried the money to protect it because he was too afraid to do anything with it. In summary, God has given you a gift. Your assignment, should you choose to accept it, is to take that gift and make the most out of it so that you can be a blessing to others. If you operate in fear, you will hide your gift and miss the assignment. I don't know about you, but I have to be about my Father's business because I want to hear Him say, "Well done, good and faithful servant." Pray with me today for a greater sense of clarity and strategy concerning your God-given assignments.

READ TODAY: MATTHEW 25:14-29

#TREATYOSELF

#TreatYoSelf – a self-care reminder literally meaning "treat yourself." This hashtag can be seen accompanying posts of people doing things for themselves such as getting pedicures or massages. It applies to any action that one may take on their own behalf.

Example: I splurged and ordered the $80 steak, and it was worth it! Sometimes you just have to #TreatYoSelf.

Do you know how to treat yourself? I know you're probably tired of hearing people talk about self-care, but I'm going to talk about it anyway because it's so important! There's no skating around the fact that stress can kill you. No, seriously, it almost killed me. I had gotten into this extremely stressful cycle that included working almost non-stop. I used to work a side-gig traveling to see patients in nursing homes. I remember being so worn out one day and then getting the call on the way down that the visit had been cancelled. I turned around, went home, and got some much-needed rest. Later that evening, I was scolded for being lazy. Apparently I should have been cleaning the house with my unexpected time off. That experience cultivated a years-long mindset that caused me to associate rest with guilt and shame. Stress had been a central theme in my life for several years, so when I popped out with diabetes, hypertension, high cholesterol, and a random autoimmune thyroid disease all in my 20s, why was I even surprised? Let's take a look at this scripture where the disciples had been working so hard that they hadn't even had a chance to eat. You will see that Jesus literally instructed them to practice self-care. If you are unsure what to do, pray and ask God to show you how to treat yourself.

READ TODAY: MARK 6:30-32

TO DIS DAY

To dis day – a phrase popularized by heavyweight champion Deontay Wilder. He was referring to the struggles that black people have been facing since the beginning of slavery, all the way up to this very day. The phrase is now being used to describe anything that continues to happen consistently.

Example: I'm 40, and I am scared to backtalk my mama to dis day!

One thing about life? It changes. People are born. People die. Jobs come and go. Friends come and go. Our bodies do weird things sometimes out of nowhere. Technology continues to advance. I still remember when video calls seemed so futuristic! With so many changes going on around you, how do you remain grounded? How do you keep yourself from being destroyed by the transitions? You have to hold on to the one thing that never changes, and that's God's love for you. Sometimes I get emotional when I think about how God has been there for me through it all. He has never forgotten nor forsaken me the way that others have. At times I have neglected my relationship with Him, but that was on me. God has remained consistent with us to dis day! The old saints would say that God is an anchor, a solid rock, and a firm foundation. The Bible says that there is not even a "shadow of turning" with God, which means He's not going to flip the script on us. His promises to us are true to dis day! Let's thank Him today for how He remains consistent in a world filled with inconsistency.

READ TODAY: ISAIAH 40:8

COUNT YOUR DAYS!

Count your days! – an angry threat of retaliation issued to an offender. It puts the offender on notice that their punishment will come soon, and that there are only a limited number of days left for them to enjoy life.

Example: I just got home and found a gold tooth in my corn!
Tyrone's Chicken Hut, count your days!

Let's talk about counting our days. When we are young, it is hard to wrap our minds around the idea of not living forever. The older we get, however, we see people that we know leaving here left and right. Mr. Jesse Simon, my godfather, always taught us to live each day as if it could be our last. When he unexpectedly passed one morning, it felt as if someone had ripped our hearts from our chests. But there was also this overwhelming sense of peace, because **everyone** knew how he lived each day without regrets. The Bible teaches us that we should learn to count (or number) our days so that we can be more strategic with our wisdom. Are you spending huge chunks of time unhappy with your situation or at odds with others? Are you procrastinating on things that you know you should be working on? Life is short and tomorrow isn't promised to anyone, so use your wisdom. If you knew that you only had a limited number of days on this earth, would you really want to spend them *that* way? Let's pray and ask God to teach us the best way to spend our days.

READ TODAY: PSALM 90:12

ENTANGLEMENT

Entanglement – a colloquialism used to describe an inappropriate relationship. The word was first used in that way by a popular actress who had been called out for having an extra-marital affair with a much younger man. She stopped short of calling the involvement a relationship and instead called it an entanglement. The internet ran with it.

Example: I'm trying to lose weight, but my cheat day somehow turned into an 8-month entanglement with carbs.

Have you ever gotten tied up in something that you knew was no good for you? Maybe it was an inappropriate relationship of some sort, an addiction, or a toxic behavior. There was a group of people in the Bible who got caught up in an extremely toxic behavior that caused them to be entangled. It's going to sound crazy, but before Jesus came, there were all of these very specific laws that people had to follow in order to show that they were righteous. Once Jesus came and did His work at Calvary, however, we were offered grace and made free from those laws that were so binding. The plot thickens! After we were set free, there were those who still tried to make people operate under the old laws! Paul referred to it as an entanglement. He warned against getting tangled up with the unachievable rules and regulations of religion while ignoring the law of liberty that was afforded us by Jesus Christ. And people still do it to dis day! Imagine being tangled up not with some pretty young thing or with Krispy Kreme donuts, but with religion! Whew chile! The point is, **anything** that prevents you from walking in complete liberty with Christ, is an entanglement that you do **not** have to be bound by. Let's pray and ask God to help us take hold of our freedom today!

READ TODAY: GALATIANS 5:1 (KJV)

#FREEGAME

#FreeGame – valuable information or knowledge that is shared without cost.

Example: If they text "I miss you," but never make time to see you, they are lying. #FreeGame.

One thing I like about Jesus is that He was always somewhere spitting some free game. He would tell these little stories called parables to help people relate with the message. One parable was about a son who asked his father to run him his inheritance early (while the father was still living). The son went and tricked all of his money away doing dumb stuff and ended up broke and having to eat pig feed. It was then that he realized that he could always go home. He pulled it together and went home to his father, fully expecting to be demoted from son to servant. In a surprising turn of events, the father was just happy to have his son back. He celebrated his return and restored him to his rightful place. So let me put you up on some #FreeGame. No matter what you have done and no matter how far you have gone, you can still return to your heavenly Father's house. He hasn't demoted you. He loves you just as much as He did when you decided to go astray. He will restore you back to your rightful place as His child. No matter how long it has been, don't be ashamed to return to your Father. He is waiting for you with open arms, and it's all for free. In what ways have you gone astray? Let's thank God today for His restoration power.

READ TODAY: LUKE 15:17-20

JUST LOG OFF.

Just Log Off. – Advice given to people who are showing obvious signs of internet burnout and fatigue.

Example: *Posting @ 3:00am* Has anyone ever tasted an actual rainbow? Does it taste more like rain, more like bows, or more like Skittles?
Friend: Hey buddy, just log off.

When I am tired, my friends can tell because I act really silly. Sometimes I begin to post random cheesy jokes on social media. That's usually when they advise me to go ahead and log off. You know who else believed in logging off? Yes! Jesus Himself had to occasionally log off of His earthly connection in order to log in to His divine connection. He often went up to high mountains to pray. One time He was gone for 40 days just a'fasting and a'praying. If Jesus had to do all of that back then, before there were phones, internet, social media, and television, how is it that we feel as if we never need to disconnect from the constant stream of content coming our way? We are grateful for technology and all of the various means of connectivity, but sometimes media and social media can be an extremely toxic environment. It's okay to get away from time to time so that you can spend time with God focusing your mind on more spiritual matters. Sometimes it's social media, and sometimes it's just certain people or certain places. If you find yourself feeling overwhelmed today, consider going up to your own personal "high mountain" to fast and pray away from the others.

READ TODAY: MATTHEW 14:23

I CAN'T GET THOSE 60 SECONDS BACK.

I can't get those 60 seconds back. – used when a person realizes that something that they have viewed was a complete waste of time.

Example: I just watched a whole video of someone eating an egg roll, and I can't get those 60 seconds back. I'm also hungry now.

Have you ever dealt with feelings of regret? Maybe you feel that if you had done a few things differently, then you wouldn't be where you are today. Maybe you feel that if you could just get one more chance, you would be able to make things right. You have to be very careful with regret because it can lead to feelings of guilt, shame, and condemnation. These are some of the most effective tools in Satan's toolbox. If he can get you focusing on the past and on the time that you can't get back, then he has done his job in slowing down or stopping your forward momentum. It's crazy because people will literally waste time sitting and wishing that they hadn't wasted time! I'm telling you the devil is sneaky. Don't fall for the banana of regret in the tailpipe. Not today Satan! Let us keep our eyes focused forward and continue to press on towards better. Let us pray today and ask God to heal us from any past trauma that could lead to regret.

READ TODAY: PHILIPPIANS 3:13-14

"HE GON' CRY IN THE CAR."

"He 'gon' cry in the car." – a popular quote from the movie *Friday*. It is used to indicate that a person has just been embarrassed in public and will probably have to cry about it in private.

Example: That man is 46 years old, and his mama just came outside and whooped him with a belt in front of his girl for leaving dishes in the sink. He's trying to play it cool, but he gon' cry in the car.

Crying is really frowned upon. I'm not sure why we do this, but we make people feel as if something is wrong with needing to cry sometimes. The men have it the worst. Most men cringe at the thought of anybody knowing that they have to cry, so you know they definitely don't want anybody actually **seeing** them cry. I wonder how many men have had to go cry in the car. The world will never know. Maybe it's just how we have been conditioned, but I'm so glad that God isn't like that. He never told us that we couldn't cry out to him. As a matter of fact, He lowkey encourages it. If you must cry, I encourage you to cry out to God specifically. The Bible tells us that when the righteous cry, He hears us and delivers us from our troubles. Don't be afraid to have a good cry with God when you need it. If there's anything you need to cry out to God about, you can do it today. He won't look down on you for it.

READ TODAY: PSALM 34:17-18

"HE NEED SOME MILK".

"He need some milk." – a phrase taken from a viral video in which a man is apparently high off of some type of hallucinogen and is throwing himself around violently. He finally hits the ground extremely hard, and the onlooker who filmed the video shouts, "He need some milk!" Maybe she thought milk would help him come down from his high. We don't know. Of course the undefeated internet ran with the phrase and now uses it whenever someone falls or hurts themselves in any extreme way.

Example: *man jumps off roof onto a trampoline and then bounces
          into the street where he is hit by an oncoming car*
          Onlooker: He need some milk!

Have you ever seen someone who looks down on others who are new to the faith? The awesome thing about God is that you don't have to pass some difficult exam in order to be saved. All you have to do is confess with your mouth and believe in your heart that Jesus was who He said He was and did what He said He did, and boom…saved! So when someone first gets saved, there will be a lot that they don't know, which is fine. We were all that way at one point. We needed some milk. Paul tells us that just as newborn babes, we should desire the sincere milk of the word which will help us to grow healthy and strong spiritually. If you are new to the faith, do not let anybody make you feel ashamed as you go through your learning process. If you have been walking this walk for a long time, never forget where you came from. Just because you can now understand revelations that are as deep as the ocean, that doesn't mean that you are any more saved than anyone else. But hey…if you need a gold star, let me know, and I'm thinking we can arrange that for you! Let's thank God today for meeting us on our own level.

READ TODAY: 1 CORINTHIANS 3:1-2

FALLBACK GAME STRONG

Fallback game strong – a phrase used to indicate that a person is comfortable reducing or eliminating their interaction with another individual at the slightest hint that their presence is unwanted or unappreciated.

Example: Oh so you were too busy to respond to my texts for two days? Cool. I won't be texting again. Fallback game strong.

Is your fallback game strong? Do you know how to retreat from or leave a situation that is detrimental to you? When someone tries to start a fight with you, do you know how to walk away, or do you continue going back and forth with them? When someone shows you that your presence is not valued, can you move along, or do you keep trying to prove yourself worthy? When you see temptation rearing its ugly head, are you able to fall back from it and go in the opposite direction? Fallback skills are extremely underrated. You'd be surprised how many people's problems would be solved simply by turning around and walking away from them. The Bible tells us that there are certain battles where we can literally fall back and let the Lord fight for us instead. Pray today and ask God to grant you the wisdom to know when you need to fall back as well as the strength to stay back.

READ TODAY: 2 CHRONICLES 20:17

DON'T FEED THE TROLLS.

Don't feed the trolls. – a warning given to remind people not to continue toxic interaction with those attention-seeking individuals online who find enjoyment in being negative, antagonistic, argumentative.

Example: Person A: Two plus two is four.
Person B: Two plus two is eight, you idiot.
Person C: Don't feed the trolls.

If you are a decent person, it may be a little hard to wrap your mind around the fact that there are people out there who find their jolly in trying to frustrate others. On the internet, these people are known as trolls. These people really do need prayer, because something is clearly wrong with them. My concern, however, is how you respond to these types of people online and in real life. Do you know someone who is so hungry for attention that they will attempt to get it in any way that they can? Is someone unnecessarily negative and nasty towards you? Do you feed them by continuing to engage? Are you allowing their negative energy to frustrate you as well? I've got news for you. The devil is the troll-in-chief. Do not feed him by continuing to focus on the negative thoughts that he tries to introduce. He loves seeing you taking your focus off of God to give the attention to him. Don't fall for it. Feed your spirit today instead by praying and meditating on God's word over your life.

READ TODAY: 1 PETER 5:8

I FEEL SEEN.

I feel seen. – a phrase used to indicate a feeling of acknowledgement after someone has said or done something that you heavily relate to on a personal level. It is usually something that is not often talked about, acknowledged, or understood.

Example: Person A: Shout out to everyone who loves the Lord but still runs to the dance floor when you hear that Cash Money Records is taking over for the 99 and the 2000.
Person B: That's me! I feel seen.

Do you ever feel like you've been overlooked? Maybe you started at the company at the same time as your peers, but they have all gotten promotions already and you haven't. Maybe it seems as if all of your friends have found happiness, love, and marriage, and you haven't. It is easy to feel like maybe God has forgotten about you, but I can assure you that He hasn't. There have been moments in my life where I have cried like a baby simply because God did something small to let me know that I hadn't been forgotten. Trust me, God sees you. Not only does He see you, but He is also concerned about everything that concerns you. He literally knows how many hairs you have on your head right now. Yup…He even subtracted the ones that fell out in the sink this morning. I just want to encourage you to hang in there. My prayer for you today is that God would in some way remind you that you are seen by Him.

READ TODAY: LUKE 12:7

#ABOUTLASTNIGHT

#AboutLastNight – a hashtag used to accompany a post highlighting the events of the previous evening.

Example: *posts video of myself crowd surfing in the club*
Caption: #AboutLastNight

What did you do last night? Hopefully you slept peacefully like a newborn baby being cradled in the bosom of Jesus all while riding in the backseat of a car that is floating on a cloud. But maybe things were a bit more difficult for you than that. There are so many people that cannot seem to achieve peaceful sleep simply because they can't get their minds to shut off long enough to rest. Maybe you are okay all day, but nighttime is when certain realities seem to set in for you. Is your pillowcase wet with tears? I may not have all the answers to all of your problems, but there was a man named David in the Bible who went through the same thing. His solution was to praise God. Yup, you can praise God even while you lay in bed. You can lift up your hands and begin to bless the Lord for all that He has done for you and for how great He is overall. When your mind is running crazy at night, you can stop it with something called meditation. Meditation is where you purposely set your mind on something for a period of time and refuse to let it wander off to other things. You can memorize a scripture and meditate on that, or you can simply think of the goodness of Jesus. That is your assignment for today or tonight. Find a scripture, memorize it, meditate on it, and praise God for it.

READ TODAY: PSALM 62:3-7

#WORKFLOW

#WorkFlow – a hashtag that usually accompanies a post about what a person is currently doing at or while on their way to work.

Example: I've read my morning devotion, and I've had my coffee. Let's get her done! #WorkFlow

Do you have something that you're supposed to be working on now? Did God give you a clear vision for…and this is literally where I stopped, got distracted, and didn't come back to writing this page for three whole days. I came back to it and was instantly convicted by my own words. Wow! God be knowin'. Okay, but that's a prime example. We often act as if we have all the time in the world to *eventually* get around to our God-given assignments. Do you really want to be one of those people who leave this world with a bunch of potential that was never realized? We dedicate so much time and energy to working and grinding for our own advancement, but what about the advancement of God's kingdom? There were some people in the Bible doing this very thing. They were so busy trying to build their own homes that they let the Lord's house lie in ruins. Do you know what the Lord told them? He said the reason why they worked so hard, yet it never seemed to amount to anything, is because they kept ignoring **His** work. Whew! You can literally run yourself ragged toiling all day and night and still be broke when you deprioritize or ignore the thing that **God** has assigned for you to do. Let us consider our ways. Take some time today to pray and ask God to give you clear vision as well as the proper strategy concerning your assignment.

READ TODAY: HAGGAI 1:3-10

#CHURCHFLOW

#ChurchFlow - a hashtag that usually accompanies a post about what a person is currently doing at or while on their way to church.

Example: *posts photo of family wearing matching church clothes*
#ChurchFlow

Church, church, church. Oh, church. What can I say about church? Some people love church. Some people hate church. Some people have a love/hate relationship with church. The church has been a beacon of light for centuries. It has been a vehicle of help, hope, change, and encouragement for so many. Unfortunately, the church has also been a vehicle of hurt, disappointment, and discouragement for many as well. The church is nothing but people. These people are imperfect human beings and are therefore subject to getting things wrong. I think one way that the church sets itself up for failure is by promoting a false image of perfection. We're so desperate to make "our way" seem the most attractive, that we think we must show forth this fake flawlessness now that we know Jesus. Imagine how disappointed, discouraged, and deceived people must feel when they discover that the church is full of people with all kinds of problems from the bottom all the way to the top. The crazy thing is that the answer is right there in the Bible. It tells us that if Jesus is lifted up, then He can draw people unto Himself. Now this was referencing His crucifixion, however, we can still tell of the powerful work that Jesus did on the cross and continue to lift Him up, even today. I have visited churches where everything and everyone was being exalted and lifted up but the Savior of the whole world! Today, let us repent for trying to fake our own perfection when all we had to do the whole time was point people to the cross.

READ TODAY: JOHN 12:32-33

#WEDDINGFLOW

#WeddingFlow - a hashtag that usually accompanies a post about what a person is currently doing at or while on their way to a wedding.

Example: Can't wait to see my best friend walk down the aisle! #WeddingFlow

       I spent several years working as a wedding photographer. Although it was rewarding, it was also extremely demanding. If you have ever been behind the scenes of a wedding, you know how easy it is for drama to arise. You may be dealing with anything from a broken zipper to a bride that's missing all together. I learned that it's much more fun to be a guest. Well Jesus was chilling at a wedding reception one day, just minding His own #weddingflow, when He was asked for help with something behind the scenes. He ended up performing His first documented miracle, which was turning some water into wine after the catering company unexpectedly ran out. Of course the guests commented that His wine tasted even better than the other wine! Why do you suppose Jesus turned water into wine as His first miracle? Since we don't know for sure, let's use our Holy Ghost imagination. Maybe Jesus was trying to tell us that He didn't come to earth to stop us from enjoying the party. Maybe He came to save us from the embarrassing reality that we didn't have enough on our own. Maybe He came to cover us so that we wouldn't have to deal with the public shame of others knowing just how unprepared we really were. Maybe, just maybe, He came to provide us with something much better to drink than what we were previously sipping on. I'm just giving you a little food for thought. Let's give thanks today simply for the fact that Jesus loves us enough to fill our empty cups with better.

READ TODAY: JOHN 2:1-5

#ISSAVIBE

#IssaVibe – literally meaning "it's a vibe," this hashtag is used to describe a good feeling in an atmosphere. It is the modern-day term for "good vibrations."

Example: I'm here at the grand opening of Jimmy's on 5th. The music is good, the food is good, and everybody looks good. #IssaVibe

Everybody is talking about vibes these days, but what are they? Vibes, or vibrations, are sort of like the energy that is being given off by a person, place, or thing. The vibes can be good, bad, or anything in between. It is left up to the person experiencing them to determine what kind of vibes they are. If you get good vibes from a certain group of people, for instance, you would be more likely to surround yourself with them. If you get bad vibes from another group, you would be more likely to avoid those people. Does this sound familiar? Have you ever heard of a thing called discernment? Discernment is a gift given to us by the Holy Spirit that allows us to intuitively feel the vibes. Have you ever gone to a place and the atmosphere just seemed off? Maybe you couldn't put your finger on it, but you knew not to stay. Have you ever met someone, and their spirit just seemed off? Maybe you couldn't put your finger on it, but you knew not to let them close to you. Don't ignore your God-given ability to feel the vibes. If the Holy Spirit is steering you closer to or away from any person, place, or thing, **please** listen and obey. Your discernment of vibes could literally be the difference between life and death. Let us pray today and ask God to strengthen us in the area of our discernment.

READ TODAY: 1 KINGS 3:9-12

THAT'S BAE.

That's Bae. – a statement of declaration that reveals the identity of your romantic partner to the world (of social media). Most people understand the word "bae" to be a shortened version of "baby," but urban legend has it that bae is actually an acronym meaning "Before Anyone Else."

Example: *posts photos hugged up with a new man or new woman*
Caption: That's Bae.

If you are in the dating game (aka not married), being on social media can get pretty wild. The internet is overflowing with people who make tons of money by claiming to be "relationship experts." There are thousands of social media accounts dedicated specifically to posting up memes about what you should do about your relationship (or lack thereof). The biggest argument of them all is whether you should make your relationship public on social media or keep it private. There are very fine arguments on both sides. But overall, it is a big deal when a person decides to share who they are dating with the rest of us. People will literally celebrate and congratulate you as if you have just gotten your PhD. The message today is to simply remind you to drown out all the noise. Don't become so inundated with social media advice that you forget to listen to the Holy Spirit concerning your relationship. Don't choose your partner based on how good the photos will look on Instagram. Don't stay in a toxic relationship simply because you already posted it, and now you don't want to disappoint the online cheering squad. We will cheer for just about anything, so don't be led by that. You must seek guidance from the Holy Spirit and not from your friends and followers. You must pray and ask God to show you what He wants you to see concerning your relationship. Sometimes you even have to hit a fast from social media for clarity on what you should do. Did **God** say that was bae? Hmm.

READ TODAY: PROVERBS 3:5-6

NO CHILL

No chill – used to describe a person who either doesn't know when to stop or just doesn't care.

Example: Y'all, my grandma just told my cousin she was too big to be going back for seconds. Grandma has absolutely no chill!

Do you know somebody who has no chill? A person who has no chill either does not know what is appropriate or simply does not care. A person with no chill does not stop when it's time to stop. I used the example of a grandmother saying something harsh because people of a certain age often feel that they have earned the right to say whatever they want to say, whenever they want to say it, and however they want to say it. Aht! Aht! The Bible never said that. There is no verse that says, "after age 60, you can become reckless with your tongue." Shoot, some of you are 30 and already there. There is absolutely nothing wrong with choosing your words more wisely. There is absolutely nothing wrong with seasoning your words with grace. Moreover, there is absolutely nothing wrong with keeping your thoughts to yourself sometimes when you know they are going to cause hurt and pain. How can we call ourselves children of the Most High if we continue to be reckless with our words? Let's pray today and ask God to help us understand when it's appropriate to just chill on out.

READ TODAY: JAMES 1:26

#brb (2)

#brb – a hashtag acronym that stands for "be right back."

Example: For some reason my job actually wants me to work today.
We will finish this conversation in just a minute. #brb

Welcome to April! We now enter the season in which many of us will be observing the Easter holiday (or "Resurrection Day" depending on how woke you are). It's only fitting that we talk about the greatest #brb of all time. Alright, so boom…God is good. Included in His goodness is the fact that He is just. Justice is important. Think about what society would be like if people knew that they could commit terrible acts against others without having to be held accountable to the justice system. Shoot…think about what society *is* like because certain people are allowed to abuse the justice system! Right. So God is good and justice is important. Now let's add on to that the fact that God really loves us. The conflict comes in when we as a people decided to get tangled up in sin and evil. The punishment that we all deserved was death. God didn't want us to go out like that, and yet He couldn't let it completely slide, because that would have compromised His just nature and therefore His goodness. So God sent us His son as a loophole. Jesus came, lived the human experience without sin, and therefore did not deserve any punishment of His own. This enabled Him to take on the punishment that we would have faced for our sin. Jesus was crucified and took the death penalty on our behalf. They laid His body in a tomb, but three days later discovered that He had risen from the dead. He had told everyone that He would be right back, and there He was! He went around showing Himself and His bruises to everyone so they would know it was Him. I said all that to say that the same power that Jesus used to bounce back from the grave is the same power that enables you to bounce back from **anything** that you may face today.

READ TODAY: 1 CORINTHIANS 6:14

#FIGHTME

#FightMe – a hashtag normally used when a person posts what they know will be an unpopular opinion or comment.

Example: I know y'all love guacamole, but I say it's trash. #FightMe

Have you ever been in a fight? Maybe you have never been in a physical fight, but maybe you've been in a heated argument with someone. I don't like fighting. Not only is it stressful, but I'm not very good at it! My voice starts cracking and then I start crying and my words become unintelligible. Ugh, it's a train wreck. The Bible tells us that when we find ourselves in a fight, it may seem that we are fighting against some other person, but we are not. Our fight is actually against Satan and all of his wickedness. I don't know about you, but it seems like the devil is always trying to find a way to #FightMe. In order to withstand this type of fight, we must prepare differently. God has supplied us with a certain type of "armor" to put on before the fights even come. We are to use things like truth, righteousness, peace, faith, salvation, the word of God, and prayer. I want you to really **study** today's passage below. It will tell you in detail how to cover yourself for every fight that comes your way, and it's not by arguing, yelling, or throwing hands. Put on the whole armor of God **today**, so that you won't be caught off guard.

READ TODAY: EPHESIANS 6:10-18

DEAD

Dead – used to indicate that something is so utterly funny that the person has died from laughter. This word is often accompanied by the skull emoji for extra emphasis. The person has not literally died but is simply trying to convey how hard they have laughed.

Example: *Posts video of a rhythmless person trying to dance*
Comment: Bwaaaahahaha!!! Deaddddd!!!!

I'm not going to lie to you, this is one popular phrase that I never say. I'm not trying to be all deep, but my words are just a liiiittle bit too powerful for me to go around saying that I'm dead. That's neither here nor there, though, because today's message isn't about that. Today's message is about grief. What happens when someone you loved is now dead? We have to be very careful with grief, because it is undoubtedly a part of Satan's strategy to defeat you. There's a distinct difference between mourning the loss of a loved one (healthy and normal) and being grief-stricken (problematic). When a person is grief-stricken, they are just that...stricken. Their lives are literally paralyzed by the pain of their loss. If the devil can use your grief to immobilize you, then he has successfully blocked you from moving forward in your purpose. I'm not trying to be insensitive about what you're going through. I think that's one of the sneakiest things about grief. We all want to be sensitive, so we will sit back and watch someone we love destroying their own lives because we don't want to hurt them any more by telling them the truth. Is grief causing you to do unhealthy or toxic things? Has grief stopped you from walking fully in your purpose? We must overcome grief by learning to worship the Creator more than we worship any creature that is no longer here with us. Is it possible that you are losing hope because your faith was wrapped up in another person's presence? I am praying for you today.

READ TODAY: 1 THESSALONIANS 4:13 (ESV)

LET'S NORMALIZE

Let's Normalize – a phrase used to suggest that something most people view as abnormal, should actually be considered normal.

Example: Let's normalize going to the hair salon and not being there for 13 hours.

That word normalize is very interesting. There are definitely some things that we view as abnormal that shouldn't be viewed that way. Seeking therapy, for example, should be considered normal in my opinion. On the flip side, we take things that should be considered abnormal, and we feel very normal about them. Sometimes we operate in dysfunction so long that it becomes comfortable. See when things are dysfunctional, it means that they are actually still functioning…just poorly. I think we get confused and even satisfied simply because we are still trucking along. The objective is just to get from Point A to Point B right? But what if your dysfunctional motor takes 5 hours to get you to your destination when it's only a mile away? Sure, you eventually got to Point B, but guess what? There was actually a Point C after Point B and now you've wasted time and missed it. Getting from Point A to Point B is life, but getting to Point C is **abundant** life. Because the devil is such a hater, he loves to see you normalizing dysfunction and forgetting that there is better. Let's not give his old ugly bubble-head self the satisfaction. Pray today and ask God to reveal any dysfunctional things in your life that you have accepted as normal.

READ TODAY: JOHN 10:10

DON'T SLEEP

Don't sleep – used to let people know that something deserves their attention. It is often referring to something or someone who may have otherwise gone unnoticed.

Example: Don't sleep on those nerdy guys in college. You might turn them down today, but they'll be CEOs and hedge fund managers with seven figure incomes and yachts before you know it.

Do you know one of the biggest differences between God and man? We sleep and He does not. If you've ever seen an infant or a toddler who has gone too long without sleep, you've seen a hot mess. When they haven't slept, they get loud, cranky, short tempered, delusional, and inconsolable. Even the most bougie babies will go to just about anybody's arms when they are sleepy. I'm not 100% sure why He did it, but God has designed our bodies to shut down temporarily for rest. If you try to ignore your body's need for rest, you become a ticking time bomb just like those babies. Most of the time, the babies are tired but fight sleep because they are afraid that they will miss something. Some of us adults miss sleep because we are up worrying about problems or trying to grind our way to the top. Do you really trust that God has it all under control, or are you too busy trying to figure out how to put the pieces of the puzzle together yourself? Can we surrender our own need for control long enough to calm down and go to sleep when our bodies need rest? Have you forgotten that God is more than able to fix it for you? Please don't sleep on Him, because He never goes to sleep on you. Pray and ask God to grant you peaceful sleep as you put your concerns in His hands.

READ TODAY: PSALM 121:3-4

YOU ATE THAT!

You Ate That! – a phrase that means a person did a great job or has pulled off something exceptionally well. It is commonly used to refer to someone who has done a better job than those around them who attempted to do the same thing.

Example: *Posts video of family doing a dance from Tik Tok*
        Comment: Yessss!! Grandma, you ate that! The rest of the family looked lost, but you ate!

We've always heard it said that you are what you eat. This applies spiritually as well. It really does matter what you ingest. If you are someone who is struggling with anger or violence issues, for example, listening to violent lyrics all day may not be a good idea for you. If you are struggling with heauxing, then maybe you should give the 90s R&B a break for a bit until you pull it together. Know thyself. When life presents you with unexpected challenges, your victory (or lack thereof) will be a reflection of what you ate. I once heard a story about a man with two dogs. One was named Flesh and the other was named Spirit. Every weekend, he would fight the two dogs and people would come to place their bets. The owner himself would place a bet as well. Sometimes Flesh would win and sometimes Spirit would win. One of the other men noticed that the owner always chose the right dog. "How do you always know which dog will win?" the man asked. The owner replied, "Whichever dog I feed the most during the week…that's the dog that will win." Which dog are you feeding the most each week? Do you let your flesh eat more than your spirit? If so, don't be surprised if your flesh is strong and your spirit is weak when trouble comes. Feed your spirit today with God's word and other things that are uplifting. Be careful though, not every "gospel" song is…never mind. Y'all aren't ready for that conversation!

READ TODAY: MATTHEW 5:6

I'M WITH YOU WHEN YOU RIGHT.

I'm with you when you right. – a much more jazzy way of saying, "I agree with you." It adds more pizazz.

Example: Person A: Raisins have no business being in potato salad!
Person B: I'm with you when you right!

The interesting thing about social media, is that people will back you up and stand in your corner when they feel that you are right. It's a two-edged sword though, because those same people might throw you under the bus, drag, cancel, and get you fired from your job when they feel that you are wrong. Nobody is perfect, but on social media there isn't a lot of room for error. I'm so grateful that God will never leave nor forsake us. He sticks beside us when we are getting it right, and He also sticks beside us when we are messing up. He never throws us away. He continues to see value in us beyond our own mistakes. Even when we turn our backs on Him, He doesn't throw us under the bus in return. This is exactly why we must stop putting so much stock in having social media friends and followers, because they will only be with you when you're right. In today's passage, the writer (David) had been wrong, yet he asked God to make him right again. He asked God not to throw Him away. Let's take time to thank God today for His mercy and for loving us unconditionally.

READ TODAY: PSALM 51:9-11

IT BE YA OWN FOLKS.

It be ya own folks. – a phrase meaning that sometimes the people closest to you, such as friends and family, are the ones who hurt you the most or treat you the worst.

Example: Person A: *posts picture that they think is cute*
Person B, C, & D: Aww! Love it! You are so cute!
Person E: You ashy! You need some more lotion cuzzin!
Person A: Ugh…it be ya own folks.

Isn't it funny how complete strangers can be your strongest supporters? People complain all the time about how their own friends and family are the least likely to support them. I am grateful for friends and family who have come through to support me, but I always tell people that if you're depending solely on your friends and family to carry your business venture, you might not make it! Jesus went through this. He was literally traveling all over the region teaching and performing miracles. But when He came home to His own city of Nazareth, they were like, "Wayment! Ain't you just a carpenter?! We know ya mama Mary and ya brothers and 'nem. You ain't nobody for real." Jesus (in essence) said, "SMH…it be ya own folks." Their faith in Him was so low that He couldn't do very much while He was there. He healed a few sick folks and taught a little, but that was it. I said all that to say, don't give up on your calling because of the friends and/or family who don't support you. Jesus couldn't even get His own folks to believe in Him, so what makes you think everyone will believe in you? It's best to pray and ask God to help you identify the places to which you are called. That place may or may not be home.

READ TODAY: MARK 6:1-6

#THROWBACK

#Throwback – the hashtag you use when posting an older picture or video. You may also see it as #ThrowbackThursday as Thursdays have unofficially been designated as the day to post pictures from the past.

Example: I just found this picture of Uncle Luke and I at Freaknik back in 1994. #Throwback

Do you ever start feeling sad about what's going on in your life right now? Do you sometimes wonder where you might be if maybe you had done a few things differently? Did some kind of deflating disappointment come along and steal your joy? It's not that hard to slip into a little (or big) bout of depression. The Bible tells us that we can actually fight depression with a #throwback. I know, I know, it sounds crazy, but hear me out! God has come through for you before, right? That last time that you thought everything was going to fall apart, you ended up being okay, right? That thing that you were sure was going to permanently ruin your life is all just a distant memory now, right? Okay then! Use that throwback! You will see in today's passage that the psalmist, David, was feeling depressed. His two solutions were to 1) praise God anyway and 2) remember the ways that God had made for him in the past. Next time you feel depression attempting to tug at you, stop and think of one of God's throwbacks, and then use your memory to praise Him. I keep mine locked at loaded, just in case.

READ TODAY: PSALMS 42:6

NATIONAL SIBLING DAY

National Sibling Day – a holiday celebrated annually in the United States on April 10th. It is not a federally recognized holiday, and nobody gets off work for it. People commonly celebrate it by posting pictures of their siblings with the hashtag #NationalSiblingDay.

Example: I just wanted to wish my sibs a Happy National Sibling Day! I still want to know who broke my Hot Wheels racetrack!

Isn't it interesting how children who come from the same parents and were raised in the same house can sometimes be polar opposites? It makes for an interesting dynamic at home and can easily lead to fights. Sometimes there will be a sibling rivalry wherein the children are constantly trying to compete for parental approval. As you can imagine, this can lead to things like jealousy, resentment, bitterness, anger, and discord. I know you think this is about to turn into some super deeply spiritual revelation, but honestly, I'm just here to let you know that tomorrow is not promised to anyone. If you are a fully grown adult and still beefing with your brother or sister over some petty stuff, I encourage you to squash it. Of course you cannot control what another person will do, but you can control your part in it. The Bible tells us that we should actively look for and pursue peace. You can seek peace by deciding to forgive…even if they never fully acknowledged what they did. If they knew how to be better, perhaps they would. Your forgiveness sets you free from the grip of bitterness. You can also take accountability for anything that you may have done that was messed up. Lastly, you can reach out and try to move forward as siblings by focusing on the future instead of the past. You may still come up empty-handed, but you never know until you try. I don't want anybody falling over a casket like a wet noodle filled with regret because they spent 20 years mad at their brother or sister over something that could have been let go.

READ TODAY: PSALM 133:1

TRY JESUS. DON'T TRY ME.

Try Jesus. Don't try me. – a phrase used to warn people that picking a fight with them is unadvised. Trying Jesus would be a better option, because well…He's still working on me, and I might just whoop you in the streets. An artist named Tobe Nwigwe popularized the phrase and idea even further with His song entitled "Try Jesus."

Example: Then Karen called herself slamming the papers down on my desk. I told her she better try Jesus. Don't try me, because I will take her to the stairwell and drag her down all 3 flights.

Okay, so as ratchet as this idea may be, there is actually so much validity to it. For far too long, people have idolized leaders and people with certain gifts. Bishops, Pastors, Elders, Apostles, Prophets, Evangelists, Teachers, etc. They should definitely be treated with respect and honored for their work in the ministry. But the problem comes in when people begin to worship these servants more than they worship the Master. We are supposed to be trying Jesus, and yet so many people are honestly just trying Bishop so-and-so. If your faith is wrapped up in a human being, what happens when that human being starts human be-ing? What happens if or when they mess up? What happens if or when they experience some sort of fall from grace, and you are now confused and/or embarrassed? Heck, what happens if they die? If you have been trying Jesus, you can pick up and continue to move forward in your relationship with Him no matter what happens to a leader. But if you have been trying Apostle such-and-such, then you are far more likely to lose faith and give up on your spiritual journey. Some of you may even be looking at me like I'm someone to try just because I write these lil' devotionals. Aht, aht! Nerp! I'm not perfect. I be messing up sometimes, so don't try me. I urge you today to give Jesus a try instead.

READ TODAY: ROMANS 10:9-11

#MCM

#MCM – a hashtag acronym standing for Man Crush Monday. On social media, Monday is the unofficially designated day to post about a man that you admire. It is usually romantic in nature but can also be used platonically.

Example: I want to celebrate my husband today. He is funny, smart, kind, and loving. My heart still skips a beat. #MCM.

You're probably not reading this page on a Monday, but I am going to go ahead and tell you about today's Biblical #MCM. This brother is known to most as "The Apostle" Paul, but let's talk a little about his origin story. Paul's mama actually named him Saul. He started out trolling and terrorizing followers of Christ. One day he had a really intense encounter with God that changed him forever. He did a complete 180 and ended up becoming one of the most (if not the most) effective ministers of the gospel in history. Because of his words, billions of people have become believers. His words are still reaching people to dis day, because he is credited with writing almost two-thirds of the New Testament! A couple of years ago, I prayed for my future husband. I asked God specifically to send me somebody who used to be a hot mess (like Paul), because I wanted somebody who had experienced God's transformative grace (like Paul), and who was therefore going to turn around and go all in for God (like Paul). What can you learn from Paul's life? Whenever I think of Paul, it reminds me that all it takes is **one** encounter with God to change the whole game.

READ TODAY: ACTS 9:18-20

#MCM

#MCM – a hashtag acronym standing for Man Crush Monday. On social media, Monday is the unofficially designated day to post about a man that you admire. It is usually romantic in nature but can also be used platonically.

Example: *posts picture of Kofi Siriboe*
Caption: My gorgeous #MCM!

Oooh…look at us doing a lil' Bible series and whatnot! Okay, today's Biblical #MCM is a brother named Daniel. Daniel found himself, a child of God, living in Babylon. Now Babylon was a bit more ratchet. They didn't worship or respect God. They worshipped idol gods and they were known to engage in a lot of unholy foolishness. Even though Daniel wasn't Babylonian, he earned respect and a place of leadership in the kingdom because of how he was able to utilize his God-given gifts of wisdom and dream interpretation. I like how he did it because he was able to advance without conforming to the Babylonian ways. He didn't worship the idols, and honestly, he didn't even eat their food. He would eat fruits and veggies while they were chomping down on pork chops and ribs and such. Of course the haters got jealous. They convinced the king, who actually liked Daniel, to make up some raggedy law that anyone who didn't worship the king himself would be executed via lions. Daniel, who continued to worship the True and Living God, got tossed in the lions' den. But the way God is set up, He shut the lions' mouths, and Daniel was in there chilling. What did we learn from Daniel? Work hard, use the gifts God gave you, be disciplined, don't sell out from what God told **you** to do, and have enough faith to know that your obedience to God will protect you from haters.

READ TODAY: DANIEL 1:8

#MCM

#MCM – a hashtag acronym standing for Man Crush Monday. On social media, Monday is the unofficially designated day to post about a man that you admire. It is usually romantic in nature but can also be used platonically.

Example: I see everybody posting their #MCM, and it's really beautiful. Meanwhile, my crush is on tacos. I'm not hating on y'all though.

Next up in our Biblical #MCM series is none other than "The Psalmist" himself, David. David was dope because he brought us one of the most fii (yes, fii) books in the Bible known as The Book of Psalms. David's story is jam-packed with drama and adventure, but let's focus on something that happened towards the beginning of his journey. There was a giant named Goliath who was literally trolling the Israelites. He kept daring somebody to fight him, but King Saul and all of his soldiers were too afraid. David wasn't even a solider for real (his brothers were). His job was at home tending to his father's sheep, but sometimes he would run some food up to his brothers at the camp. He overheard Goliath talking that noise one day and was offended that Goliath wasn't putting "respeck" on God's name. He insisted that he be allowed to fight him. He was young and a bit scrawny, but he cited the fact that God had already helped him kill a lion and a bear to protect the sheep. This would be no different. So without armor or any fancy weapons, David took one shot at the giant with a rock from his slingshot and took him clean slap out. Everybody knew from then on that David was the man. He eventually became king. What did we learn from David today? When God is on your side, there is no reason to fear a problem even if it seems huge and intimidating. God is **bigger**…and if He's done it for you before, He can do it again!

READ TODAY: 1 SAMUEL 17:32-37

#MCM

#MCM – a hashtag acronym standing for Man Crush Monday. On social media, Monday is the unofficially designated day to post about a man that you admire. It is usually romantic in nature but can also be used platonically.

Example: I want to dedicate my #MCM to the guy at Rico's Chicken Wing Shack who always makes sure I get all flats.

Today's Biblical #MCM is Joshua. You already know Joshua was lit because he has a whole book of the Bible named after him. If you're not super familiar, Joshua is the guy who took over for Moses after he died. Those were some big shoes to fill, am I right? But let's talk about how Joshua ended up receiving this position. Remember when the Israelites escaped from slavery in Egypt? They were supposed to enter into Canaan, this beautiful land that had been promised to them by God. Instead of grabbing hold of the promised land like they were supposed to, they sent 12 spies into the land to check it out and determine if the whole thing seemed doable. Out of the 12 spies, 10 of them came back saying that they'd never be able to do it. Only two spies, Joshua and his friend Caleb, came back saying that they believed in the promise of God enough to pursue the land. They were outnumbered and, of course, God was not feeling the lack of faith in the group. He told them that they would have to wander around in the wilderness for 40 years looking crazy until they all died off and the new generation was old enough to move forward without them. The only two people from that group (of well over a million Israelites) who lived to enter the promised land, were Joshua & Caleb. God bless them. What did we learn today? If God has made a promise to you, stop moving all scared and sketchy like He hasn't made a promise to you. Our lack of faith is what will have us wandering around, wasting time, and missing it.

READ TODAY: NUMBERS 14:6-9

#MCM

#MCM – a hashtag acronym standing for Man Crush Monday. On social media, Monday is the unofficially designated day to post about a man that you admire. It is usually romantic in nature but can also be used platonically.

Example: I am really getting tired of these #MCM devotions! I sure hope this is the last one.

I know you're probably growing tired of these by now, but I have one more #MCM before we move on. The final #MCM goes to none other than Jacob. I'm excited to talk about Jacob today, because Jacob is my whole mood right now. Jacob was born as the younger (fraternal) twin to his brother Esau. He famously fenagled the birthright from his brother, and years later he tricked his father into bestowing upon him the blessing that was reserved for the firstborn. Jacob later fell in love with a woman named Rachel, but her dad wasn't trying to give her up. So Jacob made an agreement to work for her father for seven years just so that he could marry the woman he loved. Jacob also encountered God in the wilderness and wrestled with Him all night long. He refused to give in, saying, "I won't let go until you bless me." God then blessed him and changed his name from Jacob to Israel…yup…that Israel. Does anybody else notice a pattern here? Jacob was playing chess, not checkers. Jacob was **serious** about his future and his blessings. In his younger days, he didn't always go about things in the right way, but he was always thinking about the end game because he knew that the full blessings of God were worth it. God honored this man's hustle. Let us go after our own blessings with the same tenacity as Jacob. Yes, you may have to put in extra work. You may have to sacrifice or suffer persecution. You may have to fast, pray, forgive, or seek forgiveness. Whatever you must do, don't give up until you see God's blessings on your life. It will be well worth it.

READ TODAY: GENESIS 32:26-28

#WCW

#WCW – a hashtag acronym standing for Woman Crush Wednesday. On social media, Wednesday is the unofficially designated day to post about a woman that you admire. It can be used romantically or platonically.

Example: Mya is my #WCW. She is 42 years old and looks just as fine today as she did when she was 22!

You had to know we were going to do women next, right? Well today's #WCW is Mary, the mother of Jesus. I like Mary because she was somewhere just minding her business and being on point. She was so on point, that God chose her (out of all the women on the planet) to birth and then raise the savior of the whole world. The angel pulled up and told her that she was going to have Jesus. All Mary did was ask a few basic questions that I think any pregnant virgin would be well within their rights to ask. But after that, Mary was just like, "Aight, bet." She wasn't 100% sure about how it was going to work, but she didn't fight it. She wasn't 100% sure about how it was going to make her look or even if her fiancé would break up with her. But still she was like, "Okay God, whatever You say." Listen! Mary is #goals okay? What can we learn from Mary today? 1) Be found somewhere minding your business and being on point. 2) When God gives you an assignment, just go with it, even if you don't know how it's going to play out. 3) Trust the process.

READ TODAY: LUKE 1:38

#WCW

#WCW – a hashtag acronym standing for Woman Crush Wednesday. On social media, Wednesday is the unofficially designated day to post about a woman that you admire. It can be used romantically or platonically.

Example: I just want to give a shout out to my lovely wife today. She works so hard every day to make sure that things flow smoothly for the children and for myself. I can never repay her, but today I surprised her with a trip to Hawaii. #WCW

Today's Biblical #WCW is a woman named Hannah. Admit it, you're starting to like these little Bible stories, aren't ya? Okay, so Hannah was married to a guy named Elkanah. Elkanah had two wives chile, so imagine the drama. Well Elkanah was actually in love with Hannah, but she couldn't have any children. The other wife, Peninnah, did have children. She knew that Elkanah was really in love with Hannah and not her, so her jealousy led her to make fun of Hannah for being barren…exactly, drama. Hannah really wanted a son by her husband. For yeeearrrrs she cried and prayed. Even her husband was like, "Bae, we love each other. Shouldn't our love be enough?" But Hannah never gave up on God. She vowed that if God would give her a son, that she would dedicate his life back to the Lord. I lowkey think this is where we get "baby dedications" from, but I digress. God did indeed bless her with a son named Samuel who went on to become one of the most on point prophets/judges of all time. So what did we learn from Hannah? For me it was the fact that she didn't give up on God when she didn't get her way. Some people are quick to get bitter and turn away from God when He doesn't grant their requests. Hannah may have been a little salty, but she **never** turned away from God. I'm not sure what you may be standing in need of today, but never forget that God is the only one who can make it happen.

READ TODAY: 1 SAMUEL 1:19-20

#WCW

#WCW – a hashtag acronym standing for Woman Crush Wednesday. On social media, Wednesday is the unofficially designated day to post about a woman that you admire. It can be used romantically or platonically.

Example: Michelle Obama is my #WCW because…well duh.

Today's #WCW is…well…they never said her name in the Bible. We just call her "The Woman at the Well." Here's the tea. One day Jesus was sitting down by a well. A woman from Samaria pulled up, and Jesus asked for her to get Him something to drink. She was like "Umm…first of all…you're a Jew and I'm a Samaritan. Y'all don't even fool with us like that, so what's really good?" Jesus was like, "Well…first of all…if you knew who I really was, you would have asked **me** for something to drink, and I would have given you some of this living water. It's not water water, but whoever drinks it will never be thirsty again." Then sis was like, "Hold up! Give me this living water then because I don't want to be thirsty no mo!" Then Jesus was like, "BINGO! Cuz you been acting real thirsty running 'round with all these different men you ain't got no business with." He went on to tell her all about herself, and she was completely blown at the accuracy. She realized that only somebody truly sent by God would know these things. She went back and told everybody to go see Jesus because He was legit. A loooot of people started believing in Jesus because of her. What did we learn? Every day, we see people who are thirsty for attention, love, or validation. Those people are honestly just trying to find someone to fill a void that only Jesus can fill. Instead of judging, we must pray that they have an **encounter** with Him. We also learned that ratchet people make the best witnesses. Everybody knew she was a mess, so when HOT GIRL SHEILA said go check Him out?! Tuh! They went.

READ TODAY: JOHN 4:13-14

#WCW

#WCW – a hashtag acronym standing for Woman Crush Wednesday. On social media, Wednesday is the unofficially designated day to post about a woman that you admire. It can be used romantically or platonically.

Example: My #WCW got married yesterday…to somebody else. I guess it's back to the drawing board for me.

Okay, it's really giving VBS 1996 vibes…am I right? Okay, today's Biblical #WCW is the woman who is described in Proverbs 31. I'm not going to lie. I used to get tired of hearing people talk about Proverbs 31, Proverbs 31, blah blah blah, Proverbs 31. It's on license plates. People use it as their IG handle…@Probers31nderful69. It was so much that I went a really long time **not** studying Proverbs 31. Well that was the trick of the enemy, so let's get into it. I pray that you'll set aside time to read the entire chapter. She was out here holding down her husband and children, making her own clothes, and investing in real estate. But today I want to highlight one of her lesser-discussed attributes. Verse 26 tells us that when she opens her mouth, wisdom comes out. It also tells us that there is kindness in her tongue. Ladies, how can you call yourself a "Proverbs 31 Woman," if you're always talking to people sideways? Our words and even our tones have power. Do you take a moment to make sure that you aren't being reckless with your lips? When your friends come to you with an issue, do you get them further riled up about it? Or do you know how to speak a word of wisdom that will keep your homegirl from slashing those tires? Men and women alike should read Proverbs 31. It gives you a much better idea of what #goals should be than the fake relationship experts on social media. Proverbs 31 is basically free game.

READ TODAY: PROVERBS 31:9

#WCW

#WCW – a hashtag acronym standing for Woman Crush Wednesday. On social media, Wednesday is the unofficially designated day to post about a woman that you admire. It can be used romantically or platonically.

Example: I am my own #WCW. I like myself.

Our final #WCW is Esther. Esther was a Jewish woman who lived in exile in Persia with her older cousin, Mordecai. The king of Persia at the time was really whack. He was a drunk and a high-level misogynist. When he was on the hunt for a new queen, he ended up choosing Esther out of all the women brought before him. As you can imagine, Esther was a beautiful woman. The king saw that she was naturally beautiful inside and out. He had no idea that she was actually Jewish. One of the government officials got into some personal beef with Mordecai. He wanted to get Mordecai back, so he convinced the king to put out a decree to have all the Jews in the kingdom massacred. Mordecai asked Esther to help by asking the king to spare the lives of the Jews. Y'all this king was so conceited that it was against the law for Esther to even approach him without being summoned. This was punishable by death. She realized that maybe God had placed her in the position specifically for this purpose. Esther put on her big girl panties, got cute, risked her life, and approached him anyway. He heard her out and spared the Jews. What did we learn from Esther? I learned that any and everything that God has given you can and should be used for His glory. Did God make you physically attractive? Use that! Are you funny? Are you an excellent speaker? Did God give you a position of authority? Esther shows us that you have to "use what you got to get what you want," like Diamond said. Don't worry about who Diamond is if you don't already know. Amen.

READ TODAY: EPHESIANS 4:15-16

THE AUDACITY!

The audacity! – an exclamation used when you cannot believe that someone feels bold enough to be as rude, disrespectful, or intrusive as they are.

Example: Sir, I have not spoken to you since high school. You didn't like or comment when I got married, purchased a home, had a baby or lost my father. But when I congratulate our new VP, Kamala Harris, on my own page…now you have something negative to say? The audacity!

We've all seen the video clips of black people minding their business yet getting harassed in a public place by some random lady, colloquially named Karen, who feels as if we're still on the plantation. I often look at those clips wondering why Karen felt so comfortable in her audacity. How is she this bold? Well, if you could stand on 400+ years of a discriminatory system that was set up so that you always win, you'd probably be just as confident. I know it's sad. But what if I told you that as a believer, you also have a system that is set up for you to win? You do! We have victory in God through Christ. Sin doesn't have dominion over you. Satan has no dominion over you. Death has no dominion over you. Racism has no dominion over you. Depression, Anxiety, and Fear have no dominion over you. The Bible tells us that if **God** is for us, everything else that tries to come against us will lose. We have all of these precious promises, yet so often, we are reluctant to share this good news with others. We lack the boldness, or the audacity, to let others know about this victory that we have in Jesus. If Karen is confident enough that her racist system will protect her in spreading hatred, should we not be even more confident that God's system will protect us in spreading His love?

READ TODAY: EPHESIANS 6:18-20

AUDACITY MUST BE ON SALE TODAY.

Audacity must be on sale today. – a sarcastic way of saying that you wonder how certain rude and/or disrespectful people have acquired their boldness so easily.

Example: Wait, so they thought they could just invade the Capitol, commit treason against a whole nation, and fly back home on a commercial flight without being arrested? Whew chile! Audacity must be on sale today! Audacity must be half off!

I don't know if you saw the slew of videos from January 2021 with people being removed from planes and arrested as they tried to return home after violently attempting to overthrow the government, but they all had one thing in common. Those being arrested absolutely could not believe that they were being treated like criminals. They literally had the audacity to commit the crime, live stream themselves doing it, brag to social media about it, and then act outraged at the fact that someone would charge them with a crime! That's just how much racist favoritism they believed was built into the system on their behalf. So let's talk again about **our favoritism** as believers. Have you ever done something that you were ashamed about? Perhaps you were so ashamed that you didn't even want to pray to God about it. Maybe you assumed that because you had messed up, you had no right to ask God for forgiveness and continued blessings. That's not how God operates. He tells us that we should still come before His throne of grace with **boldness**. This kind of audacity wasn't cheap or on sale, but it was purchased for us at full price by Jesus at Calvary. The devil wants you to curl up in guilt and shame so that you stay away from God whenever you make a mistake. Don't fall for that. Jesus paid for your audacity with His life. Let's thank God today simply for the ability to come to Him boldly.

READ TODAY: HEBREWS 4:16

YOU KNOW WHAT?!?

You know what?!? – an expression you use when you have a lot to say and nothing to say at the same time.

Example: Person A: I am crying because I just broke up with my boyfriend, and my husband wants to help, but he can't figure out what's wrong with me.
Person B: You know what?!?

My mother once told me that reading the Bible makes people smarter. She said that she had known people from rural towns with very little education who began studying the Bible. By talking to them, you would never know that they had stopped their schooling in the 5th grade. These people turned out to be well-versed in a range of topics, not just Biblical, but it all started when they picked up the word of God. The knowledge that they had obtained was simply astounding. "You know **what**?!? How did you even learn **that**?" people would wonder. I always wondered about this particular phenomenon. I have since witnessed it for myself. As great as formal education might be, God knew that everyone wouldn't have equal access to that. Well the word of God is anointed enough to overcome any barrier, including education…so there you have it. It wasn't until recently that I stumbled upon this phenomenon in the Bible. People were astounded at Peter and John's level of wisdom, knowledge, and understanding because they knew that neither one of them were actually educated. They reasoned that Peter and John knew all that they knew because they had been with Jesus. The people were right. They had spent time with Jesus, who was the word made flesh, and it elevated their minds. I say this to anybody who may be self-conscious about their level of education. Jesus chose disciples regardless of their educational status, because He knew the power of spending time with God's word. Can you spend time with His word today?

READ TODAY: ACTS 4:13

I'M IN MY BAG.

I'm in my bag. – a phrase used when a person is diligently focused on their goal in such a way that it's only a matter of time before their hard work pays off.

Example: If y'all don't see me on social media as much, just know it's because I'm in my bag.

When I originally wrote this page, I had just come home from a long day of work. I was tired, my head was hurting, and all I wanted to do was go lay down. I wrote the page anyway, and it was fire! I remember looking at the page and thinking, "Wow, I'm so glad I focused and pushed through. This page is going to help somebody. I'm really in my writing bag tonight!" Chiiillle tell me why my computer crashed, and I lost about five pages that I can't get back? There was no recovery document or iCloud backup. The Time Machine app wouldn't take me back, and somehow the autosave had been turned off. (I know I didn't turn it off, so how was it off?!) Thankfully, it had only been five pages since my last backup, but how are we losing work in the year of our Lord twenty twenty-one?! Now I'm back on the page and not even sure what I wrote. I'm frustrated, but I'm here. I may or may not be crying, but I'm still writing. I'm still in my bag. God has given us all a gift bag. Some will have one gift in their bag, while others may have two or even five gifts in their bag. He expects us to take and use whatever He has given us to produce more. When you use your gift to bring glory to God and to bless others, I can guarantee you that God will turn right around and use that same gift to abundantly bless you as well for being a good and faithful servant. It won't always be easy. The devil is going to try to throw all kinds of discouraging distractions your way when He sees you walking in purpose. That original page was lit. I don't know why it had to get deleted…but God be knowin'. I trust Him enough to stay focused.

READ TODAY: MATTHEW 25:21

THERE'S A LOT TO UNPACK HERE.

There's a lot to unpack here. – what you say when there are multiple layers of an issue that all need to be addressed in order to gain a full understanding of the matter at hand.

Example: Person A: My brother is also my uncle.
Person B: Wow. There's a lot to unpack here.

Have you ever heard of something called emotional baggage? It's when people carry heavy things around with them that they have collected from past experiences. The crazy thing about emotional baggage, is that oftentimes people are carrying around bags full of stuff that they never even packed for themselves. A lot of emotional damage is packed on to us by other people who never figured out how to manage their own. Sometimes these heavy loads are packed on by our own parents. Other times our bags are packed for us by toxic relationships or other life disappointments. Some of us carry around things like fear, anger, bitterness, envy, and insecurity. Unfortunately, so many of us waste time waiting around for the people who packed this stuff to come along and unpack it for us. Listen…you may never get closure or healing from the people who hurt you, so stop waiting around for someone else to make you whole. True healing and wholeness will only come through your relationship with the Lord. He has instructed and empowered us to unpack those ugly things so that we may have room to pack other, more beautiful, things like kindness, humility, patience, and love. I know that a lot has happened to you. I know that a lot was packed on to you. I know that you think that you are obligated to carry that stuff around, but the good news is that Jesus came to take it off your back. He wants to exchange your heavy and burdensome load with something that is much lighter. The "seasoned" saints would tell you to let go and let God! In your prayer time today, give it to Him. I don't know what *it* is for you…but surrender it.

READ TODAY: COLOSSIANS 3:8-15

IT WAS AT THAT MOMENT...

It was at that moment... – a storytelling device used to describe the exact moment in which the main character reaches an important realization. When the lightbulb goes off.

Example: ...and it was at that moment that Sheila realized why her friends told her not to eat the entire brownie.

In therapy, they call it a breakthrough. Wait a minute...they call it a breakthrough in church too! *runs lap around sanctuary* Breakthrough is that moment when a person's understanding of a matter graduates from one level to the next. Sometimes a breakthrough is needed mentally or emotionally. Sometimes a financial or health-related breakthrough is needed. Either way, breakthrough is that moment when you make it to the other side of whatever wall or obstacle was standing in the way of your forward progress. Getting to the other side is sometimes as simple as turning the knob of an unlocked door and walking from one room into another. Other times, it's like playing one of those "saferoom" games where you have to solve a difficult riddle to figure out that the key is actually under the mannequin's typewriter! No matter the type of breakthrough you stand in need of, and no matter the level of difficulty you face, one thing remains universal. You will have an extremely difficult time trying to breakthrough or unlock any door in a room that is pitch black. We waste so much time fumbling around in a dark room trying to figure out how to get out on our own, when God has supplied us with the light switch *and* has already paid the power bill. Jesus is the **way**, the **truth**, and the **light** that is needed to break you through any wall that you may encounter.

READ TODAY: ISAIAH 60:1

YOU TRIED IT...

You tried it... – a way to give somebody credit for having the audacity to attempt something that had a very low possibility of success.

Example: Modern-Day Grandmothers: No, I will not watch your kids on Friday night because you want to be in these streets doing hoodrat stuff with your friends. Grandma will be busy doing hoodrat stuff with her own friends. You tried it, though.

I'm not going to lie to you. It's not always easy doing things God's way. Have you ever gotten the bright idea that you'd be better off doing things the way that you want to do them instead? I mean, God is always trying to teach us pesky little lessons like patience, humility, gratitude, discipline, and trust. Wouldn't it be easier if we just fenagled a few things here and there? There's a story in the Bible of a son who had the sheer audacity to request his inheritance from his father while the man was still living. He thought he'd be better off in life if he could just go off and live the way that he wanted to live with his new money. It wasn't much later that life had him completely burned out, broke, busted, and disgusted. He tried it! Thankfully, he remembered that his father was yet alive and well. He returned home and was welcomed by his father with open arms. This story clearly symbolizes us with God. We run off thinking things will be better only to find out that life is a hot mess outside of the will of our Father. I'm just glad that He never stops us from coming back. I imagine God opening His arms to embrace us while saying, "Aww...you tried it." I don't know what it is you ran off and tried, but let this be a reminder that you can still come back home.

READ TODAY: LUKE 15:17-24

THE ACCURACY!

The accuracy! – an exclamation used whenever a post does a great job of depicting or imitating one of life's realities.

Example: *Posts parody video of a 5-year-old who is coming up with every reason under the sun to stay up past bed time.*
Parent: The accuracy! This is my child every night!

Imagine a target/bullseye. If I shoot at the target but sometimes I hit it, and sometimes I don't, my skills are said to be unreliable. If I hit the target every time, but sometimes I hit it at the top, sometimes I hit it at the bottom, and sometimes I hit it in the center, my skills are said to be reliable but inaccurate. If I hit the target every time and always in the center, this means that my skills are both accurate and reliable. I said all that to say, that the Holy Spirit's skills are accurate and reliable. His job is to lead us into all truth, which makes Him, by nature, very accurate. He's actually 100% accurate and 100% reliable, so why is it that we still tend to question His ability to lead is us in the right direction? Has the Holy Spirit ever been trying to show you something as clear as day, but you acted like you were still confused? Maybe it was because you didn't really want the truth. Maybe you wanted the outcome that you desired, even if it wasn't God's will. Let's put some respeck on the Holy Spirit and His accuracy by listening next time. Let's pray and ask God for help recognizing the Holy Spirit's voice.

READ TODAY: JOHN 16:13

OMW

OMW – an abbreviation for "on my way."

Example: I was supposed to be there 30 minutes ago. I sent
them a text saying "omw," but honestly, I'm still in
the bathtub.

Nobody is perfect. Don't let these people fool you. I don't
care how happy they seem on Instagram. I don't care how "together"
their lives seem to be from the pulpit. I don't care how smart, rich, or
important they look. I don't care how many life hacks they post on
Pinterest. I don't care how many matchy-matchy family photos they
post up where everyone is smiling including the dog. Nobody is
perfect, and nobody's family is perfect. We are **all** on a journey. The
older I get, the more I am realizing that life is more about the journey
than the destination. Do I have goals? Absolutely. Do I want my
business to prosper? Definitely. Would I love to sell a million books
and never have to worry about money again? Totally. I'm not there
yet, but I'm on my way. Don't get discouraged by the fact that you're
not there. Be encouraged by the fact that you are on your way. The
journey may not be easy, but it will be worth it. We have to trust God
enough to know that He is leading us on the path that is the best
possible route for us. So many of us feel that we can't enjoy life until
we get "there." This is a trick of the enemy, because as long as you are
living in human flesh, you will never reach the destination of perfection
because you aren't Jesus. Yet we must continue to press on in the
direction of perfection. I know it sounds crazy, but every single day
that you are on your way to better is a blessing and it should be
appreciated. Let's pray today and ask God to show us the beautiful
parts of the journey that perhaps we have missed.

READ TODAY: PHILIPPIANS 3:12-14

I'M SHOOK.

I'm shook. – an expression meaning that some unexpected discovery has affected you in such a way that has shaken you to your core.

Example: Y'all! They just shot Ricky Baker in an alleyway! He was only a couple of months away from leaving for college to play football. I'm shook!

When a person is shook, it means that they are troubled, confused, and often scared. If you live long enough, you will have moments where it feels like everything you have known has been shaken up and turned upside down. Pause. No lie…I just found out that my biggest crush passed away back in 2015. I'm not kidding. I literally paused while writing this paragraph to check something on IG and saw a post of his sister referring to him as her angel. No! I spent several years secretly in love with this guy back in the day! I'm really shook. Wow. Okay, God. If You want me to personally experience the devotions, just say that! Where were we? Oh, yes. If you live long enough, I can guarantee that some shaking will occur. The best way to handle it is proactively. If your foundation is solid *before* the shaking, it means that you can survive it without crumbling or collapsing amidst the turmoil. **Now** is the time to build your life on a solid foundation. Now is the time to get your prayer life together. Now is the time to get deep into your word. It's easier to secure the foundation of a building when everything is calm. It's hard to fix a foundation while the natural disaster is actually occurring. When storms come, that's not the time to be trying to remember how to pray. That's not the time to be confused about God's promises. I think the saints of yesteryear put it like this: Stay ready, so you don't have to get ready. What are you doing to secure your foundation today?

READ TODAY: MATTHEW 7:24-27

YOU BIG MAD, HUH?

You big mad, huh? – a patronizing question you ask to an angry person in order to make them even more angry.

Example: So the Falcons blew a 30-point lead against the Alabama Crimson Tide, and now you're not picking up the phone when I call? Oh you big mad, huh?

I think we can all agree that anger is a slippery slope. Although it is a natural emotion that any one of us may be subject to having, the Bible is extremely specific in telling us what we should do with our anger. That's because unchecked anger is dangerous and even life-threatening. It can cause a person to say damaging things that they can never take back. Anger can lead us to make terrible decisions with lasting consequences. It causes some people to lose control and become violent. Some anger is so intense that people lose their lives over it. People who are chronically angry can develop health issues because of their own stress. The Bible tells us a few important things about anger. It tells us that "anger rests in the bosom of a fool" and that you should not "let the sun go down on your wrath." It also tells us to "be angry and sin not." The Bible never tells us that anger itself is the sin. It's all about how we respond to it. Are you allowing your anger to rest in your bosom? Do you let it hang around for long periods of time? Are you carrying your anger from one day into the next? I've heard several successfully married couples say that they try not to go to bed angry. That's biblical. When anger comes, the trick is to get rid of it as quickly as you can. The longer it hangs around, the more damage it is likely to do. Also, we must be careful not to do anything crazy when we are angry. Don't let it cause you to sin. If you are angry, it's a good time to pause and **wait** until you are able to function rationally. Pro Tip: Prayer will cool you down real quick.

READ TODAY: EPHESIANS 4:26

…WON'T LET ME BE GREAT

…won't let me be great – a phrase used to explain what or who is preventing you from doing better; an excuse.

Example: I need to lose 10lbs, but my mama and her fried chicken won't let me be great.

Newsflash! The devil doesn't want you to be great! Oh wait a minute, we already knew that. You are sadly mistaken if you think that you don't have an adversary, aka an enemy. One of Satan's biggest goals is to keep **you** from reaching the place where you are walking in your full purpose and embracing your true identity in God. Do you feel like things are going haywire all around you? Does it seem like a million issues are hitting you all at once? Did you lose a loved one, rip your favorite jeans, find out you owe some huge bill, wreck your car, and get some bad news from your doctor all in one day? Do you feel as if there are literally demonic forces that are doing all they can do to prevent you from being great? Here is another newsflash. The devil and his demons like to hang out near doors. When he sees you getting ready to walk through a great door, he begins freaking out and throwing everything (including the kitchen sink) at you in an attempt to get you to turn around and go back. You see, Satan can't actually stop you from going through your door. But all he can do is trick you into changing your own mind about wanting to go through it. So next time it feels like all hell is breaking loose in your life, praise God! It means you are standing close to a major door. Don't turn back. Pray today and ask God for the strength to continue pressing forward. I've drawn a diagram to help.

READ TODAY: 1 CORINTHIANS 16:9

#WFH (2)

#WFH – a hashtag acronym meaning "Work From Home."

Example: Today at work, I watched three episodes of my favorite
show, did three loads of laundry, ran three miles on the
treadmill, and deep conditioned my hair. #WFH

Pray for me y'all. I need deliverance from this spirit of jealousy
that comes over me whenever I hear people talking about how much
more they can accomplish by working from home. Must be nice. Well
anyway, today I want to talk about working **at** home. I'm not talking
about your employment. I'm talking about your real job. Think about
how much work you put in for your employer. Do you keep that same
energy when it comes to working to keep your home together and at
peace? We have seen time and time again where people's careers are
taking off all while their family life is in shambles. The marriage is
falling apart, and the children are acting out and failing in school. Have
you ever heard of pastors who get so busy with their work at church
that they don't have time to pay attention to what's going on at home?
This message is a reminder that when it comes to your job, you are
dispensable. The pandemic taught us that employers are quick to lay
people off if things go awry. The pandemic/quarantine also taught us
how important it is to have a good home environment where you can
actually stand to be present. Sadly, domestic violence calls skyrocketed
once quarantine hit because people were forced to be at home. It is
possible for your home to be a place of peace and beauty, but you must
work **for** home. And no, I'm not talking about kicking everybody out!
Prayer is work. Fasting is work. Communication is work. Forgiveness
is work. Going to therapy is work. Be proactive. Don't just be lazy
and hope for the best. That's how things fall apart. And don't scoff at
this if you don't scoff at the assignments your boss gives you on your
job. Don't give up on your "homework." This was worth re-visiting.

READ TODAY: PROVERBS 24:3-4

PICK ME

Pick Me – (noun) a person who is so desperate to look superior to his or her counterparts that they are willing to throw others under the bus in an attempt to gain brownie points, usually from the opposite sex or from another race.

Example: Person A: The problem with most women is that they don't want to cook and clean for a man anymore simply because they work a full-time job and pay all the bills. I do both! Person B: Whew chile, it must be so hard being a Pick Me.

If you've ever seen a Pick Me in action, it's quite sad. It's like watching a dog doing tricks and hoping to be thrown a bone or be given a pat on the head. All they want to hear is, "you're not like all the other (women/men/black people/white people/Christians/etc.)" When you see people desperate in this way, subconscious self-hatred is often a factor. This is why they must seek validation from those who they deem to be on a higher level than themselves. I hope you aren't a Pick Me, but just in case you are a person who struggles with the need to receive validation from others, let me help. First of all, stop placing other human beings on such high pedestals. Everyone has their faults. Theirs may be different from yours or harder to see, but their validation of you (or lack thereof) is not some grand determining factor of your value. You need to understand that you were already "picked" by God. You were chosen by Him a long time ago, and that's all the validation that you need in order to know that your value is very high. Why does it matter if other people see your value or not? Have you ever thought about the fact that maybe those people need their own eyes checked? All you need to do is continue to fight the good fight to become the best possible version of yourself. If you are doing that, then you can rest in knowing that God sees how dope you are and will reward you for sowing those good seeds.

READ TODAY: EPHESIANS 1:3-4

131

DISCLAIMER

Disclaimer – a legal term that is used, usually in advance, to deny responsibility for a potentially harmful situation. On social media, it is often used to clear up potential confusion in a storyline.

Example: I dare you to go slap your mama and record her reaction! Disclaimer: I will not be held responsible for any resulting hospital bills that you may incur as a result of this dare.

I have a disclaimer that I want to give to anyone reading this book. Some of you may be new to the faith while others of you may be O.G.s in the game. My goal was to write a book that could be useful no matter where you are in your Christian journey. I think one of the biggest issues with modern-day Christianity, is that it is often presented in a way that makes people feel that once they follow Christ, their lives become perfect. I meannnn…yes and no. It's perfect in the sense that everything, whether good or bad, is being used to build you up and bless you. This doesn't mean that every day will feel like sunshine and roses with unicorns pooping out rainbows with a pot of Skittles at the end. This is where people get confused. Following Christ allows you the opportunity to be **victorious** over anything that life throws at you, but life is still going to keeping life-ing. Sadly, too many people become disillusioned and turn away from God when hardships arise. In the Bible there is a story about seeds. The seeds were planted in different environments. The ones that were planted in good soil thrived and produced a good harvest. One set of seeds initially seemed like it would thrive, but soon withered away once it had to face the harsh elements. The seeds represent God's word, the ground represents our hearts, and the environment represents life. I wanted to give this disclaimer, so that you can be sure that you are receiving God's word and following Christ from a pure heart. It's not a magic pill that prevents you from ever having problems, but it is the answer to them.

READ TODAY: MATTHEW 13:3-8

...AND ION LIKE DET.

...and ion like det. – a popular phrase that literally means, "...and I don't like that." It is usually preceded by something that has been a source of disdain for the user.

Example: Some of y'all still use the bathroom and don't wash your hands, and ion like det.

Let me tell y'all a story about something that ion like. In the year 2020, we experienced a pandemic. A global health crisis hit due to this extremely dangerous and contagious virus that was spreading rapidly across the world. The pandemic led to...you guessed it...pandemonium. And do you know what these people did? People in America started fighting over toilet tissue. Yes, toilet tissue! ToylaTisha! People were freaking out because many of us were asked to quarantine at home, and the stores were running low. Chile it was a mess. Some people were getting into physical altercations with strangers. Other super greedy people started stockpiling the tissue in their homes. While others were really in need, they had a year's supply in their basement, which made the problem worse. Other morally corrupt people were buying up the tissue to price-gouge and re-sell it for some ridiculous amount to get rich, which made the problem even worse. But what takes the cake is a video of a young woman with a cart full of tissue trying to snatch more tissue out of some poor elderly woman's hands. We acted a fool, and ion like det. I **really** don't like how we, as individuals and as a nation, responded to crisis. I'm lowkey embarrassed and ashamed about how we acted over that tissue! When you find yourself in the midst of a crisis, do you start acting desperate and crazy? Do you forget that God has taken care of you this whole time and will continue to do so? Next time you find yourself on the verge of freaking out about something, remember how foolish those people looked fighting over...tissue. Bye!

READ TODAY: PSALM 37:25

IMMA SIT THIS ONE OUT.

Imma sit this one out. – what you say when you feel that it is wise not to interject yourself into a discussion.

Example: Person A: Hey, what are your thoughts on Beyoncé?
Person B: Imma sit this one out.

A wise person once said, "We ain't gotta know what you think about every single thing." Okay, it's me…I'm the wise person, and that's the delusion of social media. It confuses people into thinking that their (often uninformed) opinion on every single issue must be shared with the public. This is how and why people get "canceled." All it takes is one ignorant tweet or FB post from 10+ years ago, and someone can find it and use it against you. People have lost contracts, jobs, elections, and sponsorships this way. It doesn't even matter that you were 19 and didn't know better. You may very well have evolved since then, but once you have put something out there, it's very hard to take it back. This goes for social media posting as well as life in general. The Bible talks about the importance of having a disciplined tongue. If you live long enough, life will humble you. You were so sure about how Tracy should have handled her situation, and you talked about her like a dog. It was clear cut and completely black and white. But now that you find yourself in the exact same situation, you are suddenly able to see all of the gray areas. I understand that there may be a "hot topic" that you want to weigh in on, but don't get in such a rush to jump into the conversation that you forget to exercise wisdom. Allow the Holy Spirit to guide you. There will be times when you want to add your two cents so badly, but the Holy Spirit says to sit it out. There will be times when your voice is needed, but there is nothing wrong with pausing and taking time to hear from God to make sure that your words reflect Him. You don't have to be first. Let's practice this today.

READ TODAY: PROVERBS 21:23

WE ARE NOT THE SAME.

We are not the same. – a phrase used to highlight the differences between two opposite ways of thinking.

Example: Y'all are worried about looking rich. I am busy creating my business plan so that I can actually build wealth that will last for generations to come. We are not the same.

Have you ever noticed that some people get uncomfortable when they see you trying to do or be better in life? It's like they want us to stay the same, but when the truth of God's word starts transforming your life, there is no way that you can continue to see things the same way that you did in the past. Maybe you used to fight, but now you simply de-escalate and walk away. Maybe you used to trick your money off in the club buying bottles for everyone. Now you are saving up for a down payment on a new home. Maybe they used to be able to text you at 3am and you'd throw on some sweats and be in their bed in 15 minutes flat. Now at 3am, you are good and sleep with your phone on the "Do Not Disturb" setting. It seems like people would be happy about your growth and maturity, but this is not always the case. Sometimes your foolishness was benefitting them in one way or the other or making them feel more comfortable about their own foolishness. The main thing you need to do is be mentally prepared for the changes. It can be hurtful to know that certain people who you have known forever will now reject you for trying to improve yourself. Don't take it too personally, these were probably the people that you didn't need in your immediate circle anyway. God be knowin'. We are no longer the same, and for this we give God praise. Let's pray today and ask God to send us the friends who will encourage us to strive for greater.

READ TODAY: ROMANS 12:2

MAKE THIS PUBLIC!

Make this public! – a comment made by a person who wishes to share a status on FB but is unable to do so based on the author's privacy settings. The person is requesting that the post be made "public" and therefore shareable.

Example: Person A: *posts an inspirational message or meme*
                Person B: Make this public!

Vegans won't shut up about being vegan. Keto people won't shut up about Keto. Sports fans won't shut up about their team. People in love won't shut up about their partner. Can someone explain to me why we can speak openly about almost everything except our relationship with the Lord? Do people even know you're a follower of Christ? People who **claim** to follow Christ have given Him such a bad name over time, that we now feel as if mentioning Jesus is like cussing. Sadly, so many people use "Christianity" as the vehicle to spew their judgement, hatred, and condemnation, when Jesus was actually all about loving people. It's really one of the biggest shames of all time. The Jesus that they have shown the world is truly not the Jesus of the Bible. How do we fix that? How do we make the real Jesus public? It's up to us to let our lights shine in such a way that the love of Jesus is easy to see. It's not just making social media posts. It's not even standing on the corner with a megaphone. We have to tighten up on our own **example** if we are hoping to make Jesus public. We have to love more and give more. We have to follow God's word and ensure that we walk in our purpose and receive our promises. We have to build real **relationships** with people. Once they see how your walk with Christ has worked for you, they will be much more likely to give Him a try. We all have an individual responsibility to represent Jesus well and to make Him public for someone else to see.

READ TODAY: MATTHEW 5:16

TELL US HOW YOU REALLY FEEL.

Tell us how you really feel. – a response to someone who has shared their true feelings on a matter without holding back.

Example: Person A: I can't stand this job, my co-workers, or my boss.
Person B: Oh wow. Tell us how you really feel.

Do you know what really grinds my gears? There's something about being around fake people that I just can't get jiggy with. Maybe that's why I worked so hard to be self-employed. Having to share space with people who are fake will run you low. You never know if what they are saying is sincere or if they are just being disingenuous. They may act like a friend while in your presence yet talk about you like a dog in your absence. Do you ever wonder why phony people are the way that they are? My theory is that fake people can't tell you how they really feel because they know that they are wrong. Think about it. If you operate from a pure place in your heart, there is no reason to fake the funk. But if you operate from a place that is messy and filled with things like jealousy, bitterness, and prejudice, then you obviously want that to remain hidden. Fake people are dishonest people who know that they are wrong but are not willing to do the work required to purify their hearts. If you find yourself consistently having to be fake with people, my advice to you is to find a way to operate in truth and **love**. Don't allow yourself to create a "safe space" for lies and resentment. My advice to everyone else is to stop being enablers. If they are being a fake friend to someone else and talking about them behind their back to you, guess what! They are probably talking about **you** behind your back too! Do not enable them by listening. Let's pray today that God would reveal any fake friends or acquaintances and also that we might have the courage to operate in truth and love towards one another.

READ TODAY: PROVERBS 12:22

"SORRY TO THIS MAN."
– KEKE PALMER

Sorry to this man. – a phrase that became popular on social media after actress Keke Palmer participated in a lie detector test for *Vanity Fair* Magazine in 2019. She was shown a picture of former Vice President Dick Cheney but said she did not know who he was. She pushed the picture away while saying, "Sorry to this man." The internet ran with it.

Example: My ex tried to speak to me in Target, but I kept walking like I didn't see him. Sorry to this man.

Have you ever owed someone an apology? Perhaps you owe someone an apology right now. I think we all know what it feels like when someone has done us dirty but refuses to acknowledge it. Why is it so hard to apologize? Some people find it difficult because of pride. It requires a certain level of humility to admit that you aren't a perfect person. Others prefer to be "non-confrontational" and feel as if it's better to just sweep things under the rug than to deal with them head on. These are all tricks of the enemy because he knows how powerful a simple apology can be. Do you know how many relationships could have been mended and how many homes could have been kept together if people would have simply humbled themselves and sincerely apologized for their mistakes? Do you know how much unity has been disrupted by people's refusal to apologize? Actually, it may be written somewhere in the Black parent's handbook never to apologize to your kids. But let's talk about just how important it is. Jesus Himself was preaching one day and basically said that if you pull up to church with your offering, but remember that you have beef with your brother, just put the offering down, go make things right with him, and then come back and give the offering. I mean daaaag! God don't even want your lil' stanky offering till you apologize. Think about that!

READ TODAY: MATTHEW 5:23-24

SIPS TEA

Sips Tea - used to indicate that a person is intrigued by some sort of drama going on amongst others. The sipping of the tea indicates that you are ingesting the gossip.

Example: Person A: They act like the perfect couple on IG, but she just found out his side chick is pregnant and keeping it!
Person B: Wait a minute! Say what now?! *sips tea*

Okay, so "the tea" is another name for gossip. It comes from the idea that women in England would sit around drinking tea and chatting about the affairs of others. One of the most popular memes of all time surfaced in 2014 when a photo of Kermit the Frog sipping tea and saying "but that's none of my business..." went wildly viral. There are three different kinds of people when it comes to tea. There are those who literally ask for the tea, those who supply and pour the tea, and those who don't ask for the tea, but sip it anyway when it is offered to them. All three of these people are dead wrong. I'll be the first to admit that I may not request or pour the tea, but I don't always turn it down when it's piping hot and being offered. I am **much** better than I used to be though. Do you know what helped me? It was that moment when I became the tea. When I went through a divorce almost no one talked **to** me, but I found out that people had shonuff been talking **about** me! I didn't find out until later that the tea about me had been contaminated with false information, slander, people's own conspiracy theories, and flat-out lies. It was very hurtful to know that people were having entire conversations about me and enjoying it, yet never took the time to reach out and ask if I was even okay. God had to show me through experience how important it is **not** to spread gossip or even enable it by listening. It may not be as entertaining, but consider praying for people and checking on them instead of providing more wood for the fire.

READ TODAY: PROVERBS 26:20

BUT THAT'S NONE OF MY BUSINESS...

But that's none of my business... – an addendum used as a way to throw shade and then absolve yourself from the responsibility of it.

Example: Some of y'all brothers can't go swimming because your "haircut" will smudge, but that's none of my business...

How do we determine what is our business and what is not? This is an extremely important conversation. Most of you have probably experienced a time when you regretted ever involving yourself in a situation. It wasn't until you were knee deep in the cow manure that you realized that none of it had anything to do with you! There were other times, however, where maybe you regretted your nonchalant attitude. You saw all along that your friend was headed for trouble, yet you said nothing and watched them get hurt. This is where it really comes in handy to have an ongoing relationship with the Holy Spirit. Don't be so quick to jump into everything, but don't be so quick to turn a blind eye to everything either. Pray and ask God to show you whether this is something that He has deemed to be your business. Sometimes God will give you an assignment, and it may be your words of wisdom that help save a life. Other times the whole thing is just one big distraction from Satan to get you off course. Pray, and then follow the Holy Spirit's guidance. It's not as complicated as it may seem. It's just the fact that we are so busy looking at things naturally, that we don't take those necessary spiritual steps to make the best call. Let's pray today that God would reveal to us exactly which business belongs to us.

READ TODAY: PHILIPPIANS 1:9-10

AND I'D DO IT AGAIN!

And I'd do it again! – a storytelling device in which a person describes a wild story using the 3rd person point of view, only to reveal a plot twist in which the narrator was actually the main character.

Example: Y'all, so I'm in the grocery store and I see this young woman trying to snatch some toilet tissue from an elderly woman's hands. Another lady saw the whole thing, got angry, snatched the young woman's wig off, and said, "How does it feel to get your stuff snatched?!" The whole thing was crazy...AND I'D DO IT AGAIN! *holds up wig*

Okay, today's message is really simple. Do you find yourself continuing to make the same mistakes over and over again? Is it always some girl with a big butt and a smile that gets you caught up? Is it always a tall, dark, and handsome brother that has you running through your savings? The old saints used to say, "When you know better, you do better." The Bible tells us that in all things, we should seek to gain an understanding. Superman **understood** the effect that kryptonite had on him, so he knew to stay away from it. Do you really understand the effect that certain things are having on you? Perhaps if you truly understood how the bacon was clogging your arteries, you wouldn't keep eating those double bacon cheeseburgers wrapped in bacon. If you find yourself struggling to get out of bad cycles, take some time to do a deep study. What about me makes me susceptible to falling into that trap? What is the bait? Where is the switch? What triggers should I avoid? What are the residual effects that this cycle has on me? Is it worth it? Am I being a fool? Is my continued participation distracting me from something better? Do I need to speak to a professional about this? Write these questions down somewhere and refer to them as needed! You're not stuck, you just need strategy.

READ TODAY: PROVERBS 26:11

...HIT DIFFERENT

...hit different – used to highlight how changing variables effect a particular situation.

Example: That light bill hit different when ya kids home for the summer.

I know it's bad grammar, but relax. It's just social media...we do this. But let's talk about life. One thing I have learned about life...it's gonna hit. Y'all why is the spellcheck giving me those red lines and trying to tell me that "gonna" isn't a real word? I don't receive that! I digress...life...it hits. If you live long enough, you'll understand that sometimes life comes at you swinging uppercuts. If you aren't careful, it will knock you out. The fact that you may have to deal with the trials and tribulations of life is not a reflection on how much God favors you. Don't let anybody tell you that. The Bible says that it rains on the just **and** the unjust. What's important is your relationship with Him. He didn't say that rain wouldn't come, but He did promise that He would be a safe place for us run to in the time of a storm. I promise you that life will hit different with God. I can put two people in identical situations. One gets to go through it with the help of the Lord. The other rejects God and has to go through it alone. Whew chile, just typing that gave me chills. I can't imagine how much harder life must be when people reject their Help. I just want to encourage you today. Your life may not feel like sunshine every day, but it's okay. You have the perfect umbrella.

READ TODAY: PSALM 91:1-7

"IT'S ABOVE ME NOW."
-Craigory Levon Brooks II

It's above me now. – a quote from a viral video in which a hotel employee calmly refused a room to a woman who had chosen to use a racial slur when speaking to him. She begged to be given a room, while the employee let her know that her case was now "above" him and would have to be dealt with at another time by upper management. He politely informed her that there was a Best Western next door.

Example: Parent: So how did you do on your final exam?
　　　　　Student: It's above me now.

This quote swept the nation. If you have never seen the video, just Google it. Countless memes, songs, and dances were created to celebrate the fact that it's above us now. This was ministry. Millions of people were reminded that instead of freaking out over situations beyond our control, it is better to put them in the hands of the Lord. Like the gentlemen in the video, we can rest easy and remain unbothered knowing that the Man Upstairs will fight on our behalf. We only make matters worse by freaking out or trying to fight battles that don't even belong to us. Think of it like someone on a lake who has gone too far and doesn't know how to swim. If they kick, fight, and lose their cool, they will surely drown. If they let go, lean back, and relax, they can float. I don't know who needs to hear this, but whatever it is, give it to God and rest. Stop tossing and turning and losing sleep trying to figure out how you can get the outcome that you prefer. Trust that God will take care of it and you. In your prayer time today, surrender those burdens up to God and leave them where they belong…above you.

READ TODAY: 2 CHRONICLES 20:15-17

SUNDRESS SEASON

Sundress Season – also known as "sundress szn," this is a time of year when it gets warm enough for women to begin wearing their sundresses. Men get especially excited for sundress season because sundresses typically help accentuate a woman's figure, particularly her booty.

Example: I'm grateful that the Lord allowed me to live to see another sundress season!

This one doesn't need a whole lot of explanation. It's beginning to warm up. The temperatures are going up, and the amount of fabric is going down. Sundresses are super cute and comfy. Women love them, and so do men. I just want to issue a warning about sundress season. It's not harmless. Be extremely careful, guys, that you are not allowing your eyes to get you in trouble. Now you may not be able to help but notice a beautiful woman and her figure, but don't let it cause you to slip and fall into lust. Lust can lead to some terrible situations. It happened with David in the Bible. As much as David loved the Lord, he still let his eyes get him caught up. He just so happened to see Bathsheba when she was bathing and next thing he knew, he had fallen down an entire rabbit hole of even more sin that led to the death of two others. If David wasn't immune to the foolery, what makes you think that you are? You're only human. Lust can happen to the best of us. Be very intentional about how you enter into this season. If you are single, please do not let lustful eyes choose your partner for you. If you are married or in a committed relationship, please don't put that on the line trying to follow after some nice-looking sundress booty. And ladies, if he didn't slide in your DMs until after you posted that sundress…oh ok. Go ahead and pray today that sundress season doesn't catch you slippin'.

READ TODAY: 2 SAMUEL 11:2-5

HEY BIG HEAD...

Hey big head... – how people who are no longer in your life greet you when they miss you and want you back.

Example: Y'all, Rodrick just slid in my DMs talking about, "Hey big head." I rebuke you Satan. Not today!

Have you ever been in a situation where somebody did you dirty? I have. A big reason why I never seek my own revenge is because I know that God's got me. I also know that it's only a matter of time before my absence does the work on my behalf. When a person begins taking your presence for granted and harming you in the process, they have lost sight of how much favor is being added to their life because you are in it. Don't be surprised if they try to pop back up. It may be weeks, months, or years later. By now, they have tried other stuff and realized that it simply doesn't compare to how they were being blessed when they were with you. Here is my advice to you...because you may be the good thing, or you may be the one who lost a good thing. If you were the one who was treated badly, first of all, forgive. Always forgive because harboring resentment and unforgiveness in your heart can turn you into someone that you don't want to be. Secondly, seek God's guidance in all things. Sometimes people make mistakes and need to experience your absence in order to better appreciate your presence. Other times, that "hey big head" is nothing more than Satan's strategy to pull you back into the same old cycle of foolishness that keeps you distracted from your purpose. If you are wondering whether to allow someone access into your life, prayer and even fasting may be in order. If you were the person who messed around and lost a good thing, my advice to you is to seek God's guidance as well. If that relationship is meant to be restored, God can give you wisdom and a strategy on how to enter through the front door instead of trying to slither in through some partially cracked window on the side of the house.

READ TODAY: MATTHEW 10:13-16

HOW IT STARTED VS. HOW IT'S GOING

How It Started vs. How It's Going – a social media challenge in which a user posts two images side by side. The first image shows the beginning of a thing such as a relationship, a physical transformation, or a business venture. The second image shows the present state of that thing, usually highlighting growth or change.

Example: Photo A: High School sweethearts taking mall pictures in matching Tommy Hilfiger outfits and herringbone chains. Photo B: Same couple 25 years later, now married with 3 grown children, a beautiful home, and still in love. Caption: How It Started vs How It's Going

If your "How It Started" continues to look identical to your "How It's Going," we have a problem...unless, of course, you are a vampire, and we are talking about aging. Well...we're not into preaching perfection over here, but we do preach progress. There was a man in the Bible who suffered from an infirmity for 38 years. He stayed in the same place, doing the same thing, for a long time...with no results. Jesus saw the man lying there and had to ask him if he even wanted to be healed? Instead of giving a straightforward answer, he began to tell Jesus his excuse for not making any progress by now. Such are some of us. When Jesus comes into our lives, we don't take hold of what He is trying to offer us. Instead, we offer Him excuses as to why we cannot do better. The simple truth is that we **can** do better with the help of the Lord. A practical thing you can do to keep progress at the forefront, is to set realistic goals that have specific timelines as well as progress that can actually be quantified. Today, let's pray and ask God to show us the areas in which we need to grow. Let's also ask Him to show us His vision for our progress so that we can write it down and continue to keep track of it.

READ TODAY: JOHN 5:5-8

#BLESSED

#Blessed – a popular hashtag often used when people are grateful for something happening in their lives.

Example: I just bought myself a brand-new BMW! #blessed

What does it mean to be blessed? Let's explore that, shall we? If you post up a picture from your vacation in Santorini, Greece and say that you are #blessed, you did not lie. But does that mean I'm not blessed if I couldn't take a vacation this year? If you post up a picture with your new shiny engagement ring and say that you are #blessed, you (hopefully) did not lie. But does that mean I'm not blessed if I'm still single? See how confusing that might be for an onlooker who is living an opposing reality? I love that we express gratitude to God when favorable things happen in our lives. That is in order. But let's be careful not to attach the label of being blessed only when we have material things to show. Blessings come in so many forms. For a person who was struggling with inner turmoil, finding peace was the biggest blessing they could have ever hoped to receive. There's no photo to post for that. You may be wondering what my point is. I want you to live a life of more gratitude and less comparison. When you are walking with God, you are blessed, period! On the good days, be thankful. On the hard days, be thankful. For the small things, be thankful. For the big things, be thankful. Gratitude is a posture. You are not blessed because of what you have, you are blessed because of **who** you are connected to. Just open up your eyes to see it. When you pray today, just start thanking Him for any and everything you can think of. Sometimes I do this, and it gets out of hand. I just start off thanking Him for things as innocuous as gas money...and hands that can pump gas...and a car that works...and eyes to drive with...the next thing you know, I'm in the floor rolling around and crying like a baby.

READ TODAY: 1 THESSALONIANS 5:18

#SELFCARE

#SelfCare– a hashtag used to promote the idea that people should be more intentional about doing good things for themselves.

Example: Today I will be turning my phone off and enjoying a day at the spa. #SelfCare

Okay, so if you have spent any time at all on Al Green's internet in the last decade or so, you probably know that everybody is talking about self-care. Do you know whhhyyyyyy everybody is always talking about self-care? It's because we need to hear it! Some of us do, anyway. Some of us get so utterly wrapped up in taking care of others, that we neglect to take care of ourselves. Have you been so busy taking other people do their doctor visits that you haven't set your own? Have you been so busy making sure that everyone else has the clothes and shoes that they need, that you don't have the energy to shop for yourself? I think what happens for many of us, is that we give the love that we honestly just wish to receive. We treat others how we wish to be treated. That's really beautiful, but I think the problem comes in when we sit and wait for someone to do the same thing for us. If you are naturally nurturing and/or a caretaker, it can be hard to understand why you don't seem to be getting that same treatment in return. I used to wait around for someone to take care of me like I take care of others, and whew chile, I was **sorely** disappointed! Let me help you. The Bible tells us that we must love our neighbors **as** ourselves. Yet we are too busy loving on our neighbors to even love on ourselves. It's admirable, but it ain't biblical at all. And then you wonder why you're feeling rundown and raggedy all the time. Am I preaching to myself today? Absolutely. Today, let's pray and ask God to show us practical ways to achieve better self-care.

READ TODAY: MARK 12:30-31

LINK IN BIO

Link in bio – a phrase used to refer people to the biographical portion of your online profile (usually on Instagram). From there, they can click on a hyperlink that will re-direct them to a website containing further info.

Example: My new devotional book is now available! Link in bio!

Is there a link in your bio? No, I'm not talking about a link in your social media bio. I'm trying to ask a really deep and existential question here! Go with it! When people learn more about you (your figurative bio), do they also learn more about God? Are you linking people back to your Source? When people praise you for your accomplishments, are you re-directing those praises to God, or do you receive all of the glory for yourself? I'm sure you already know that God blesses us to be able to achieve certain things and even to attain certain positions so that we may be better able to show forth glory on His behalf. Do you chalk it all up to your own hard work and discipline, or do you let people know where all of your help comes from? If it weren't for God's grace in granting us certain abilities and opening up certain doors, who knows where we might be? Don't ever let success go to your head. Don't ever forget to use your platform as an occasion to link people to God. Don't ever get to a place where you are ashamed to let your connection to God be known. If you have people looking up to you, make sure to share your special link and re-direct them even farther upward…to the hills from whence cometh your help.

READ TODAY: PSALM 121:1-8

#BODYGOALS

#BodyGoals – a hashtag often used to indicate that someone's physique is admiral and worthy of imitation.

Example: I'm watching these Olympic sprinters, and all I see are #BodyGoals.

Let's talk about #BodyGoals. I'm not talking about our physical bodies. I'm talking about the body of Christ, also known as the church. That's right. We, the followers of Christ, make up the church. The church is much bigger than your local assembly, and it is not a physical location. You and I are the church. Jesus is the "head" of the church, and we are known as His "body" because it is up to us to carry out the functions necessary for the movement and advancement of the gospel. Just like a physical body, each body part has a different, but important function. All parts are needed for a healthy and effective body. Problems arise when certain members of the body do not understand the job that they are in place to do. For instance, my job is not to pastor a church. My job is not to minister through song. My job (a part of it) is to write these lil' daily messages to help strengthen believers and get them in the habit of seeking God on a daily basis. That does not make me any more or less important than any other member of the body. Our #bodygoals should be to familiarize ourselves with the roles that God gave us, commit to functioning in them properly, and most importantly, to operate in **unity and love**. Do you know what your contribution is supposed to be to help move the body of Christ? Are you currently operating in that assignment? If not, what is stopping you? You already know I'm going to suggest that you pray and ask God to make your assignment clear and that He would also grant you the boldness to walk in it without fear.

READ TODAY: 1 CORINTHIANS 12:12-20

IN MY FEELINGS

In my feelings – an expression meaning that a person is currently under the influence of some sort of strong emotion. It usually refers to hurt feelings.

Example: I'm really in my feelings this morning. My baby girl started Kindergarten today, and I have called in sick. I'm just staring at a wall and listening to Sade. I'm not okay!

Feelings are very interesting thangs. We all have them. Feelings are a very important part of the human experience. Without them, what would life even be? But...why are we always so focused on our feelings and not on our knowings? See...spellcheck just proved my point! It's giving me a red line under the word "knowings" but not under the word "feelings." I suppose the plural of knowing isn't even an actual word. Perhaps it's because so many of our lives are steered by how we feel and not by what we know. The problem with being led by your feelings is that feelings a) change b) change and c) change. Today I may feel like giving up on everything. Tomorrow I may feel like being great. So how do we do a better job of being led by our knowings? First, it's important to know where our knowings come from. Everything that we know **for sure** comes from the truth of God's word. If it's true, you will be able to trace it back to what God said either in His written word or in the word that He has spoken to you. What does that tell you? It tells me that it's more important to be in my word than in my feelings. When I'm unsure about something that I'm feeling, I intentionally submerge myself in the word **because that's where my promises are.** I will literally disable my social media and click on the Bible app instead. I won't even watch TV...I'll watch people preaching on YouTube (shoutout Dr. Charles Stanley & G.E. Patterson). I'll pray and then listen for God to speak. The word...get out of your feelings today and into the word!

READ TODAY: JOHN 15:7-8

SUBSCRIBE, SUBSCRIBE, SUBSCRIBE!

Subscribe, subscribe, subscribe! – an expression commonly used by YouTubers who are attempting to increase their viewership in order to generate revenue with their YouTube channel. When people subscribe, they receive notifications when new videos are posted.

Example: YouTuber: Thanks for watching, and don't forget to subscribe, subscribe, subscribe! See you next time!

When you decide to subscribe to something, it means that you believe in it enough to actually follow it. It means that you would like to receive updated content from that particular source on a regular basis. When I was in high school, my older brother gifted me with a subscription to *Black Enterprise Magazine*. A new magazine would come every month, and I would read them cover to cover. That magazine was quite influential in my life, because it showed me the benefits of entrepreneurship. Years later, I am completely self-employed. I said all of this to say, watch who and what you subscribe to. It's very important to follow things or people who will sow positive content into your life. There is no shortage of people who want to tell you how to live your life. One of my friends was, for a time, obsessed with finding love. She read books, listened to a bunch of different relationship podcasts, and followed relationship pages on IG. She wanted to be knowledgeable and prepared. She almost blew a fuse trying to follow the advice of some of these so-called relationship gurus. Half of them can't even keep their own relationships together but want to advise others for views and money. Still others are sincere and gifted by God to help. How do you know the difference? It's best to compare the content with God's word. Does it line up? Don't be fooled by bits and pieces that sound good. Even a broken clock is right twice a day. Pray and ask God for the spiritual discernment to know the difference.

READ TODAY: 1 JOHN 4:1

SEARCH RESULTS

Search Results – a phrase that you will see accompanying a listing of possible answers to your query. Search engines, such as Google, have made it easy to find most people, places, or things.

Example: The search results brought up 5 different wing joints within 5 minutes of here.

Do you have a question? Are you searching for something? Do you need to figure something out? Think of Jesus as the ultimate search result. I know it sounds corny, but hear me out. In 1998, Larry Paige and Sergey Brin founded a company called Google. They are now the 6th and 7th richest people in the world, respectively. The company itself is still going strong and in 2020, reported $182,527,000,000 in revenue! They currently employ almost 140,000 people. All of this because they figured out an easy way to help people find the information that they were looking for. I, for one, am quick to ask Google something. Shoot, I don't even argue with people anymore. I just google it and squash it. As a matter of fact, I just asked Google if the verb "google" (meaning to google something) should capitalized or not. So clearly, we place a high value on answers. Meanwhile, we have Jesus, who has/is the answer to literally everything, yet we often forget about Him. He told us point-blank that we could ask, and it would be given. He told us that we could seek, and we would find. He even said that if we knock on a door, it would be opened for us. Don't get me wrong, Google is an awesome tool, but it is no match for Jesus. Google takes on no responsibility for what you do with the answers you find there. Google makes no guarantee that what you find there is even 100% true. But you can rest-assured that if God gave you an answer, it is true and in the very best interest of your life and future. It is better to trust in God than to have confidence in Google.

READ TODAY: MATTHEW 7:7-8

#WINNING

#Winning – a word popularized by Charlie Sheen around 2011. Although going through a tumultuous time in his personal life, he used the word multiple times, across several different interviews, to refer to himself. The internet ran with it.

Example: They just gave me an extra nugget by accident! #winning

When Charlie Sheen repeatedly announced that he was "winning," it seemed quite ironic to many of us. He had been dealing with drug addiction, rehab, and even some domestic violence charges. Perhaps he was in an advanced stage of denial, but maybe we can still extract a lesson here. We have to understand that our victory is not determined by whether or not things are going "well" for us in the moment. Our victory isn't even determined by our own good performance in the game. We are winning and have already won for one reason and one reason only. God pre-determined our victory through His son, Jesus, a long time ago. This means that even on the days that things look bleak, you are still in the winner's circle. We win in life, and then we win again in death. It's a win-win situation for those of us who love the Lord. It's important to keep this simple idea at the forefront of your mind. It helps, when things don't seem to be going your way, to remember that God is using all of those same things to work together for your good. This means that you are always a winner, even when you don't feel that way. Even when it feels like you've lost, it's a win. Did someone leave you? You win. Did your job let you go? You win. Did your plans get cancelled? You win. Did people turn their backs on you? You win. It's literally just a matter of time before you figure out exactly **how** your situation will play out as a win, but I'm just here to encourage you to keep your head up until you do. Let's thank God today for always giving us the victory.

READ TODAY: ROMANS 8:28

#TWINNING

#twinning – a hashtag usually used to accompany a photo of people dressed similarly. It may also refer to a picture of actual twins.

Example: I showed up to my ex-boyfriend's wedding wearing the same dress as the bride. Whoops, my bad! #twinning

Do you remember back in the day when people used to wear those W.W.J.D. bracelets? They were all the rage. If you aren't familiar, W.W.J.D. stands for "What Would Jesus Do?" Millions of people were wearing them, and they came in so many great colors and designs. The bracelet was supposed to serve as your reminder to think about how Jesus might handle a situation before you respond to it. While that's really great in theory, I think a lot of people may have skipped an important step. It's hard to know what Jesus would have done if you've never spent time actually getting to know Him. That's no shade to anyone. I'm just saying that if you plan to mimic someone, it's really helpful to learn more about that individual. The most admirable thing in the world to me, is for a person to want to live after the example of our precious Savior. But how can you be #twinning with Jesus if all you know is what other people have told you about Him? If you go read the gospels for yourself, you will realize that He may or may not be what you were taught. He was loving, but He also knew how to get people together when He needed to. He was humble, but He also knew exactly who He was and the kind of authority He had. He told the truth in love. He made it easy to understand, but He didn't sugarcoat it. All I'm saying is don't assume. If you haven't read the gospels in a while, now might be a good time to spin the block on them to see what new revelations you can find about the person we should be hoping to imitate.

READ TODAY: 1 PETER 2:21-24

NOTED!

Noted! – an expression used to indicate that you have observed someone's behavior or handling of a situation and have made a mental note that you will hold them accountable to in the future.

Example: So you're saying that storming the Capitol building in an attempt to overthrow the government isn't really a crime? Oh okay…noted!

Do you have a journal? I will admit that I need to step my journaling game up. When I was in college, I did a much better job of it. Many years had passed when I found an old journal that I had written in as a young college student. Reading my own words brought me to tears. I think I was more upset that I had let the distractions of life keep me from journaling for so many years. Why is it important? Journaling helps you to take note of the things that God is doing in your life. It helps you to keep track of the prayers that you have prayed and how they were answered. Sometimes God will subtly answer prayers that we have forgotten all about. If you grew up in church, you may be familiar with the hymn *Yield Not To Temptation*. There is a line in the song that says, "…each vict'ry will help you, some other to win." My goodness that's powerful! My memory of one victory, helps me in my next fight. When I can recall a time that God came through for me in the past, it boosts my confidence and therefore my faith in Him for my current situation. I know we're all young and sharp, but relying on our own sketchy memory banks may not be a good idea. If I can walk into a room and forget why I went in there, will I remember in great detail that time 10 years ago when I almost lost my mind and God delivered me from my troubles? God even told the Israelites to write down His commandments and what He had done for them because He knew that they'd forget. God is actually doing some pretty dope things in your life. You just have to take note.

READ TODAY: DEUTERONOMY 6: 10-12

MAY 31

SEE FRIENDSHIP

See Friendship – a tool in which Facebook users are able to see their history of interaction with another person dating back to the inception of that FB friendship.

Example: I just found out that one of my FB friends passed away. I clicked on "See Friendship" and realized that we never missed a year wishing one another a happy birthday.

Wouldn't it be cool if we had "See Friendship" buttons in real life? It seems like it would be quite helpful to be able to step back and see certain friendships for what they are. I think we take some friendships for granted. We don't appreciate just how important they have been. Certain friends have been consistently loyal in our lives for many years, and we don't even stop to express our gratitude. Other friends have been inconsistent, untrustworthy, jealous, and fickle. Perhaps they seem to disappear when you need them the most. Still others have been bad influences and distractions from our goals. We spend so much time focusing on romantic relationships, but let's be clear. Platonic relationships can be toxic as well. Your choice of friends can make or break you. It's important to be very intentional about the company you keep. I understand that you've known him since 6th grade, but that doesn't mean he is supposed to follow you into every season of your life if he is hindering your forward progress. I know you used to ride the bus with her, but that doesn't mean you are supposed to keep getting half-naked and drunk and fighting in the club with her well into your 40s. Diamonds are forever, but friends may or may not be. That doesn't mean turn your nose up at anyone. It simply means pray and ask God to allow you to "see" your friendships more clearly. Ask Him to send good friends into your life. Pray that God would help you to set boundaries around people who are not supposed to be as close to you as they are.

READ TODAY: PSALM 1:1-3

WELL THAT ESCALATED QUICKLY...(1)

Well that escalated quickly... – a common phrase used when a matter, usually a conflict, increases in seriousness at a faster rate than expected.

Example: Person A: So I was walking my dog in the park when he ate somebody else's dog. I ended up in a knife fight with the other owner who happened to look like a younger version of me. Turns out, I have a son! He's now in the hospital. Person B: Wow...well that escalated quickly.

Do you ever wonder why God doesn't just bless you overnight with all the things that your heart desires? I mean, we know it's not a question of whether He's able. We also know that it's not a question of whether He loves us. It's not even a question of whether He wants us to have good things. So why on earth does it feel like it's taking so long to get off the starting blocks? Well I don't have all of the answers. I don't know exactly why God is choosing to make you go through a lengthier process instead of granting you a quick escalation. But let's just be honest, rapid elevations can be dangerous. Think about the lottery winners, pro athletes, and entertainers who go quickly from rags to riches. It's not always pretty. Some of those people simply can't handle it. They may end up broke again or worse. Did you know that it's possible to climb a mountain too fast? Yup. As you go up the mountain, your body needs time to adjust to the lower oxygen levels and atmospheric pressure. If you climb too fast, you can end up with something called "altitude sickness" which causes trouble breathing, nausea, and difficulty walking. I don't know about you, but I don't want to be on the edge of some cliff falling all out and junk. The key is to take your time, allow yourself to master the level that you're on, and then continue to climb. Instead of complaining, let's strive to master the place where God is trusting us to be currently.

READ TODAY: ISAIAH 40:31

WELL THAT ESCALATED QUICKLY... (2)

Well that escalated quickly... - a common phrase used when a matter, usually a conflict, increases in seriousness at a faster rate than expected.

Example: Adult Child: *posts on FB* I really love my daddy!
Mother: Been meaning to tell you...that ain't ya daddy.
Onlooker: Oh my! Well that escalated quickly...

Do you know what else escalates quickly? Sin...sin escalates quicker than a snicker. Okay, that doesn't make a whole lot of sense, but I think you get my point. One minute you're just "innocently" flirting in someone's DMs, and the next thing you know, you're caught in an extra-marital affair and losing the house, the car, the kids, and the dog in a nasty divorce. When it comes to sin, my mom would always tell me that sin takes you farther than you want to go, keeps you longer than you want to stay, and makes you pay more than you planned to pay. I think the best thing to do when it comes to sin is to avoid having a prideful or arrogant spirit. We look at certain sins and think, "How could they be so foolish?! Tuh, I would NEVER!" That's exactly how sin sneaks up on you. The truth is, you were just never placed in that situation. Of course you weren't heauxing around. Nobody was checking for you! It's better to be intentional and prepared by understanding that it's God's grace that keeps you and not your own strength. I used the example of flirting in the DMs, but what kind of flirting do you do? Do you use liquor as a solution to your problems? You're flirting with alcoholism. Is food becoming your best friend? You're flirting with gluttony. Are you considering doing something unethical for money? You're flirting with greed. Please be careful to nip these things in the bud, because you have no idea how quickly they may escalate. Ask God to show you any seemingly small ways that you could be flirting with sin.

READ TODAY: ROMANS 6:23

COOKING FOR BAE

Cooking For Bae – this phrase is often seen as the hashtag, #CookingForBae, and normally accompanies photos of food that looks terrible. There is an IG page @cookingforbae, solely dedicated to finding and sharing these images from across the internet, especially around the holidays.

Example: *posts picture of undercooked chicken, mac n' cheese from a box, and burnt biscuits* Caption: I love cooking for bae!

Okay, let me explain this one a little more. "Cooking for Bae" is when a person gets in a new relationship and wants to prepare meals for their partner. If you are like me, you understand that one of the best feelings in the world is watching someone enjoy a meal that you have prepared for them with love. So it doesn't surprise me that people in new relationships get that urge to cook. The problem comes when people who never took the time to learn how to cook, begin to share their "creations." It's wild to the rest of us, because we don't understand how completely oblivious a person must be to proudly share these culinary monstrosities with the public. Sadly, some of these people end up being embarrassed when their meal becomes a viral laughingstock. I'm using this as an example to underscore the importance of wise counsel in your life. If you don't know how to do something, it's okay to ask for help! If you don't know anyone who will help, in this age of information, there are many other resources that you can take advantage of. And before you go presenting something to the world, it's okay to run it past a few people who you trust to be honest with you. It could save a lot of headache or embarrassment later on. If God placed an assignment on your heart, but you're not sure how to go about it, don't be lazy. Study, practice, and ask for help.

READ TODAY: PROVERBS 11:14

#UNAPOLOGETIC

#Unapologetic – a hashtag used when a person is doing something boldly and has no qualms about it.

Example: I know every line of every episode of *A Different World*, and I'm not sorry about it. #Unapologetic

One Satan's slickest tricks is something called shame. That's right, he figures that if he can make you feel ashamed about something, then it cannot be used to bring God glory nor propel you into your destiny. We all have life experiences that perhaps we aren't proud of. We've all done things that we wish we could take back now that we know better. But what do you do with that information/knowledge that you have gained? Are you too ashamed to use your testimony to help someone else? Didn't God's word come along and set you free? Wasn't it a big game-changer in your life? Why then, do we clam up in shame, sweep it under the rug, and keep it to ourselves. Are we worried about what people will think when they find out that we haven't always been perfect? Well, newsflash…you still aren't perfect, so maybe it's time to stop trying to put off that image. The key is that you must allow the Holy Spirit to guide you. Your story isn't for everybody! Some people are just nosey and hoping to run and tell your business. Others could truly benefit from knowing just how God brought you out of that horrible pit. The Holy Spirit helps you to discern who is who. Don't apologize for how awesome you are now, and although you are still a work in progress, don't try to hide the fact that God has already brought you a mighty long way. Be unapologetic about giving God the glory that is due unto Him!

READ TODAY: ROMANS 1:16-17

#THECUTLIFE

#TheCutLife – a hashtag used to accompany a photo of a woman with short, beautiful hair.

Example: I love my short hair. It's so easy to maintain! #TheCutLife

    About two weeks ago, I cut my hair. For the first time in my life, I am wearing a short cut hairstyle, and it is amazing! It's giving me Halle Berry in Boomerang vibes if you need that visual. But let me tell you about the **real** cut life. So there was this time in the Bible where Jesus was talking, and He used the analogy of a vine with branches and fruit to describe the relationship between Himself and the rest of us. He is the main vine. As such, He provides us with the life-giving nourishment that is the word of God. We are the branches that feed off of Him. As branches, our job is to grow fruit. Jesus said that even branches that bear fruit, will sometimes need to be pruned (or purged) of excess vegetation that could hamper the growth of said fruit. This tells us that sometimes things will need to be cut away from our lives. Did a romantic partner walk away and leave you without explanation? Did you have a long-term friendship that ended? Were you terminated from your job? Any time you are struggling to deal with a loss of any sort, consider that perhaps those things or people needed to be cut away from your life in order for you to bear more fruit. If God needed those things or people to bless you, they wouldn't have been able to leave. But since they did, just know that their absence won't break you. The pruning process may be painful at first, but just understand that the emotional pain is only temporary. Things and people will come and go, but God is blessing you with fruit that will **remain**. When I cut my hair, I instantly felt liberated! Instead of becoming an emotional wreck over what is gone, let's thank God today for the new freedom that #TheCutLife has afforded us.

READ TODAY: JOHN 15:1-3

#BOOKEDANDBUSY

#BookedAndBusy – a hashtag used to describe a person whose business is in demand and doing well.

Example: Hair Stylist: I am no longer accepting new clientele.
Me: Okay boo!!! Guess you #BookedAndBusy, huh?

Did God give you some sort of dream or vision? Maybe it was a business venture. If you are anything like me, you probably thought that all you had to do was build it and they would come. Oh the dear, sweet, naïve little Lori that I was! I opened my optometry clinic fresh out of optometry school. It was truly something that God gave me a vision to do. He also gave me the provision for it through a miraculous turn of events (remind me to tell you that story one day). Imagine my surprise when all of Birmingham, AL didn't knock down my door to get in. Some days, I would sit and watch *Fresh Prince* in my office because there were no patients to see. I had to take a part-time job working at a men's federal prison just to pay my bills. I would often pay my employees while wishing I could pay myself. I cried a lot. I wondered if I had made a mistake. It was a great day when I could **finally** work at my own office full-time! Now, not only am I working there full-time, but as of today, the next available appointment slot is about seven weeks out. I'm still shocked that people are like, "Seven weeks?!! Okay...put me down." There is literally a waiting list of people hoping that other people cancel. I am now able to refer countless others to friends of mine with newer practices. In other words, I'm booked and busy. I shared this testimony to encourage you (and me too). If you know God gave you that vision, don't stop until you see it manifest. Keep your hands on the plow and continue to put in the work. Things may not be taking off as quickly as you had hoped, but continue to operate in excellence and love. Sow good seeds by doing right by others. Keep the faith, and God will grant the increase.

READ TODAY: HEBREWS 11:1

BLOCKED

Blocked – when someone's privileges of electronic contact have been revoked via one or more methods of communication.

Example: Blocked people will create a whole entire fake profile just to see what's on my page. Don't worry, I'll block that too!

The ability to block people...where do I begin? It is truly a blessing. Some people block their exes. Others block scammers and internet trolls who are always looking for drama. I have even had to block people for making inappropriate sexual advances. Al Green's internet can still be a pretty scary place, but blocking makes it a little better. If social media can do us this grand favor by blocking what we deem to be undesirable, just imagine how much more effective God is in that same regard. The Bible and Fred Hammond tell us that no weapon formed against us will prosper. The problem is that we freak out because we see the weapons forming, but don't trust God enough to know that He will block them before they can get to us and do the damage. This is usually about the time that we start running around like a chicken with its head cut off trying to come up with some sort of cockamamie solution. That's because we lack faith. When you abandon your faith to take matters into your own hands, you are actually playing right into Satan's plot against you. He can't make the weapons prosper, so he must rely on **you** to do something foolish out of fear and desperation. Instead, we should trust that God's got everything under control like He always has. Your faith in God is like a protective shield that keeps you safe. Keep your eyes focused on Him and block out the crazy weapons forming around you.

READ TODAY: EPHESIANS 6:16

SHOOT YOUR SHOT.

Shoot Your Shot. – an expression that encourages people to attempt something that may or may not be successful.

Example: Person A: I don't know. She's so beautiful and she
probably has a thousand guys trying to holler...
Person B: You never know...shoot your shot!

Shoot your shot is basically the modern-day way of saying, "you never know until you try!" There is a really cool, black-owned watch brand named Talley & Twine that I follow on IG. I really like listening to their CEO (@ceorandy) as he shares his gems about success in business. I once heard him talk about how he "failed" at business for 10 straight years before experiencing success. What I heard him saying was that he kept shooting his shot until the ball went in. Some people shoot one brick and are ready to give up on all sports forever. I highly doubt LeBron James came out of the womb shooting nothing but net. Actually, that may not be a good example...he probably came out shooting his own diapers into the trash, but I digress. People will advise you all day long to "shoot your shot," but what they don't tell you is that sometimes you have to keep on shooting. Don't get me wrong, your target/goal may very well change. Don't keep inboxing that same girl for 10 years if she's asked you to leave her alone, king. Just clarify your goal. Don't get stuck on Sheila...the goal is love. Don't get so stuck on Business Idea A...the goal is success. Don't let one, two, or even ten years of missed shots cause you to wad up in depression and check completely out of the game of life. The best thing to do is pray (or even fast) and ask God to give you a strategy and a better shooting technique. Also ask Him to help you extract wisdom from the shots that didn't make it.

READ TODAY: ROMANS 5:3-5

SO I DID A THING...

So I did a thing... – a caption used to accompany a picture of you doing something out of your norm. The photo is self-explanatory, and therefore nothing more has to be said.

Example: *posts picture of myself skydiving from a plane*
          Caption: So...I did a thing.

Let's talk about mistakes. We all make them. Even the Bible says so! What do you do after you've made a mistake? Do you fall into a depressed state of guilt and shame because you did a thing that you shouldn't have done? Aht! Aht! That's the flaw embedded in some of the Christian education that you may have received from parents or from church. Fear is often used as a way to get you to do the right thing. The crazy part is that this isn't even how God operates. He draws us with love and not fear. God's love is powerful enough that it doesn't need scare tactics to win us over. I remember going through a divorce (very ghetto, zero stars, do not recommend...fast and pray for 40 days and 40 nights alone up in a high mountain and make sure you hear from God before you walk down that aisle!) and thinking that God would be so mad at me for needing one. I figured that He would no longer want to show me His favor. As a matter of fact, I was told that He wouldn't. I was even told that I should watch my back as if God was just going to strike me down all together! Whew chile. Imagine my reaction when God's love for me didn't change. As a matter of fact, He pulled me even closer and showed me even more favor. I think He wanted it to be **undeniable** that He was still with me. From that, I learned that God hates divorce (because it brings out the worst in some people), but that He didn't hate **me**. So you did a thing...I get it. Repent, learn from it, grow from it, and do better next time! God isn't going to throw you away, so snap out of it. Guilt is just another one of Satan's tools in his strategy to defeat you.

READ TODAY: ROMANS 6:14

LET'S START THERE...

Let's start there... – a phrase used when clarification of a contributing factor is needed before addressing the matter at hand.

Example: Person A: I got fired from my job today, and I don't know why! I think it's because I'm black!

Person B: Didn't you call in sick and then post live videos of yourself at Essence Fest? Let's start there...

I'm no counselor. I check people's eyes and dassit. But sometimes people come to me for advice. I think I get on their nerves because I am always challenging them to dig deeper to find the source of their own issue. Sometimes we have to tap into a little thing called personal accountability. I'm not very good at giving people a magic bullet to resolve their situations, but I do specialize in helping you to see where **you** went wrong so that you can avoid the same pitfalls in the future. I can't make RayRay act right...but I can ask you why you felt that loaning your car to an unemployed man with a suspended license while you rode the bus to work was a good idea. I can't get your money back for you, but I can ask you why you gave all your account information to some internet stranger you never met. I know, I'm such a party pooper. Here you are wanting to go off about your mama's ridiculous rules, but I'm trying to figure out why you're 45 and have never moved out of her house. I suppose the point that I'm trying to make today is that someone who cares about you will tell you the hard truth about yourself...in love. It will never be in a mocking or judgmental way. You will be able to see their true concern for your well-being and for your future. These people are very valuable. Do not get offended and toss them away. Listen, and begin to ask the Holy Spirit to show you any incorrect thought processes that you may have. Ask God to show you what **you** should be doing differently. Let's start there.

DOING THE MOST (1)

Doing the most – a phrase used to indicate that a person is clearly trying too hard to gain attention.

Example: This girl keeps trying to DM my man about his business, but is trying to flirt with him on the sly. She is doing the most and has no idea that I answer all his messages for him!

Let's talk about doing the most. Back in the Bible days there was some confusion over what makes a person holy. Back in the Old Testament days, there were a bunch of laws that had to be followed to a T in order to be considered holy or righteous. Jesus came to make it very simple for us. Because of His work at Calvary, we were liberated from those cumbersome laws of sin and death. Jesus was the fulfilment of every law, and therefore all we have to do is accept the free gift of grace that He has given us. Yet there were (and still are) some people who just couldn't accept that. They carried on thinking that they could be considered holier than everyone else by doing the most. It doesn't work like that anymore. If it did, we would be able to take credit for the righteousness that was simply imputed to us (put on us) because of our faith. When people feel like they can depend on their good works, they are sadly mistaken. As a matter of fact, the Bible says that you could literally be doing the most down here in the name of holiness yet get up to heaven and God not even recognize you. Whew chile! You can't interchange good deeds for a personal relationship with the Lord. The good deeds and righteous actions will come naturally the closer you get to Him anyway. What are some ways you feel you can strengthen your relationship with Him?

READ TODAY: MATTHEW 7:21-23

DOING THE MOST (2)

Doing the most – a phrase used to indicate that a person is clearly trying too hard to gain attention.

Example: Tiffany is always playing the teacher's pet. She is really doing the most right now.

Have you ever met a person who thinks that everything is a competition? Maybe you bought a new car, so they had to buy an even newer car. Maybe you went on vacation, so they had to go on an even fancier vacation. Perhaps you had a dream wedding, so they had to be lowered into their wedding via helicopter and then carried to the altar in a palanquin. They were always trying to do the most. There was a situation in the Bible where the mother of disciples James and John got it in her mind to ask Jesus if her two sons could be the ones to sit on his right and left hand in heaven. Jesus shut it down respectfully and let James and John know that they ain't ready for all that, and plus His Father would determine who sits where anyway. The other disciples overheard it and they were offended that James, John, and their mama were trying to do the most as if heaven was some kind of competition. Jesus told them they were all worried about the wrong thing anyway. I think when people feel the need to compete, it is a form of insecurity. They are busy comparing themselves with others and trying to find a way to one-up someone because they need that validation. Meanwhile, the person they are trying to compete with is often just minding their business and authentically enjoying their life. Social media has amplified this. There are people so obsessed with capturing perfect photos to show that they are having fun, that they aren't actually having any fun. If you are this way, staaaawp it! Be grateful for what you have and make the most of **that**. Don't worry about what another person is doing, because just as Jesus told James and John, you really don't know what it takes to sit in that seat.

READ TODAY: MATTHEW 20:20-28

169

WHEELS UP!

Wheels Up! – an expression that people post just before placing their phone into airplane mode for a flight.

Example: Chicago, I'll see you soon! Wheels Up!

If you have ever been on a plane getting ready for takeoff, then you know that the flight attendants always remind the passengers to make sure that their baggage is stowed away properly and that their seatbacks and tray tables are in the "upright and locked position." I quicken violently every time I hear that, because I'm a little churchy sometimes. But also, it's because I think about the things required for takeoff. First, it's important to place all of your baggage in its proper place. Is your baggage preventing you from being ready for takeoff? Are things from your past falling all over the place and hindering your ability to go higher? There is a proper place for all that you have experienced. You don't have to throw it all away. You can use those difficult experiences to become stronger and wiser. You can also use them as a tool to help others who may be going through similar experiences. The flight attendant also instructs you to lock into the upright position. An upright person is a person whose focus and therefore position is raised upward. An upright person is so busy looking to the hills and focusing vertically up to God, that they aren't distracted by the random things going on around them horizontally. Sometimes we get so encumbered with the people, places, and things around us (horizontal), that we take our eyes off of God and lose our upright position (vertical). In summary, get ready for takeoff by managing your baggage properly and by keeping your focus upward to God.

READ TODAY: PSALMS 84:11 (KJV)

THE NEGRO SOLSTICE

The Negro Solstice – a much anticipated Black Twitter event that took place on 12/21/20. On this day, black people all over the world were able to unlock their superhuman powers due to a planetary alignment that would activate melanin particles to their full capabilities.

Example: Hey guys! I just received my Negro Solstice powers. I just used my new laser vision to fry some chicken! Woohoo!

If you weren't on Twitter during the Negro Solstice of 2020, I feel bad for you, son. 12/21/20 and the days leading up to it was probably the best time I've ever had on Al Green's internet. The jokes were top-tier. We laughed nonstop about the powers we had received. I could barely work. There was so much unity! Can you believe that something similar happened in the Bible? It was called The Day of Pentecost. This was a day, about 50 days after the resurrection of Jesus, where about 120 believers had gathered in the upper room of a house. They were praying together, and the Bible says that they were all on one accord, meaning that they were extremely unified. Suddenly, there came a sound from heaven. They say that it sounded like a mighty rushing wind, and it filled the whole house. They were all filled with the Holy Ghost at this time, and it was really wild because they began to speak in other languages. The people who were living in Jerusalem at the time were from all over the world and spoke varying languages. Yet, each one of them could understand what these disciples were saying, because every person heard them as if they were speaking in his or her native tongue. Craaaaaazy!! Imagine getting that power activated! Well...that wasn't the only power that was activated that day. God's Holy Spirit now dwells inside of us as well and enables us to do a whole slew of things that wouldn't otherwise be possible. I dare you to spend some time today learning what kind of power we get from the Holy Spirit.

READ TODAY: ACTS 1:8

SELFIE

Selfie – a photo of one's own self that is taken by one's own self, usually with a cell phone.

Example: Is it normal for people to post a selfie every single day?

I'm not going to lie, I enjoy selfies. It's really all about hitting a good angle and finding the proper lighting. My selfies are usually pretty good, but when other people take a picture of me, I always look a hot mess. Sometimes I'll take a selfie just to see what I look like. Well back in the Bible days, they didn't have cell phones…or cameras. And they definitely didn't have cell phones with cameras on them! They had mirrors. That's it. That's all. If they wanted to see themselves, they'd go look into a mirror. The first chapter of James says that when people hear the word of God but do nothing about it, it's like taking a good look at yourself in a mirror and then instantly forgetting what you look like. That's deep. The word of God really is like a mirror in which we can see ourselves…a selfie, if you will. If you've ever spent time studying the Bible, you will see that it's not just random stories about other people. It gives you insight into your own life and allows you to gain a better understanding of things that you may experience. If you look into a mirror, or take a selfie, and see that there is something stuck in your teeth, don't you try to fix it? Well, when the word shows us the truth about ourselves, we should take heed and apply the wisdom that we gain to fix areas that may be messed up in our lives. I think of people who sit up in church every Sunday for years but remain the same. Let's not be those people. One awesome thing that you're already doing is studying it daily. Now it's just a matter of taking it and putting it into practice!

READ TODAY: JAMES 1:22-25

…HAS ENTERED THE CHAT.

…has entered the chat. – a system message displayed when a person enters a "group chat" conversation.

Example: Person A: You know, maybe I should stop letting Rodney stay with me rent-free.
Person B: Yeah, and maybe I should stop putting people with no jobs on my cell phone plan.
System: *Common Sense has entered the chat.*

Do things change when you step on the scene? They should. Have you ever walked into a breakroom at work, and it seemed as if the conversation suddenly changed because you entered the room? Don't feel bad. It's not always because they were talking about you (although sometimes it is). Sometimes it's because your very presence commands a certain level of decency and respect. They had to straighten it up. I hate to be the one to break it to you, but just because you don't understand how anointed you are, doesn't mean that others won't still see it all over you. When you enter an environment, the climate is *supposed* to change. What is the point of your faith if it doesn't have an effect? I went down to Orlando once with some friends to visit Disney World. Apparently, Orlando had been in a severe drought at the time, having received little to no rain for two straight months. As soon as we arrived, the bottom fell out. We experienced heavy, nonstop downpours of rain for almost the entire trip. We never even made it to Disney. We were disappointed but joked that our presence and our anointing had ended the drought and blessed the people of Orlando! I said all of that to say, don't be ashamed to let your anointing be the difference-maker in any situation. You never know whose drought might end simply because you have entered the chat.

READ TODAY: MATTHEW 5:13-16

…HAS LEFT THE CHAT.

…has left the chat. – a system message displayed when a person exits a "group chat" conversation. A person may leave a chat due to disinterest in the subject matter, excessive message notifications, or because they were offended by the group in some way.

Example: Person A: I like sugar on grits!
Person B: Hey, me too!
System: *Lori Croom has left the chat.*

Your words are extremely powerful. I know we hear it all the time, but it's true. Think about it. God literally used His words to create the whole earth, and Jesus is literally God's word that was made into flesh. So since we were created after the image of God, it stands to reason that our own words hold a lot of weight as well. I am seriously trying to do better about watching what I say and how I say it, so certain chats I have had to leave. If people around you are trying to pull you into conversations that are not edifying (conversations that don't build you up), maybe you shouldn't participate. Is there someone who always wants to talk about others negatively behind their backs? You can and should leave that chat. Is someone always talking to you about their wild sex life while you are struggling to treat your own body like a temple? You can leave that chat too. Is someone always complaining to you about the job while you are trying your best to remain positive, upbeat, and grateful every day? Once again, you can leave that chat. Be careful about hanging around those who always want to pull you into some negativity. That stuff is contagious. Use your words to speak life into dead situations. Use your words to frame a better world for yourself. How can you start today? Pay close attention to the words you speak and the conversations that you participate in.

READ TODAY: HEBREWS 11:3

THAT'S A LOADED QUESTION.

That's a loaded question. – what you say when someone asks a trick question with the intent to use the answer against you like a loaded gun.

Example: Woman A: So how do you actually know my boyfriend?
Woman B: Uhh…that's a loaded question. Gotta go!

Jesus was the most loving person to ever walk the face of the earth. He really was. But the more you read the gospels, the more you see that He knew how to get people together too. From time to time, the religious leaders would try to trip Him up with loaded questions. Jesus would peep game and answer their loaded question with an even more loaded question. So much so that they'd have to walk away embarrassed. I think this is half the reason why they wanted to crucify Him. They couldn't get any real dirt on Jesus, **and** He continued to make them look silly. What does this have to do with you? From time to time, you may encounter some people who will hate on your faith. All over social media, you will see people who get all in their feelings whenever somebody even mentions the name Jesus. I mean they lose their entire minds and want to argue back and forth all day (I never understood that…if you don't believe in something, why are you **so** passionate about it? I don't have time to argue all day about things that I know aren't true…but I digress).   Mainly, I just want you to learn the difference between a troll questioning you about your faith just to argue vs someone who is asking questions because they really want to understand. Use the Holy Spirit to help you discern which is which. It should be pretty easy. Don't allow yourself to be dragged into a futile argument with someone whose heart is not ready or willing to receive anything you say. Protect your peace like Jesus did in today's scripture!

READ TODAY: MARK 11:27-33

YOU A WHOLE FOOL.

You a whole fool. – a phrase used to let someone know that they are very silly.

Example: Person A: Popeye's had us waiting in the drive-thru for so long that I got out, went in the kitchen, put on some gloves, said "excuse me," and made my own chicken sandwich!
Person B: Did you really?! You a whole fool!

My grandmother told me never to call anyone a fool. I think it's in the Bible somewhere…please hold. Okay, I see it. It's derived from Matthew 5:22. I'm glad we cleared that up. It's crazy though, because although it says not to go around calling people fools, there are **several** instances in the Bible where fools are referenced extensively. I guess God can call people fools, but not us. That makes sense though, because He's the only One who fully knows what's in a person's head and heart. So let's talk about one of the **many** ways that the Bible identifies a fool. The Bible says more than once that a fool can be identified by his or her mouth. No one really knows whether a person is foolish or not until they speak. Have you ever thought someone was attractive, but as soon as they opened their mouth, you were turned off? I'm not talking about poor dental hygiene, silly! I'm talking about the foolish things that they said. The Bible tells us that a foolish person says whatever comes to their mind, but that a wise person waits until they can think things through. This tells me that even wise people can have foolish thoughts from time to time. That's why press conferences get so wild. People get put on the spot and try to give quick answers. Everyone wants to look so smart, but a wise person knows how to say, "I'm not sure. I'll get back to you." I think this is something that should be a daily prayer. "Lord, help me not to say anything foolish today that I can't take back. Help me to think things through before I blurt them out."

READ TODAY: PROVERBS 29:11

KANYE SHRUG

Kanye Shrug – describes an action wherein one responds to a matter by simply shrugging their shoulders while extending their hands outward like Kanye West did in 2009 after interrupting Taylor Swift's acceptance speech at the VMAs. He apologized later that night.

Example: I ate the whole pizza by myself. *Kanye Shrug*

If you remember the 2009 MTV Video Music Awards, you will recall that Kanye West was seriously out of line that night. As Taylor Swift accepted her award, Kanye barged on stage and took the mic from her mid-sentence to proclaim that Beyoncé had the best video. The crowd cheered initially, but Beyoncé was horrified, and Taylor was embarrassed. Once the crowd realized that this wasn't a part of the script, they were also quite disturbed and felt sorry for Taylor. Kanye shrugged as if to say, "Sorry, but I'm not sorry." So crazy! But do you know why the crowd initially cheered? It was because Kanye wasn't lying, and everybody knew it. Beyoncé should have won. And although it was rude, I give credit to Kanye for having the courage of his convictions. He thought Beyoncé was being discriminated against. He went, spoke his peace, didn't care who was mad, and left knowing that he told the truth about something he believed so strongly. The Bible tells us that as believers, we should have the courage of our convictions as well. We should be bold enough to share the gospel that we believe so strongly…in love of course! But if people don't receive it, it's okay. You tried. Don't be sorry. Just shake the dust from your feet, do a little Kanye Shrug, and be out. When you shake the dust from your feet, it means that you don't even want the residue of that failed experience to remain with you. Don't get angry. Don't try to force Jesus on them if they don't want to receive Him. And don't let it discourage you from sharing with someone else. Just keep it moving on to the next.

READ TODAY: MATTHEW 10:14

I'M GOOD LUV, ENJOY.

I'm good luv, enjoy. – a phrase used to kindly decline participation in something, while still wishing the other person well in their own enjoyment of it. It is often used sarcastically.

Example: Sharon: Hey! Come down to the breakroom for the company potluck! I made my raisin infused potato salad! Tisha: I'm good luv, enjoy.

I really want us as a people to have better balance. I joke a lot about people who put sugar on grits having psychopathic tendencies, but it's really just a joke. The truth is, I don't care what **you** do with **your** grits. People will literally fight all day long over how somebody else chooses to live their life. I have seen people cuss each other clean out in comment sections because a woman, that neither one of them knew, proposed to a man. I have my thoughts on what eyyyyeeee would or wouldn't do, but I'm not about to fight over what someone **else** is doing. And it's not just online. It happens in real life too! Families and friends now have estranged relationships for no other reason than theoretical philosophical differences. Listen…if it doesn't affect me, and it's not going to put you in danger of eternal damnation…do you boo. My blood pressure will **not** be raised for this. This is why I say we need balance. I'm not going to be a pushover and do something that I know doesn't work for me (like eating potato salad that was licked by a cat) to please others. But I'm not going to judge you for doing something that works for you either. Even the Bible tells us that a lot of these hard and fast "rules" we place on each other aren't even legit. It's my job to be obedient to what God has called **me** to do and to do my best not to let my example or my actions be the reason someone else falls. Outside of that, who am I to judge?

READ TODAY: 1 CORINTHIANS 8:8

BEFORE & AFTER

Before & After – used to display contrasting images that demonstrate the effects of a certain kind of change. The change may be anything from weight loss to a remodeled home.

Example: Before: *photo of a woman with a flat booty*
          After: *photo of same woman with a round booty after
          having the Brazilian Butt Lift (BBL) surgery*

So today I want to talk to you about a very important before and after. Have you ever needed a serious blessing from the Lord? I know I have. Perhaps you needed to pass a class to graduate. Maybe someone you really loved was gravely ill in the hospital. Maybe you needed a job to come through or were facing an eviction. When I am in the process of petitioning God for something, I go all out. I mean a sister is praying all the time, fasting, present at church every Sunday, praising, worshipping, and sowing every good seed I can think of. I'm probably listening to only gospel music in my car! I even limit my social media and what I watch on TV. But how do I act once God has granted my request? I'll be the first one to say that I don't always keep the same energy after as I had before. This happened in the Bible once. Jesus healed 10 lepers, but after the blessing, nine of those guys went on about their business not thinking about Jesus. Only one actually turned back to simply say, "thank you." All I'm saying, is let's not be like those nine guys. Let's not be all about Jesus before we get blessed and then forget about Him after. You may not be in need of a miracle today, but let's continue to love on God just because He's worthy!

READ TODAY: LUKE 17:12-18

IKTR

IKTR – an acronym that stands for "I know that's right."

Example: Person A: Dating these days is not for the faint at heart!
Person B: Listennn! Okay?! IKTR!

Do you know what's right? That wasn't rhetorical. I really want you to ask yourself if you know what is right. Has anyone ever taught you? It wasn't until I went off to college, that I realized that everyone didn't have what we in the south like to call "home training." To be fair, some of the training that my friends had, I didn't have. I never even knew what ramen noodles were, for example, until I moved into the dorms. No, I wasn't raised in some uppity bourgeois home where ramen noodles were beneath us! NOPE! We just never had em…shole coulda used some though. Anyway, my point is that the way you were raised has a lot do with how you view the world. It has a lot to do with how you perceive right vs wrong. When people move away from home, they are confronted with people of varying viewpoints who have been raised differently. It's great to keep an open mind, but my advice to you is not to give up on the things that you know are right just to be accepted by others. You were blessed with something called a foundation. It's up to you to learn, grow, and build upon it. If your house is built on the solid rock of your faith, and you know this is right, don't let anyone come along to tear it down. My old Sunday School teacher, Ms. Bessie Corley, would always tell me, "If you don't stand for something, you'll fall for anything." This is exactly why we must begin showing our children at early ages how important it is to have a **personal** relationship with the Lord. We should communicate this to them not only verbally, but also with our example. When they see you walking uprightly, operating in love, and leaning and depending on Jesus, you are helping to build their foundation. When the rain and wind come, they will be able to stand on what they know is right.

READ TODAY: 2 TIMOTHY 3:14-15

"PUT SOME RESPECK ON MY NAME."
-BIRDMAN

Put some respeck on my name. – a statement/warning issued by Birdman to the hosts of The Breakfast Club Morning Show.

Example: Karen, I prefer to be addressed as "Dr." when we are in this clinical setting. I worked hard for it, so put some respeck on my name. Thanks!

We don't know what set Birdman off that fateful day in 2016. He and his entourage were only in the studio for about two and a half minutes before storming out. Unfortunately, the hosts of the show could never get him to explain why he entered the room in such a hostile manner. Perhaps he had just been stung by a bee. All we know is that he wanted more respeck to be placed on his name. We can only assume that he felt disrespeckted somehow. His quote became a meme, a mantra, and even a song. What does this have to do with anything? I'm glad you asked. The Bible tells us that there will come a day, when every knee shall bow, and every tongue shall put some respeck on the name of Jesus. The name of Jesus alone carries so much power that the Bible tells us that when we pray for things, we should name drop and ask in the name of Jesus. The Bible also tells us that demons tremble upon hearing the name Jesus. I know this is true. Go on social media and say something about Jesus. You can literally say something as simple as "I love Jesus," and hateful trolls will get all bent out of shape, darn near cuss you out, and tell you that Jesus was just made up by white slave owners to oppress you. Whenever I see it, I know I'm watching a trembling demon. My point is, don't be afraid to call on Jesus. His name is so powerful that the world has made us feel like it's a cuss word. Don't fall for that trick from Satan. Jesus has the most powerful name ever…put some respeck on it.

READ TODAY: PHILIPPIANS 2:10-11

I'M READY TO TELL MY STORY.

I'm ready to tell my story. – a phrase indicating that a person is getting ready to share their personal testimony about a situation.

Example: Surviving the Financial Aid Office of an HBCU…I'm ready to tell my story.

Do you have a story? I'll bet you do. I bet you have a story about some kind of hardship that you have experienced, and how you made it through. Perhaps you dealt with the loss of a loved one wherein the grief nearly caused you to lose your mind, but God kept you and is continuing to heal you day by day. Perhaps you dealt with a health issue that almost took you out of here, but God turned it around and you're still here to tell it. Maybe you were in a relationship with a narcissist who was emotionally or perhaps physically abusive, but you finally escaped and got out of it with your life. Maybe you had some kind of addiction that you broke free from, and now you're clean. Maybe you attempted suicide. Lord!!! I know all of my examples are always so drastic. Maybe you're young and it's not this deep. Maybe you simply learned how to deal with a bully or how to have self-confidence. Maybe your parents split, and you learned how to deal with the difficult transitions. Trust me, if you live long enough, you will have a story to tell. The problem comes when people are too ashamed to share their story with others. The devil wants to trick you into sweeping it under the rug because he knows that your testimony is where all the power is. I could preach to you all day about Shadrach, Meshach, and Abednego, but perhaps there's someone who could relate more to Shantay, Mesha, and Ahmad. The key to unlock someone else's chains might just be in your own mouth. You must exercise wisdom, because your story may or may not be for everyone to hear. It's best to pray and ask God to show you how and when to use your testimony for His glory.

READ TODAY: REVELATION 12:11

CAUGHT ME SLIPPIN'

Caught me slippin' – a phrase indicating that a person has experienced a momentary lapse in judgement often due to a lack of preparedness.

Example: Ugh! That half-off sale caught me slippin' and I spent a little too much money. Now my cell phone is about to be cut off.

The world seems so backwards at times. It often seems like up is down and down is up. It's almost as if good is bad, but bad is great. When you look at the news, it's the bad news that seems to get reported on the most. When you look at social media, it seems like the people with the most followers are the ones who have no clothes on. There's even a social media site where people can become millionaires overnight after users pay money to see them naked. Even now, I bet some of you are thinking...hey, what's wrong with people getting naked for social media?! Me even mentioning that is more offensive than the fact that we are showing our impressionable young ladies how great it is to capitalize off of lust for money. Nobody tells them about the spiritual repercussions for any of that, but I digress. It seems like the people who sell drugs and kill people to get rich are our heroes. What I'm saying is that it gets very tempting to go those routes when you're barely making ends meet. I just want to encourage you not to get distracted by what's going on to your left and right. Continue to stand firmly and keep your eyes focused forward, so that your foot does not slip. Remain committed to doing whatever God told **you** to do. The other options may look appealing, but understand that the instant gratification may not be worth the way that it will affect your spirit. Continue to hold to God's unchanging hand, and don't let the things of the world catch you slipping.

READ TODAY: PSALM 73:2-3

NOTIFICATIONS

Notifications – an alert issued to you by either your cell phone or a social media app. Notifications can alert you about things like news updates, new messages received, or that another user has communicated with you in some way.

Example: I fell asleep and woke up to 30 new FB notifications.
What's going on?!

I have a weird relationship with notifications. On one hand, I love to see them because I enjoy when people communicate with me, particularly if I feel bored or lonely otherwise. On the other hand, notifications can be overwhelming especially during times when I'm super busy. I get this irrational feeling that if I don't respond to people right away that they are somewhere mad at me. It's anxiety-inducing, lowkey. That being said, to protect my peace, I have the majority of my phone's notifications set to OFF. One thing I love about the Holy Spirit is that He also has a way of notifying us of things that we need to know. He sends messages that help us to better navigate the situations that we face. Sometimes these notifications are actually warnings. Have you ever found yourself at the end of a situation wishing you had trusted that "intuition" that would have helped you to avoid it? Yup. You had a notification from the Holy Spirit, but you set it to OFF and kept speeding right past every red flag. Turning off notifications on your phone is one thing, but turning off notifications from the Holy Spirit ain't what you want. The more quality time you spend with God, the more easily you will be able to differentiate the Holy Spirit's notifications from the notifications that you receive from your flesh. Yes, your flesh sends notifications too…but that's a different devotion for a different day! Y'all be safe out here.

READ TODAY: JOHN 16:13

HAND ME YOUR PHONE!

Hand me your phone! – what you get told by your friends whenever you do too much or act crazy on the internet.

Example: Person A: ...and to this triflin' little girl Tameka Jenkins, who was smiling in my face and messing with Jason behind my back, guess what? You might want to go to the clinic to get tested boo!
Friend: Delete this and hand me your phone, sis.

We all have that one friend who gets super emotional and starts posting stuff that they probably don't need to post. Some people get drunk and post things that they later regret. Sadly, most social media friends aren't real friends. Most social media friends are there cheering you on in your craziness because...well...it's entertaining, and they don't really care what happens to you as a result. A true friend doesn't want to see you go out like that. A true friend knows you well enough to understand that you are not in the proper mental state to be posting statements to the public. If you aren't already aware, some potential employers will secretly browse through a candidate's social media profile before making a hiring decision. If they see certain red flags about your personal life, that might cost you the job. Good friends know this, and also they just don't want to see you get embarrassed. I said all this to say that a true friend will hold you accountable when they see you doing foolish things. And while we're on the subject, let's talk about personal accountability as well. If I asked you to hand me your phone, would you have to go through frantically deleting things first? Are you using your phone to engage in sneaky activities that you wouldn't want anyone to find out about? Who holds you accountable? If you don't have any friends who could take your phone, pray and ask God to send you someone who can be an accountability partner and a prayer partner. There is strength in accountability.

READ TODAY: JAMES 5:16

IS THIS THE HILL YOU WANT TO DIE ON?

Is this the hill you want to die on? – a question posed to someone who is passionately defending a position that will inevitably lead to their own demise.

Example: Person A: R. Kelly didn't do anything wrong! Those girls made their own choices! Free R. Kelly!
Person B: Is this the hill you want to die on today?

Every single day, people on the internet and in person, take stances and fight battles for causes that don't…really…matter for their lives. You see it all the time in relationships. Let's just say that Person A and Person B in the example above are in a romantic relationship. I'm not saying that Person A is a terrible monster, but perhaps he or she simply has not thought their ideas through. Perhaps they don't realize that they are victim-blaming minor children to defend a sexual predator and statutory rapist. But let's just say that I am person B. By asking this question, I'm giving you a chance to evaluate what you're saying and maybe retract it. Because once you stand ten toes down to fight for this particular cause, there is no coming back. I will no longer see you as a person I'd like to raise children with, and I'm breaking up with you. In other words, "choose your battles wisely." Every opinion that comes to your mind isn't worth dying for. I've seen people dying on hills for celebrities that wouldn't even stop to give them the time of day. Yet when battles arise that are worth fighting, they are silent. When causes that do matter require a voice, they don't want to get involved. I want us to check on our priorities. Jesus died for us on a hill called Calvary, and that was a cause that was well worth it! Rev. Dr. Martin Luther King, Jr. famously stated that, "If a man hasn't found something he will die for, he isn't fit to live." The things that you are going to the mattress for…in life, in love, and on social media…are you sure that's it?

READ TODAY: MATTHEW 12:36-37

I'M PLAYING CHESS, NOT CHECKERS.

I'm playing chess, not checkers. – an old expression used to mean that a person is operating strategically to make decisions based on long-term satisfaction as opposed to instant gratification.

Example: In high school, people made fun of me because I didn't own any expensive clothes and shoes. Now I'm 20 years old, and I just closed on my first investment property. I'm playing chess, not checkers.

The difference between chess and checkers, is that a chess match usually takes longer to play and requires more strategy. In chess, you have to visualize what you intend to do several steps ahead of actually being able to make those winning moves. Don't get me wrong...there is some strategy involved in checkers as well, but in checkers you are making decisions that seem to have the best impact short term. In chess, by contrast, you can appear to be losing for a long time when in reality, you are just busy setting the stage for the checkmate. Sometimes God will give you a vision that requires patience. Sometimes God will give you a vision that requires you to set the stage and appear to be losing in the process. Don't get distracted by the people around you who appear to be playing checkers and winning. Their assignment is their assignment. It's okay if the gratification isn't instant. Just keep in mind the vision and the strategy that God has shown you and have faith that your focus and dedication will soon pay off with a win. Be patient, and don't fall for the banana in the tailpipe trick where you take an unauthorized move out of frustration. Abraham and Sarah did this in the Bible when they got frustrated with their waiting process. They ended up creating a mess if you want to go read about it. I just want to encourage you today that it's okay to play the long game. Let's pray today and ask God to grant us extra patience to keep the faith.

HE/SHE BELONGS TO THE STREETS.

He/She belongs to the streets. – a way to describe a person who bounces from bed to bed and has no intentions of being faithful in a relationship.

Example: I don't know why I tried to have a real relationship with Linda. She belongs to the streets.

Y'all really have to get into this Bible tea. This whole story was a mess. So there was a lady who they said belonged to the streets. Apparently, she had been caught in the very act of adultery. To me that means somebody walked in on them getting it in. *Kanye Shrug* Well, they wanted to stone her to death, because apparently this was a stone-worthy offense. Now as Ricki Lake used to say, "It takes two to tango…" So now I'm trying to see how they got sis out there but not the guy who she was doing the no-pants dance with. Shouldn't he get stoned too since y'all know who he was? Hmm…moving right along. The religious trolls brought her to Jesus because they were hoping to trip Him up with another loaded question. This is when Jesus stooped down and wrote his (now famous) saying on the ground. "Whichever one of y'all that ain't never did nothing wrong in ya life, how about you throw the first stone at this girl?" (No, you will not find that translation anywhere.). Chiiiileeee…they couldn't even say anything after that! All they could do was walk off because they knew they had dirt too. Jesus told the lady she was good to go, but to get out of them streets. What did we learn here, class? I learned that Jesus came to save us from the death penalty that should have accompanied our sin. I learned that even when we **are** guilty, God's grace is…amazing. I also learned that we owe it to Him to honor His sacrifice by getting out of the street life that tried to kill us, and get into the will of God instead.

READ TODAY: JOHN 8:3-11

GOTS TA BE MO' CAREFUL!

Gots ta be mo' careful! – an exclamation of regret used when one realizes that the issue that they are experiencing could have and should have been avoided.

Example: Yeah, turns out the African prince I fell in love with was just a guy in Omaha trying to scam me for money. Gots ta be mo' careful!

I think intentionality is underrated. It seems like we romanticize the stories where "things just fell into place somehow." We love a good story where there was no planning and no preparation, but everything just worked out some kind of way. We call it organic. Don't get me wrong, there is absolutely nothing wrong with things that fall into place organically. But let's not forget how effective we are when we use wisdom to do things carefully and intentionally. Why are we always throwing Hail Mary passes when there is actually time on the clock to draw up a real play and execute it? That's no way to operate. That's how people end up with regret. What is it that you are hoping to see happen in your life? Are you hoping to buy a new home? Perhaps you should take care to tighten up on your spending habits and fix your credit. Do you want to be married one day? Perhaps you should seek healing and stop running good people away with your bitterness. Do you want to go into business? Perhaps you should improve your craft, do research on what you're trying to do, and find a mentor. Social Media will have you fooled into thinking that all these people just became a success overnight (ahem…but if y'all wanna make my books go viral overnight, that's also fine, cough cough). The majority of people who you see excelling are people who have been careful, strategic, and intentional. Would a miracle be nice? Absolutely! But simple wisdom application might be the miracle you were looking for all along. You just gots ta be mo' careful.

READ TODAY: EPHESIANS 5:15-17

"WHO ARE ME TO JUDGE?"
-Anthony Caldwell

"Who are me to judge?" – this quote went viral after social media personality, Anthony Caldwell, said it multiple times in a live video. The internet ran with it.

Example: Personally, I wouldn't let a grown, able-bodied man stay with me rent-free for 4 years, but who are me to judge?

Listen, if there is one scripture that everybody and their mama will quote, it's the scripture in Matthew chapter 7 about not judging. "Judge not, that ye be not judged." Folks that don't even believe the Bible...they believe that scripture! But I want to challenge us today to think about it a little bit deeper. Almost every other translation clarifies the verse to mean, "Don't judge others if you don't want to be judged yourself." The passage goes on to talk about people trying to judge and correct other people's small problems when they haven't addressed their own big ones. It says to fix your own problem first, so that you can see clearly to fix that of another. So wait...is it true that we should never make a judgement? No. Because how can you ever help anyone you love if you are too busy feeling as if you can't tell them the truth? The Bible in John 7:24 tells us that we should judge "righteous" judgement. But we have been backed into this "don't be judgemental, don't say anything to anybody" corner, which is a part of Satan's strategy to keep us from shining our light. The truth is that we just need to get **ourselves** together first if we want to be able to offer good, sound judgement that will help others. We must tell the truth to **ourselves** first, so that we won't be out here dishing stuff to others that we are unprepared to take. Pray today and ask God to help you see and fix any unrighteousness that's going on within yourself, so that you may be able to be a vessel that is fit to help others.

READ TODAY: MATTHEW 7:1-5

ON TO THE NEXT

On to the next – a phrase used when a person has decided to move on after a disappointment such as the loss of a relationship, a job, or an opportunity.

Example: Bob and I broke up last night. I guess it's on to the next!

Our generation is different from the one that came before us. People would stay at one job for 30+ years and then retire. They would live in the same house for 40+ years and actually pay it off. They would be married for 50+ years and throw a 50th anniversary party. Heck, they would be funeralized in the same church that they were baptized in. Nowadays, we marvel at anyone who is able to keep that level of consistency, because it is so rare. Now, we are quick to move on to the next thing. I'm not sure if it's because we value advancement over stability, but longevity is just not one of the dominant traits for us. However, this can lead to feelings of instability, especially if we are comparing ourselves to our parents. The best thing to do is to pray and ask God for direction. It's not that we want to bounce around from job to job or from relationship to relationship. It's just that we haven't been able to find people, places, and things that make us feel at peace. As I have said many times, pray about everything. If you are feeling unstable, and if you are starting to feel tired of starting over, maybe you aren't paying attention to the guidance of the Holy Spirit. When things end in one place, maybe you should take time, pray, and ask God to order your next steps. It's not wise to just hop on the next train leaving the station when you have no idea if it's even traveling to your destination. I pray that God would lead and guide you on to the next that **He** wants you to have.

READ TODAY: 1 PETER 5:10

WE OUTSIDE.

We Outside. – post-quarantine slang used to celebrate the fact that people have left the confines of their home.

Example: Person A: That looks like fun! Where are y'all?
Person B: We outside!!

I am in no way, shape, form, or fashion, claiming to be an outdoorsy type of person. Where I live, it seems like the weather is always doing extreme stuff. It's either super hot, super cold, or tornado weather. There are only a few days out of the year that I can say being outside in Alabama is comfortable to me. It's a shame, really. However, I do love and appreciate God's creation. As I write this, it's raining, thundering, and lightning. I am staring out of a window at the wind swaying the trees. It's so beautiful to me. No, I am not high! It's just that you can't help but notice how plant and animal life continues to survive even the most severe storms. So if God thinks enough of the plants and animals to take care of them throughout their storms, why is it that we worry about whether God will take care of us in ours? Why do we worry about whether God will provide for us, when He provides for all outdoors? Worry and fear can be paralyzing. It can also cause you to act erratically which will only make matters worse. When you know that God will take care of you, you can move different(ly). When you know that God will take care of you, you can go to sleep at night. Next time you go outside, take a look around you. Look at all of the beautiful things that God is taking care of and use it as a reminder that He will take care of you too.

READ TODAY: MATTHEW 6:25-33

DUE TO PERSONAL REASONS…

Due to personal reasons… – an excuse to do what you feel like doing without having to explain it to anybody.

Example: Due to personal reasons, I will be eating all of the leftover mac and cheese from Thanksgiving…by myself.

Have you ever been in a situation where you struggled to perform on the level that you were expected to perform on? Because we live in a capitalist society, a lot of emphasis is placed on performance and productivity. In 2021, Simone Biles (the greatest gymnast of all time) decided to drop out of competition in the middle of the Tokyo Olympics. She was slated to win several more gold medals for Team USA but cited "personal reasons" as to why she chose not to continue. She said that her reasons were physical and emotional but didn't go into further detail at the time. This decorated, world-record breaking gymnast was dragged by critics who called her weak and said that she let her whole country down. Meanwhile…black folks and, well, anybody who is a decent human being…cheered her on for her strength in standing up for herself to protect her body and mind. The message in this is to always remember that your life is led by the Holy Spirit and not by the high-pressure expectations of others. I am not telling you to be reckless, but if the **Holy Spirit** is telling you something, don't let anybody else override that, even if it's on the biggest stage in the world. This is why I continue to hammer home the importance of developing a close and personal relationship with the Holy Spirit, so you can tell the difference between His voice and your feelings. If you move based on your own emotions, there's no telling what may happen. But if you move based on His voice, you will have peace and protection no matter the outcome. Somebody reading this needs to pray and ask God if you're doing "it" because people expect you to or because He told you to.

READ TODAY: JOHN 16:13

THEY GONE DRAG YOU...

They gone drag you... – a phrase used to warn an individual about the onslaught of negativity that is about to come their way.

Example: Person A: I don't like Beyoncé.
Person B: They gone drag you...

If you are a newcomer to social media, you may or may not be aware that there are certain things that we simply do not say. Certain things are the equivalent to being a Red Sox fan in a room full of Yankees. It's best to just play it cool, and rep for the Red Sox when you get back to a safe place in Boston. Expressing certain viewpoints in certain places is like lighting a cigarette inside of a powder keg. When a person does this, they are literally asking to be dragged by the multitude. There is, however, another individual who seeks to drag you just for dragging's sake. You don't even have to do or say anything to provoke it. Satan is always **looking** for opportunities to take you and pull you down to the ground. That's why it is extremely important not to flirt with anything that he tries to offer you. It may seem like a good idea at first, but I can guarantee you that it will end with you being dragged...drug...druggen? Either way, when you play a game with the devil, I can guarantee that it is rigged against you. It may look like flirting with that woman at work is fun and harmless, but you're married. It's a setup to drag you. It may seem like getting involved in that sketchy, illegal business enterprise is a good idea, but if things go sideways, they already have a plan to let you take the fall. It' a setup to drag you. This is why you have to be careful. Please don't be lulled into thinking that you don't have an adversary who literally spends time looking for ways to drag the very life out of you. Don't worry, this is not to make you afraid. Satan has no real authority over you. He can only do what you allow, so don't give him the opportunity.

READ TODAY: LUKE 22:31-32

MY LITTLE BROKE BEST FRIENDS

My little broke best friends – describes one's own children.

Example: Having a blast at Six Flags with my little broke best friends!

If you have children in your life, you know that taking care of them is hard work. It can be so utterly exhausting, especially when they are young. You put them down for bed just as your body and mind are involuntarily shutting down and threatening to collapse. Yet just before you pass out from the exhaustion, you think to yourself, "gosh, I love those crazy little muckrakers." I think it's interesting to see the cultural shift wherein people now refer to their kids as their little broke best friends. Back in my day, parents would **constantly** remind you that, "I **ain't** one of your little friends." I think there is room for both ideas to be embraced. Maybe our children can be our friends. I think the problem comes when parents allow their children to say and do things that are out of line because they don't want to lose their "friendship." We've all seen the parent who is afraid to discipline their child because they don't want to fall from the child's good graces. They don't want their child to get angry, cry, storm away, slam doors and yell, "I hate you, Karen!" They are more worried about keeping the child's "friendship" than they are about teaching them what's right. Is that true friendship? If you don't tell someone the truth because of how it may affect **you**, are you really a friend? Are you doing that child any favors by allowing them to grow up with a false sense of reality? Are you doing them a disservice by not preparing them for the real world in which throwing a temper tantrum at age 23 is stupid? Is that even love? If you are struggling with balancing this with the children in your life, use God's example. He loves us, we are His children, and yet the Bible says that He calls us His friends. But when we are wrong, He will chastise us, not out of anger, but out of love. Being a friend is more than just letting someone have their way.

READ TODAY: HEBREWS 12:11

SCREENSHOT

Screenshot – a way to capture a permanent picture of whatever is being displayed on the screen of your device.

Example: Randy was on FB posting racist comments. I took a screenshot and sent it to his boss.

Screenshots have gotten people in so much trouble over the years. Our phones have even upped the ante by allowing us to not only capture pictures, but now videos of whatever is coming across our screen. But for some reason, people continue to forget that screenshots exist. Pastors, politicians, professionals, and others who are supposed to have some sense, have been caught up in scandals because of screenshots and screen recordings. I think people get lulled into trusting people with their foolery. It's all well and good until that person gets upset and decides to use screenshots of what you thought was a private conversation to destroy everything that you have built. You think those people are covering you, but they are not. They are laughing at you in the group chat with their friends. This message isn't to condemn you. Do you need to be delivered from certain areas where you struggle? Absolutely! Yet we know that perfection doesn't always happen overnight. For many of us, change and maturation is a process. But for those of you who carry an assignment from God over your life, I want you to exercise wisdom because Satan's plan is to steal your effectiveness as a witness. Don't walk into a trap wherein you expose your weakness simply because you trusted someone who has absolutely no reason to cover you in your mess. If you wouldn't want the others to see it, don't send it. Be intentional. Ask yourself if someone were to screenshot this and share it, would I be in trouble? I really want you to overcome whatever sin has got you bound, but in the meantime, stop being foolish about it.

READ TODAY: MICAH 7:5

I'M SORRY FOR YOUR LOSS/LOST.

I'm sorry for your loss/lost. – an expression used to offer condolences to someone who has lost a loved one. Although the conventional phrase ends in the word "loss," there are many people who either don't know or don't care and instead offer condolences for someone's "lost."

Example: Person A: My Big Mama gained her wings this morning.
Person B: I'm sorry for your lost. You are in my prayers.

I too, am sorry for your loss. I really am. One of life's greatest difficulties is having to experience some sort of loss. People can lose loved ones, relationships, friendships, jobs, possessions, and even pets. But my advice to you is not to allow your loss to make you lost. There are those who experience a loss, mourn it in a healthy fashion, and keep it pushing. Yet there are others whose whole entire life stops at the point of their heartbreak. We've all seen the person who becomes grief-stricken and can no longer operate because of that person or thing that is no longer there. After the loss, they are literally lost. Everything is hazy. They have no clarity or direction anymore. They may stop caring about their own life or get sick themselves. Their work performance may falter, and they may lose their job. They may sabotage healthy relationships and embrace toxic ones. If you have experienced a loss in any form, I just want you to be aware that it's more than just a loss. It's a part of Satan's strategy to defeat you. If he can get you to be paralyzed with grief and pain, he knows that you will not be able to walk in your true purpose and destiny in the earth. If he can get you to start idolizing and obsessing over the thing that was lost, he can get you to take your eyes off of God. The solution is to trust God regarding the things and people that come and go in your life. I'm sorry for your loss, but I will not stand by and watch you get lost.

READ TODAY: PROVERBS 3:5-6

SPONSORED AD

Sponsored Ad – a label placed on a social media post to alert a viewer that the message is a paid advertisement.

Example: I lost 10 lbs. just by drinking this new tea! (Sponsored Ad)

There is a reason why social media began to label things as sponsored ads. They would have been in big trouble if they were receiving money to make certain posts appear more prominently in your feed without telling you. Even celebrities are now disclosing the fact that they are being paid to post certain things, because it absolves them of certain liabilities concerning the product that they are endorsing. But can I tell you this? There are still millions of dollars being exchanged **without** notification to you, for people to influence you to do something or buy something. If you are spending time on social media, I urge you to keep your eyes open for manipulation. I understand the importance of marketing, and I think it's a really cool tool. But some marketing is underhanded, deceptive, and manipulative. It's not always to get you to spend money, sometimes it is used to get you to believe an idea. This is why it's so important to put on the full armor of God. There is a piece of armor known as the Helmet of Salvation. Helmets, as you know, are designed to protect your head, which includes your brain. Have you been inundated with other people's manipulative content? We can and should refresh the browser of our minds by allowing ourselves to be renewed daily by the word of God. This means that we should fill our heads with what God says so that we don't have room to be easily swayed by things or people who are looking to take advantage of us through manipulation. This doesn't just apply to money and sales. It applies to every area of our lives. We must guard our thoughts by meditating on what God has said.

READ TODAY: MATTHEW 24:4

PRAY FOR ME! NOTHING'S WRONG…

Pray for me! Nothing's wrong… - a phrase used to solicit prayers for things that might be deemed as frivolous.

Example: Pray for me! Nothing's wrong, I just didn't have to time to stop at Starbucks, and Glenda from accounting is already asking me questions that she should know the answers to.

When someone asks for prayer, our antennas instantly go up. What's wrong?! What happened?! Are you okay?! Where are the kids?! Is your mama alright?! For some reason, we have equated prayer with peril. And although we can and should reach out to God in times of despair, prayer is so much more than that. The Bible tells us that God is concerned about everything that concerns us. That includes things that may seem frivolous. Pray about as much as you can. Don't assume anything. Congratulations on receiving the job offer! But that doesn't mean you should accept it without praying first. I know you are upset with that loved one. But that doesn't mean you should hit send on that 10-page text message at 3am without praying and asking God how to approach the situation. I know that man got down on one knee in front of all of your family and friends to propose, but how do you know if God is giving you the go-ahead if you've never prayed to ask Him if this guy was meant to be your husband. I think you see where I'm going here. Nothing is too frivolous to pray about. There doesn't have to be something "wrong" to pray. Sometimes prayer is simply preventative. Praying for God's guidance can keep you out of the trouble that will have you flailing and desperate to pray later on. I think M.C. Hammer once told us that we needed to pray if for no other reason than to make it today!

READ TODAY: 1 THESSALONIANS 5:17

MAKING MOVES IN SILENCE...

Making moves in silence... - what people say when they want to tell people that they are up to something. Most don't realize the irony of the statement.

Example: Person A: I'm busy making moves in silence!
        Dr. Lori: Umm...not anymore.

Has your mouth ever gotten you in trouble? I know mine has. There have been times where I would have been much better off had I never said anything to anybody about anything. Maybe it's just that we are getting to that age now, but there seem to be a lot of people who now understand this point. There was a guy named Joseph in the Bible who had been given a very vivid dream about some things that were to come in the future. Joseph told his brothers about the dream, and they got jealous. They were already jealous of him to start off with, but that's neither here nor there. Once they heard about the dream, they began to plot against him. I think that I am sometimes like Joseph. I can be naïve in thinking that everyone would be happy to see me advance. I get excited when I see people winning, but I have to remember that everyone isn't like that. Now that we have social media, we have people following us who may be fake friends. For the life of me, I don't understand why people follow folks that they dislike, but people do it. If you post about the dream house that you have found, don't be surprised if someone from your own friend list goes and gets it before you can. If you post about a business idea, don't be surprised if someone from your own friend list copies it and does it before you do. If you post about someone you're dating, don't be surprised if someone from your own friend list slides in their DMs in hopes of gaining their attention instead. When God gives you a vision, keep your head down, do the work quietly, and let the Holy Spirit tell you when it's time to make an announcement.

READ TODAY: 1 THESSALONIANS 4:11-12

SNATCHED

Snatched – used to describe a woman's slim waistline.

Example: Yesss honey! Have you been working out? That waist is snatched!

I know I can come off as all deep and spiritual sometimes, but all I want is a good life, someone dope to share it with, and a waist that is snatched! When we say that a waist has been "snatched," we are saying that it has been gathered up and pulled inwards away from chaos and disorder. Some people's waistlines are naturally snatched. Others must do workouts that target the fat around their midsections. Still others make use of contraptions such as corsets, body shapers, or waist trainers to achieve optimal snatchedness. Speaking of getting snatched, has God ever snatched you out of a situation? I mean has He ever just taken you, gathered you up, and pulled you inwards and away from chaos and disorder? There are certain situations where God will wait for you to get your mind right and exit on your own. But there are other situations where God will straight **snatch** you out of the hand of the enemy. He sees and knows that if you stay where you are, you are headed for trouble. He knows that perhaps you don't know enough to leave the situation on your own. When you experience the snatching of the Lord, it's not much longer until you can look back and see exactly what he spared you from. Have you ever been in a relationship with someone, and it ended abruptly? You may not have wanted it to end when it did, but now you can look back and see that God was helping you to dodge a whole entire bullet. Your parents may have made you go to college or the military after high school. Maybe you weren't too keen on going, but now you can look back and see that all the guys who stayed around the neighborhood ended up dead, in jail, or strung out on drugs. God delivered you from evil by snatching you out of it, and for this we give God praise.

READ TODAY: PSALM 40:13

THAT THANG THANGIN'.

That thang thangin'. – a compliment, usually referring to a woman's backside that is particularly impressive in size, shape, and movement.

Example: *Woman with nice booty posts video walking in sundress*
          People in Comment Section: That thang thangin' today!

When we say that a thang is thangin', what we are really saying is that it is doing exactly what it is supposed to be doing. We are saying that it is operating on a high level and precisely as intended. You reach a whole new level of self-awareness when you can turn your identity into an action verb. I love it when my friend Adrienne is somewhere Adrienne-ing. When Adrienne (the noun) gets a chance to Adrienne (the verb), it is a beautiful thing. To "Adrienne" is to be loving, caring, giving, productive, creative, focused, organized, and happy. That's who she is, that's what she does, and that's how God designed her. She knows it and I know it. So when anything comes along trying to stop Adrienne from being able to Adrienne, it must be handled or eliminated. Are you self-aware enough to know whether your thang is thangin'? Do you know if your you is you-ing? Are you operating in the way that God has designed you to operate, or are you allowing things to come along and steal that from you? Are you a happy person who is always crying? Are you a giving person who has had to scale back due to people taking advantage of you? Are you a smart person who has to play small for the insecurities of others? If your thang isn't thangin', you are doing a disservice to the world. We need your you. God put you here for a purpose. How will you ever fulfill it if you're spending time trying to be something that you're not? Let's pray today that God would help us to find the environments in which we are able to thrive as our true, authentic, anointed selves.

READ TODAY: EPHESIANS 2:10

GLOW UP

Glow up – describes a transformation in which a person who once looked dusty and dim now looks like a bright and shining star.

Example: Did y'all see Belinda at the class reunion? Her glow up was real!

I love to see a good glow up. I gain a lot of encouragement from glow ups because they remind me that my current state doesn't have to be my permanent state. They also remind me that my greatness is already inside of me, and that all it takes is some vision and some effort to bring it out. Glow ups don't happen unless someone first visualizes themselves as new and improved. The best glow ups, however, are the ones where the change is more than external. We place so much emphasis on the physical transformations, that sometimes we forget about the spiritual ones that matter the most. Honestly, when you see people glowing externally, it is usually because they have first changed their heart or mind in some way. There is a difference between a makeover and a glow up. A makeover may be some better clothes, hair, and contouring makeup to cover a person who is still miserable. A true glow up is when the Holy Spirit begins to lead and guide you into a better way of existence. He teaches you how to make better decisions, how to take care of yourself better, how to treat others, how to forgive, and how to protect your peace. When things like these occur on the inside of you, it is only a matter of time before the glow shows up on the outside of you. Allow the Holy Spirit to become your personal mentor, and the glow up will be bright and visible to all. Your assignment, if you choose to accept it, is to go watch the 1985 film *Berry Gordy's The Last Dragon* and find your glow.

READ TODAY: EPHESIANS 5:8-9

GO GHOST

Go Ghost– to abruptly disappear from another's life without any warning or communication.

Example: Everything seemed to be going well with Ricky. I have no idea why he decided to go ghost on me.

I don't know who needs to hear this, but people who "go ghost" are the worst. I haven't experienced it myself, but I know people who have, and it's very hurtful. Going ghost is not a situation where you've had an argument with someone and decide to cut them off out of anger or fear. Oh no, going ghost is when everything seems to be going perfectly fine to the other individual, but you decide that you are no longer interested for one reason or another. You don't communicate that, though. You simply stop answering their calls, texts, or DMs. Some even go as far as blocking the individual who they literally just ate dinner with or maybe even slept with the night before. I guess it's a lot easier to go ghost than to simply communicate that you are no longer interested. But what kind of lazy sociopathic mess is that? I've known people who have called around to hospitals in a panic thinking that maybe there has been a terrible accident or that their acquaintance is dead. How do you literally break bread with someone one day and be that cruel to them the next? It's traumatic to have someone special in your life one day who is dead to you the next. And I know some of the "saints" do it too! Remember, I'm not talking about people who are abusive or toxic. You can say, "I'm no longer interested in pursuing this relationship and prefer not to explain my reasoning." After that, block/ignore them to your hearts content, but gosh darn it, be decent! If you are going to go ghost, **go Holy Ghost**. He teaches us how to do things decently and in order, and He also teaches us how to treat people with love and compassion. Maybe it's not ghosting for you, but catch the overarching principle: do unto others as you would have them do unto you!

READ TODAY: MATTHEW 7:12

OH NO. OH NO. OH NO NO NO NO NO.

Oh no. Oh no. Oh no no no no no. - lyrics to a song/sound often used on TikTok. It is usually dubbed over video of someone making a mistake.

Example: *Video of someone falling UP a flight of steps*
        Song: Oh no. Oh no. Oh no no no no no.

Have you ever asked God for something, but the answer was just no? How did you respond? Did you accept the answer and move forward? Or did you throw a tantrum while trying to get what you wanted some other way? When God's answer is no, it is in your best interest to chill out and fall back. I understand that you had a way you wanted everything to turn out. I understand that you wanted that exact house, car, man, woman, or job. I even personally understand that you wanted healing for that parent or grandparent. But let's be clear. Not only does God know what will make you happy in the long run, He also knows what will make you miserable. There will be times in life where you will reach a crossroads. If God says bear right, but you decide to speed ahead in the other direction, swerve past the cones, and jump the barricade...He might just let you go ahead and do it. But I can guarantee that it ain't what you want. Don't be surprised when you bend that corner and end up in a fiery crash because you didn't know that the road was ending and that you'd fall over a cliff. That pain is going to be a lot worse than the slight pinch that would have been required to accept God's no. If you can't accept a no from God, do you really trust Him? He's not some genie in a bottle. He sees, knows, and cares for you. Do you really believe that if He can't tell you no? A no from God will show you just how strong or weak your connection to Him really is.

READ TODAY: PSALM 26:2

MESS AROUND AND FIND OUT.

Mess around and find out. – a warning to let others know that if they keep poking at you, they will be surprised by the outcome.

> Example: This lady at work got disrespectful with me today. I may have this PhD now, but I came out the projects…she finna mess around and find out!

Have you ever been a recipient of God's grace? Well of course you have! We all are, but if you've ever been in a situation where you **knew** that you were wrong and that God did **not** have to allow you another opportunity to get it right, then today's message is for you. God has had your back way more times than you are even aware of, but let's focus on the times that you know about. Maybe nobody ever found out about that pregnancy scare. Maybe you were unfaithful in your marriage, but God saved your family and gave you another chance. Perhaps all the chili cheese fries finally caught up to you, but the doctor caught the blockage just before you would have had a massive heart attack. You see, life would be scary without God's grace, but I don't want to mess around and find out. There is nowhere in the Bible that says that we should carry on with our foolishness because we can always count on grace. If you hear the Holy Spirit continuing to warn you about something, don't ignore it. Sometimes we get comfortable simply because nothing happened the first 20 times. It's like I tell my contact lens patients who insist on sleeping in their contacts every night: "It's all fun and games until you wake up with an infection that has eaten through your cornea and blinded you while you were asleep." They get a false sense of security because they have "gotten away" with it so many times. But I try to let them know that when them consequences hit, baybehh??! Irreversible. All I'm saying is don't mess around and find out that grace may not always be the case. Do not ignore the Holy Spirit.

READ TODAY: ROMANS 6:1-2

#POSITIVEVIBESONLY

#PositiveVibesOnly – a hashtag signifying that negativity is unwelcome in a particular space.

Example: I don't know why people feel the need to screenshot what my ex does and send it to me. Stop it! #PositiveVibesOnly

There's something about getting that three in front of your age that makes you allergic to the bull shiggidy. If you are 30 or above, you probably know exactly what I'm talking about. Of course there are people who are too attached to their negativity to receive this amazing revelation. But for the rest of us, baby, we got set free! We stopped caring so much about people's opinions, and we developed something like an allergy to negativity. For some of us the allergy is so strong that we can't even stand to be in the room with it, much less listen to it. Once we catch a whiff of a negative vibe, we are ret ta go! The crazy thing is that we are often reluctant to fully submit ourselves to God because, deep down, we think that it will suck or be negative in some way. Just admit it. We've been tricked into thinking that obeying the desires of our flesh is the happy, fun, exciting, and pleasurable thing to do…that those are the positive vibes. Meanwhile, we view obeying God like the bachelor who feels that one day he'll settle down with a ball and chain only after being free and enjoying the streets. It's so backwards because God is the originator of the positive vibes. The thoughts He thinks toward us are good and not evil. Yet we act like He's the one out to make us miserable when it's the exact opposite. God's ways are there to make us free, and it's Satan who is using our flesh to make us slaves. It's Satan who thinks evil thoughts and tries to set us up for a life of misery. He's the one with the negative vibes, not God. God is able to make all things work together positively for our good. Do not be deceived. God is good **all the time** and all the time, God is what? **Positive.**

READ TODAY: JEREMIAH 29:11

#MOOD

#Mood – a hashtag describing how someone feels currently.

Example: *posts picture of The Grinch Who Stole Christmas*
Caption: #Mood

Is there a difference between happiness and joy? Back in the day, one of my Sunday School teachers told me that happiness is more of an emotion while joy is something that you possess inside. In other words, happiness is really a "mood" because it can be temporary. If you realize that the wing spot accidentally gave you a 12pc instead of the 8pc you ordered, for example, it might make you happy. But if you get home moments later and drop all those wings on the floor of the garage before you could eat any of them, the happiness quickly fades into sadness, disappointment, and hunger. As human beings, we are bound to experience a plethora of different emotions, sometimes all within the same hour. I don't think any of us are completely immune to feeling all the feels of life. Sometimes you will be happy, and other times you just won't be. But the problem comes when you don't have your joy. Joy isn't a mood. It feels good, but it isn't an emotion. It is a sense of gladness that persists and prevails without regard to fleeting circumstantial or situational occurrences. Where does the gladness come from? Well joy is a fruit of the Holy Spirit. The Holy Spirit not only teaches us stuff, but He also helps us to remember the things that we have learned. Joy happens because you have learned who God is, how much He loves you, and how He will always take care of His children. Joy happens when you refuse to let the frustrations of life cause you to forget what you have learned. When you have Joy, there's only so down you can feel before you realize that with God, you're still straight. Some people have become so caught up in their pursuit of happiness that they don't realize that what they really need is Joy, which is everlasting.

READ TODAY: GALATIANS 5:22-23

208

ISSA

Issa – slang term literally meaning "it is a…"

Example: Issa doctor! My niece just graduated from med school!

Hello! Happy whatever day this is! I pray that your day is going well. Today we will have story time. Yesterday my seven-year-old daughter had what she called a "horrible day." She explained that she had wasted milk on her pants at breakfast and that her whole class had gotten in trouble during P.E. even though she was not one of the ones acting up. She had wasted some water from her water bottle in the car on the way home and had also been scolded for rushing through her reading assignment. Not only that, but I made her and her sister go to bed 15 minutes early for not cleaning up behind themselves. I guess that was just the last straw because baby girl broke all the way down as if I had just told her she was going up for adoption of something. I told her that she should get some rest and that we'd make sure to pray for an easier day tomorrow. Well today, as we were headed to the car, a huge dog (that was literally bigger than all three of us combined) comes out of nowhere jumping all over the children and myself. It scared the living daylights out of us and my daughter exclaimed, "This is already a horrible day too!" I quickly rebuked her and said, "No ma'am, we will not speak that over our entire day." I told her that her words had power, and that if **she** says issa bad day, it will be a bad day. I said all of this to say, issa good day. Do your best to speak well over your day and define **for yourself** what it's going to be. It's important to confess positive things and speak God's promises over your days. Issa blessed day. Issa prosperous day. Issa peaceful day. Do not other people's foul mood or some unfortunate circumstance define the day for you. What kind of day will it be for you today? Speak it out loud, and even if things don't go your way, speak it again tomorrow. Keep believing that things will turn around in your favor.

READ TODAY: PROVERBS 18:21

#GOALS

#Goals – a social media label given to things or people whose example is deemed worthy of becoming a model for others to follow.

Example: This kid worked at a fast-food restaurant since age 15, saved his money and purchased his first rental property by age 21. He is now 25 and a real estate mogul. #goals.

My older brother is the first person who told me that I was a very "goal-oriented" person. I had never really thought about it until he said it. He said that I set goals that are SMART (Specific, Measurable, Attainable, Result-Oriented/Realistic, and Time-Bound). Some of you are goal-oriented as well. God give you a vision, and you set SMART goals to help make that vision a reality. But let me drop the real 4-1-1 of what it's like to be a goal-oriented individual. This is the part that nobody like to talk about. *record scratch* It's hard! It's hard because Satan knows how effective a person like this can be. When you have a vision and a goal-oriented pathway to achieve it, you are one dangerous son of a gun! Let's be clear. The attack on you is strong, and the closer you get to achieving your goals, the more frequent and intense the attacks will be. Does this mean that you shouldn't set goals and works towards them? Absolutely not. But it helps to be aware. When you sit down and write out your goals and your vision, go ahead and write out your "spiritual defense" plan too. How are you going to protect your goals as well as yourself? Be careful about who comes in and out of your life during this time period. Pray about any potential connections to make sure they aren't just distractions. Cover your goals in prayer, and protect yourself by putting on the whole armor of God. Lastly, ask God to send you someone who will offer accountability. You need someone who will get you together if they see you falling off. Any questions? Oh wait, this is a book. I can't answer. Ask the Holy Spirit!

READ TODAY: PROVERBS 3:6

WON'T HE DO IT?

Won't He Do It? – a church cliché used when God performs something great in your life. It has been adapted for social media use.

Example: I knew I wasn't prepared for the exam, and I just got an e-mail from my professor that it was rescheduled until next week! Won't He do it??!

To answer the question…yes He will. God will do it. God **will** do it. God will **do** it. God will do **it.** God will take care of you. There's something about being in the midst of a crisis that seems to make us forget who God is. God will do it because He has always done it. Whether you realize it or not, things continue to work out on your behalf. Sure, you may feel disappointed at times, but when you extrapolate whatever it is that you're going through over a long period of time, it becomes more and more apparent that God really is doing exactly what He said He would do. This is what you must keep in mind whenever you are tempted to freak out about one of life's less than ideal circumstances. Life changes can happen unexpectedly and rapidly. Think about how quickly life can change when people find out about an unexpected pregnancy or even a death. The only true constant in our lives is God. His love towards us is unfailing and unchanging. He said that He will never leave nor forsake us. He never said that everything in life would go exactly how we think it should go, but He did say that He would always be there, which is more than enough. His presence alone is what is "doing" it. The truth is that if God doesn't do it, it simply will not and should not be done.

READ TODAY: PSALM 37:25

#RELATIONSHIPGOALS

#RelationshipGoals – a hashtag often used to describe a couple and/or relationship idea that is admirable and worth aspiring to.

Example: My parents are #RelationshipGoals. They have been married for 40 years, and they still flirt with each other and go on dates!

Whenever I see someone use #RelationshipGoals, it makes me nervous. I think a part of me knows that relationships can be hard, and we don't know what's going on behind the scenes. A couple can take the cutest IG pics and be living in turmoil at home when cameras are off. And even if the relationship is dope, you have no idea how hard the process may have been for them to get to that point. That's why I'm reluctant to look at people and establish relationship goals based on things that are superficial. Similarly, we have to be careful about making goals out of people who seem to be super deep and spiritual. A person can go to church every Sunday, dance, shout, and preach the sermon but still go home to live comfortably with their demons. And even if their relationship with God really is dope, you have no idea what kind of process got them to that point. When it comes to your own relationship with the Lord, don't try to compare yourself to anyone else. Just do your best and continue to grow closer to God each day. When life hits, your relationship with God makes all the difference in the world. When your connection is strong, life still hits… but it'll be more like a slap in the face than an uppercut resulting in a TKO. If you want to model your spiritual walk after anyone, use Jesus. His connection to the Father was #RelationshipGoals by definition. Study how Jesus remained connected to heaven while on earth. Today's scripture is an excerpt of a very powerful prayer that Jesus prayed to His father (on our behalf). I want you to really get into it. Pay attention to how Jesus prayed for Himself and for us. It was all about completing assignments and being "one" with God. That's #RelationshipGoals.

READ TODAY: JOHN 17:1-11

DO IT FOR THE VINE!

Do it for the vine! – a phrase used to egg another person on/encourage them to do something that they may not otherwise do, specifically for the purpose of entertaining others on a (once popular, but now defunct) social media platform called Vine.

Example: Person A: I would never slap my mama!
Person B: Do it for the Vine!

Vine was a social media platform where users could make and upload very short (six-second) video clips. It became so extremely popular that it was purchased by Twitter for around $30 million. People thought of the six-second time constraint as a challenge and somehow came up with much of the best social media content of all time. Some users even became famous because of their creative "vines" that had gone viral. People would do things like backflip from a roof into a pool, slap people, dance, sing, and do crazy things in public, all for the Vine. Sadly, other platforms, like Instagram, saw the success of Vine and added their own short video sharing capabilities that would soon overshadow Vine. So my question is, if all of those people were willing to come out of their comfort zones to perform for Vine, why is it that we clam up with fear and anxiety when it comes to the assignment given to us by God, who is the True Vine? We have already talked about the fact that He is the Vine, and we are the branches. As the Vine, He supplies us with everything we need to be fruitful. There is nothing that God will ask of you that He hasn't already given you the tools to do. Are you supposed to be writing a book? Starting a business? Ministering to someone who is heartbroken? He's already placed the capability inside of you. Don't let fear stop you. Just do it for the Vine. He will cover you.

READ TODAY: JOHN 15:5

I AIN'T GONE DO IT.

I ain't gone do it. – a quote from a viral video in which a cute little girl in ballet clothes initially refuses to dance for the Vine. She said, "I ain't gone do it," but before she knew it, she was hitting some seriously awesome dance moves for the Vine. The internet loved her.

Example: Mother: Do it for the Vine!
　　　　　　Daughter: I ain't go do it! *hits dance moves anyway*

Do you ever struggle with setting boundaries for yourself? My friend Adrienne and I have decided that we would literally vote for boundaries if they were running for president. We'd probably even donate money to the campaign and knock on doors for boundaries to become president, because they are just that important. You may not be aware of this, but there are people out there who don't give a flying flip about your well-being. I'm not saying that they do it maliciously with an intent to hurt you, but some people are far too wrapped up in themselves to see, know, or care when something they want or need is too much for you. I went through a period of time where I was really struggling to hold it all together. I kept thinking that eventually someone would see me, take pity on my desperate state, and help me. Instead, I got people who would continue to push for their own wants, needs, and desires at my expense. Imagine my disappointment and my fatigue. As it turns out, the problem was with me. I didn't know how to say, "no" or "I ain't gone do it," because I didn't have healthy boundaries in place. Our assignment is to do the things that **God** has instructed us to do. He is the one who holds the reins in our lives. Sometimes He will instruct you to say yes, and other times He may tell you that a particular task does not belong to you at all. It's our job to stick to what He says and stop being moved by some guilt trip placed on us by others. Continue to be led by the Holy Spirit today.

READ TODAY: PSALM 16:7-9

NO CAP

No Cap – a popular phrase that means, "I am not lying or exaggerating." To lie or exaggerate is called "capping."

Example: My ex has been trying to get me back every single day since I left her, no cap!

When someone says "no cap" they are asking you to believe that what they are saying is true. There's a movie called *A Few Good Men* in which Jack Nicholson famously delivers the line, "You can't handle the truth!" It became one of the most well-known lines in movie history. Today, I want us to ask ourselves if we can handle the truth. Did you know that there are people out there who really believe that if they ignore the truth that it will simply disappear? It doesn't seem like the logical thing to do, but if I'm honest, I've done it myself. I have seen red flags and sped right past them hoping that I could make it to my destination without crashing. Who was I kidding? God has set certain principles in motion, and I'm not sure why we think we can just override them. Let's take seed time and harvest for example. The truth is that if you sow a seed, you will reap the harvest of **that** seed. You won't sow sunflower seeds and reap a harvest of fried chicken. When people are afraid of the truth, it simply means that they don't trust God to take care of them. When you choose to seek protection within a lie, you have chosen to trust Satan, because He is the father of lies. He is the originator of all cap that was ever capped in the history of capping. My advice to you is to stop lying to yourself and to others for temporary comfort. Use the truth of God's word to your advantage. All those lies will eventually take over and have you living like a prisoner. But if you know the truth and embrace it, you can be free. No one can hold anything over your head. No one can make you live in guilt, shame, or condemnation. Always remember that God's truth is to help you, not hurt you.

READ TODAY: JOHN 8:32

NAW NII…

Naw nii… – a slang term literally meaning, "no now…" that is used to express either disagreement or disbelief.

Example: Person A: Yeah girl, and when I went to the doctor for my stomach cramps, I found out I was eight and a half months pregnant and already in active labor. I had no idea!

Person B: Naw nii sis, how do you miss a whole pregnancy?

In 2017 a photo of my siblings and I went viral on Al Green's internet. We wore our college gear showing that we represented five different colleges and 4 different HBCUs. Between the five of us there are 9 different degrees with 3 of us receiving degrees on the doctorate level. We didn't grow up rich, but my mom prayed/prays **a lot**. I was surprised at how viral the post went. Most of the comments were kind, but there were many, many negative comments as well. A lot of people said the photo was fake and that we weren't real siblings. Others criticized college education as a waste of time and money. Still others assumed that we were all in massive amounts of debt. I remember one comment where someone said, "Naw nii…ain't no way it would be that many colleges in one family." Another said, "There's probably a brother they don't talk about that's locked up." Some people's minds were so limited in how they viewed black families that they couldn't believe that God would do this great work in answering my mother's prayers. After Jesus was risen from the grave, one of his own disciples wouldn't believe that it was really Him. "Naw nii…" Thomas said, "I won't believe it's Him until I see the scars for myself." I'm no prophet, but today I'm speaking to you prophetically. God is going to bless you in such a way that people won't believe it. "Naw nii…ain't that the same one who used to cuss, fight, and run the streets?" Don't let negative words from the doubters take root. God has the final say-so over your life.

READ TODAY: MARK 11:22-24

NOBODY:
ME:

Nobody:
Me: – a social media trend in which a user states what is
on their mind that nobody asked to know.

Example: Nobody:
          Me: I have a structured settlement and I need cash now!!

We've all heard it said that you are what you eat, but I wish
more people understood that you are what you think. Where does
your mind go when it wanders off on its own? When things are quiet
and there are no external voices telling you what to think, where does
your mind end up? Do you find yourself thinking unhealthy thoughts?
Are you replaying the mistakes you've made? Are you worrying about
how bills will get paid? Are you thinking about how much farther
along you should be right now? Are your thoughts consumed with
lust? Did you know that some people go to sleep with the TV on just
so they won't have to be left alone with their own thoughts? As an
introvert, it's hard for me to imagine not wanting to hear myself think,
but it's really a thing for many people. If you are struggling with an
unhealthy thought life, I challenge you to be more intentional about it.
Instead of allowing our minds to wander off aimlessly, the Bible tells us
that we should **set** them on things above. This is a deliberate action
called meditation. Instead of going to sleep to some horror movie of
raunchy sex scenes on TV, why not find something uplifting to
memorize and repeat to yourself until you fall asleep? The Bible is full
of great stuff, but honestly you just need to inject yourself with
something positive to drown out the negativity. Spice it up and learn
something different each day or week. Today's scripture is a good one
to memorize and meditate on.

READ TODAY: PHILIPPIANS 4:8

YASSSSS QUEEN!

Yasssss Queen! – How women like to hype up other women when they are doing something great.

Example: Woman A: I just got into medical school!
            Woman B: Yasssss Queen!

I've heard people mention the Queen of Sheba, but I never knew what she was famous for. Apparently, she was this black boss chick queen lady in the Bible who paid a visit to King Solomon. She traveled to see him and brought a huge treasure to give as a gift. She had heard how wise he was and came to see it for herself. The Bible says she came at King Solomon with "the hard questions," and he answered them all with wisdom and understanding. She acknowledged that King Solomon was the real deal and gave him her gifts and her blessing. What lesson can we extract from this queen? Although she wasn't attempting a romantic gesture, we can still glean some romantic advice from this. Women, when it comes to identifying a true king, do you just take their word for it? Do you ask around town about his reputation and accept what other people say as proof? Or do you find out for yourself? Do you ask the hard questions, or do you shy away from them because they may be uncomfortable? Many of us have played ourselves because we were too afraid to ask certain questions. Do you give your treasure away to men who haven't proven themselves to be kings? Remember, the Queen of Sheba didn't give hers away until after Solomon's responses proved his legitimacy. Men, if you are claiming to be a true king, can you answer those hard questions, or do you let pride and arrogance cause you to be offended by them? Brothers, there should be nothing to hide. If there is, then maybe you should begin to ask yourself the hard questions first. Ladies, let's not be so desperate that we gloss over important questions. La la la la la. This is just food for thought. Have a great day!

READ TODAY: 1 KINGS 10:1-7

PUSH THROUGH!!

Push through! – a compliment given to indicate that a person's efforts have paid off. It is usually referring to a superlative physical appearance.

Example: Person A: *posts photo in beautiful outfit, hair & makeup*
Person B: *Yassss Queen!! Push through!

Have you ever been in a situation where you had to keep going even when you didn't feel like it? Have you ever been in pain but couldn't stop or sit down? The world didn't stop going because you were hurting...or grieving. You had to continue to show up, smile and perform all while holding back tears. You had to push through. It seems unfair. Does no one in this self-centered, capitalistic, money-hungry society care that it's taking every muscle you have not to let a tear roll down? Are you no more valuable than your ability to perform on-demand regardless of how much pain you're in? Do you remember the 1996 Olympics where gymnast Kerri Strug had to vault with freshly torn ligaments in her ankle so that Team USA could win gold? With a seriously injured ankle she did an amazing vault and had to literally crawl off the mat. After winning gold, she was literally carried away by her coach while the crowd went wild with cheers. I watched that again a few minutes ago, and I literally broke down in tears. Was there no adult to say, "No ma'am, you are a child and you are injured. The gold doesn't matter as much as you do..."??! Now that I have wiped my tears, I just want to ask why we are so quick to push through for things that don't even matter, yet we are so quick to give up on God? The moment we feel disappointed or let down by God, we turn away from Him in anger. Why do we persevere so hard for our bosses or even our families, yet don't have any endurance when it comes to spiritual things? If we are going to push through for anybody, it should be for God first and foremost, because He be knowing.

READ TODAY: PSALM 27:13

POP OUT THEN!

Pop out then! – an exclamation used when a person who is usually low-key does something that grabs attention. This can refer to a woman who is normally a plain jane, but today is dressed to the nines. This could also refer to a couple that usually keeps their relationship private but has now shared that they are together on social media.

Example: I didn't even know you had a man, and now you show up with a boo thang and an engagement ring?! Pop out then!

I love a good pop out. We've all seen people who secretly changed their eating habits, killed it in the gym, and then popped out 50lbs lighter and looking great. I've seen people pop out with new homes and new businesses. Just recently, I had a friend from college who popped out with a whole baby, and we didn't even know she was pregnant. But just like my friend Erin was pregnant without anyone knowing, so are many of you. You are pregnant with something great that God is taking time to develop in obscurity. He is taking time not only to develop the "baby" that's inside of you, but He's also taking time to shape you into that person who can care for, protect, and raise the great thing that is growing inside of you. Think about David in the Bible. He spent a good bit of time alone, tending to his father's sheep, writing, singing, worshipping, and fighting off wild animals. But when the time finally came for him to pop out, he was confident and prepared to slay the giant and to eventually become king. I just want to encourage us today. Just keep working hard and sowing good seeds. Stay on the "Potter's wheel," and allow God to shape you in the way that He sees fit. Don't give up simply because your harvest has not popped out just yet. People may think you're crazy, but you're not. When the time is right, that baby will pop right out like Erin's did.

READ TODAY: HABAKKUK 2:3

#PROTECTYOURPEACE

#ProtectYourPeace – a hashtag that means just what it says.

Example: If they know this is your off day, why are they still calling
and e-mailing you from the office? Don't answer.
#ProtectYourPeace

Peace is truly something that requires protection. If you go
about life with a nonchalant attitude about your peace, I can guarantee
you that it will be disrupted. Peace is so valuable that there are people
out here willing to disrupt yours in order to keep theirs. There are
people who will literally say, "eff yo peace!" if it means preserving
theirs. Wake up. Protecting your peace means setting boundaries and
sticking to them. It means breaking any codependency you may have
with another person, place, or thing. When you are codependent, it
means that your peace is literally dependent on someone or something
else. It's very easy in a relationship, for example, to lose your peace
when the other person has lost theirs. When you love someone and
you see them upset, it upsets you. I get it. But what happens when
your peace is tied to a person whose emotions change like draws?
What happens when your mood is tied to a person whose mood
fluctuates up and down like the stock market? Is your peace tied to
how much money is in your bank account? When you start getting low
on funds, does your peace go right out the window too? All I'm saying
is that protecting your peace has to be mad intentional. Think of it like
a Fabergé egg…that sits in a case…surrounded by laser beams…in a
building that is secured by men with guns…and a sniper on the roof
across the street. Yeah. That's it. Protect it like that. Protect it by
saying "no" to anyone or anything that tries to place their chaos on
you. Protect it by rejecting any assignment that is not being given by
God. Protect your peace by keeping your mind on a consistent God
and not on the inconsistent world.

READ TODAY: ISAIAH 26:3

HEY STRANGER

Hey Stranger – what people say to throw microshade when they haven't seen or heard from you in a while.

Example: My Ex: Hey Stranger…
　　　　　Me: *does not respond*

I always find it funny when people say this, because it's always tinged with a bit of shade. Imagine going to your hair stylist or barber, and they greet you with a "Hey Stranger!" when you walk in the door. Now everybody knows that you haven't been to the shop in a while. Meanwhile, the people so quick to call you a stranger have no idea what you may have been going through behind the scenes. You may have experienced a major loss, such as the death of a loved one or a difficult breakup. You may have lost your job or had your home foreclosed on. Perhaps you couldn't afford to do certain things for a while. You may have had to step away for some time to fast, pray, and focus on your God-given assignment. A health issue may have popped up. You may have gone through a depressive episode that you narrowly escaped with your life. This list goes on. My point is that you never know exactly why a person's presence has been scarce, so maybe throwing shade isn't the best idea. If you are truly concerned about a person, you can check on them. It's that simple. I remember going through a very difficult time in life, and people who I thought were my friends and who knew I was going through a tough time, didn't even bother to check on me. They talked about me behind my back but never checked to see if I was okay. Sometimes all it takes is saying, "Hey, you were on my mind. You good?" We have to stop being so self-centered. We convince ourselves that someone's absence is about us and that we have the right to be offended by it before we even seek to understand it. That's not Christ-like. Love and compassion should be at the forefront of all we do.

READ TODAY: GALATIANS 6:1-2

STEPDADDY SEASON

StepDaddy Season – a celebration of men who can and will love a woman who already has kids. Not an actual season.

Example: Y'all can miss out on these amazing women if you want to, but I'm over here playing Fortnite with ManMan, teaching him to ride his bike, eating his mama's fried chicken, and happy. #StepDaddySeason.

I think we can all agree that a man having to raise another man's child wasn't the original design. But once things went south for Adam and Eve, there arose some things/issues that humanity deals with as a result of that fall. One of those things is the attack on the family unit. Satan knows how powerful a strong family can be, and so that is one of the main things that he seeks to destroy. And as beautiful as it might be to have a traditionally nuclear family with 2.5 kids, that's not always going to be the case. Between unwed pregnancies, unexpected divorces, and death…a lot of us are having to blend families together in the best way we know how. Some of you are the products of blended families and others of you have had to create them. Is God condemning you to hell for not having the perfect family? He is not. All I want is for you to understand the level of **intentionality** that is required. Satan doesn't stop his attack just because a family is blended. That family can be just as, if not more powerful than a traditional one. He still sees it as a threat, and therefore you must watch and pray. If you are a single parent, don't let anyone in your life out of desperation. Don't get so caught up in trying to find a new man/woman that you begin to neglect the children. Don't let the children manipulate you with guilt. And lastly, don't be afraid to seek counseling so you can be healed and whole enough to maintain a healthy relationship and home filled with love. If none of this applies to you, congratulations! Share this with someone who may need it, and then pray for that person today.

READ TODAY: 1 JOHN 4:1

HEY GIRL, HEY!

Hey girl, hey! – a greeting amongst women, the meaning of which can change drastically based on varying tones, inflections, or contexts.

Example: Woman A: *sees woman B walking through the mall and holding hands with a gorgeous man that she's never seen her with before* Hey, girl hey! I see you boo!

Bible story time! Jesus was out and about one day, and a guy named Jairus pulled up on him. He was a religious leader in the synagogue. Most of the religious haters weren't very fond of Jesus, but Jairus was desperate for help because his young daughter was back at home dying. He begged Jesus to come to the house to touch and heal her. Jesus was like, "Aight, bet…" and they started heading to the house. On the way there, Jesus got stopped by a lady who had been on her period for 12 years straight (that's another story for another day). But while this was happening, Jairus got word that his daughter had already died. Well Jesus ignored that and told Jairus not to be scared, but to believe. When they walked up to the house, the folks were up there falling out and acting a fool because the girl was dead. Jesus told them that she was only sleeping, and they thought it was funny. He put everybody but the parents out, grabbed her hand, and said, "Hey girl, hey…it's time to get up boo." She got up immediately and started walking around like nothing happened. Everybody started trippin' out. What are the lessons? 1. Don't let your haters fool you. They know you have power…they just don't like it. 2. Sometimes all you have to do is get where Jesus is and ask for what you need. Maybe you have not because you ask not. 3. God can do anything. 4. Positive vibes only. Faith is required, and there is no room for doubt even if it's your own people. 6. What looks dead to you might simply be in need of a word from the Lord. Alright, that's good.

READ TODAY: MARK 5:39-42

SHARE, SHARE, SHARE!

Share! Share! Share! – what people say when they want you to repost their online content or pass it along to your friends.

Example: We are giving away fish plates on the east side until 6pm! Share! Share! Share!

Have you ever paid attention to the type of content that gets shared online? Funny things get shared rather easily, because who doesn't enjoy a good laugh that's free? Half-naked or whole-naked women get shared easily because...well...lust. Drama and/or physical fights get millions of views because people see that as entertainment. Pictures of mouth-watering foods get shared easily because we be hungry. The list goes on, but these are the kinds of things that get shared and subsequently go viral. Sadly, it is the good news and the more positive aspects of life that don't receive as much attention. I saw a post on Instagram the other day celebrating Bessie Stringfield, who became the first black woman to ride a motorcycle all the way across the country in 1930. One of the commenters said that this wasn't worth celebrating because "it's not like she invented the motorcycle or anything special like that." Yes, that's right. Not only are people quick to share bad news and slow to share good news, but there are also trolls who can't stand to hear positivity at all. It's no wonder that so many believers are reluctant to share their own personal testimonies about the good news/gospel. Sometimes God will do something great in our lives, and we deem it as too personal to share. Yet, when the devil is trying his best to hinder us, we don't mind complaining publicly about him. All I ask is that **we** become more intentional about glorifying God. Even when we do share a tribulation, we can share it from the perspective of faith and victory in Christ. If you are quick to share negativity, but don't deem the positive to be worth a share, then perhaps your mind has been conditioned too much by this world...just food for thought.

READ TODAY: ROMANS 1:16

I FEEL PERSONALLY ATTACKED.

I feel personally attacked. – when someone says something that makes you feel singled out and judged.

Example: Person A: Your dryer is not an iron.
Person B: Says who? I feel personally attacked.

I'm sorry to tell you this, but you don't just feel personally attacked. You are personally attacked every day. I know that sounds all scary and whatnot, but it's better for you to know than for you to be oblivious to the facts. As followers of Christ, we have a known enemy whose sole mission is to steal, kill, and destroy us. Eww...I know. As much as I want to tell you that we skip through meadows once we submit our lives to Christ, we do not. As a matter of fact, it seems like the attacks get more intense the closer you get to the manifestation of your purpose. Shooooot, my life has been under a constant attack ever since I began writing this here book. I'm gon' be real mad if it doesn't set at least one person free, because ya girl been going through it over here! Tuh! I just got done crying a few minutes ago. Blow after blow I am sustaining on behalf of my purpose. The attacks are personal. But I am having to understand that it's because I am a threat. I just want to encourage someone today that if the attacks seem to be getting stronger, don't give up. You are closer than ever to your destiny, and you pose a threat to Satan's kingdom of darkness. Some days it won't seem worth it. Some days you will feel like quitting and being regular just to escape the punches. Understand that it's so much bigger than you. What's inside of you...the thing that the devil is so scared of...is meant to save lives and even families. While he seeks to steal, kill, and destroy...your mission is to help restore, revive, and rebuild. Let's pray for the strength to persevere. Let's also pray that He send us a special blessing today...doesn't matter what it is...just something to remind us that we are not forgotten.

READ TODAY: LUKE 22:31-34

CLAPBACK

Clapback – a quick-witted and stinging response issued to someone who is attempting to throw shade upon you.

Example: Auntie Faye tried to come for me at Thanksgiving because I'm still single with no kids. She wasn't ready for my clapback about her husband Uncle Kevin and the two kids that she doesn't know about.

Whhhyyy is maturity so hard sometimes? Being a grown man or woman is nice and all, but some people make you wanna reach back to those middle school days when anybody who dished it out was subject to get a piece of your mind. But alas, we know Jesus now. We are all saved, sanctified, and filled with the Holy Spirit and whatnot. And even though we are fully capable of "putting people in their place," we have to operate differently now. I know it's hard, especially these days. There are literally people on social media who have enough unmitigated gall to sit up and make fun of some beautiful dancer's crooked pinky toe, all while sitting in their own profile picture looking about as dumb as "Pinky" without "The Brain." It would be so easy to clapback and drag some people in return, but the Bible tells us to turn the other cheek instead. This is not always an easy thing to do, but let's think about it this way. Some people's satisfaction lies in knowing that you are no better than they are. They do certain things just to get a rise out of you and to see you dropping down to the level that they are on. Don't give them that satisfaction. Act like what they just said or did is too far beneath you to even elicit a reaction. Let God Himself handle your lightweight. "Clapbacks are mine, I will repay," saith the Lord. Don't ask what translation that was!

READ TODAY: ROMANS 12:19

FACTS!

Facts! – how you respond when someone is telling the truth. It is the modern-day version of saying, "Amen."

Example: Person A: If you use property taxes to determine funding
for school districts, you are automatically placing kids who
live in low-income areas at a disadvantage.
Person B: Facts!

Some of y'all won't agree with this, but for the believer, there is a difference between a fact and the truth. You're probably wondering how this can be. You see facts are descriptors. They are used to paint an accurate picture of a situation. Facts are useful tools to aid in our ability to assess what is going on. They help us to be knowledgeable so that we can know how to apply wisdom properly. On top of wisdom though, we must also apply faith. You see, there will be times when the facts don't really line up with the truth. The facts say that this mountain is too big for you to move. The truth says that a small amount of faith is enough to move an entire mountain just by speaking to it. The facts say that you are sick and that there's no coming back from this kind of illness. The truth says that by His stripes, we are healed. The facts say that you don't have enough money to send that child off to college. The truth says that Jehovah Jireh is our provider and that all will be well. So the next time you are confronted with some scary facts, don't just accept them at face value. Compare them to the **truth** of God's word to determine how to apply your faith and your wisdom. Let's take the time today to pray (in faith) over the facts.

READ TODAY: MARK 11:22-24

SOMEBODY'S SON

Somebody's Son – terminology used to describe a theoretical future boyfriend/husband whose name you don't know yet.

Example: I can't wait until the day that I am honeymooning in Greece with somebody's son.

Okay, we are back in our Bible story bag today. Let me tell you the story of how Abraham, who is known as the "Father of Faith," started out doubting. God had **clearly** promised he and his wife a son, but they were old and having trouble getting pregnant. They tried for a really long time without success. Although they knew what God said, Abraham's wife Sarah came up with this bright idea to circumvent the process by telling Abraham to have "secks" with her handmaid Hagar so that he would have a descendant. Well Hagar did get pregnant with a son named Ishmael, but it made her get in her feelings about Sarah. She had a stank attitude, and Sarah returned that same energy. That started this whole windfall of drama that is apparently still going on today. The thing is, God didn't tell Abraham and Sarah to go and have just anybody's son. He made a promise, and when it didn't come in the timing that **they** thought it should, they decided to "help" God out by taking matters into their own hands. They ended up creating more of a problem than they ever could have imagined with somebody's son. God did keep His promise and allowed Abraham and Sarah to conceive their own son, Isaac, in their old age. But wars are still raging to this day because the descendants of Ishmael and Isaac stay at each other's throats. The lesson here is not to let your impatience with God's process cause you to create something with somebody that God did not ordain. If God's promise to you was clear and specific, stop trying to fenagle your way into some low-faith, generic brand of blessing.

READ TODAY: GENESIS 16:1-4

SOMEBODY'S DAUGHTER

Somebody's Daughter – terminology used to describe a theoretical future girlfriend/wife.

Example: Y'all ladies who ignored my DMs...don't be mad when you see me in Cabo with somebody's daughter who responded.

If "I seeee it! I want it!" was a person, it would be Jacob in the Bible. All it took was for him to see somebody's daughter one time, and he was ready to settle down. Rachel must have been extra fine, because Jacob **immediately** promised her father Laban that he would work for him seven whole years just to be given Rachel's hand in marriage. Well Jacob worked for seven years only to be tricked into marrying the older sister, Leah! It turns out that Laban wouldn't give Rachel up because the custom of the country called for the first-born daughter to be wed before the younger. But Jacob loved and wanted Rachel so much, that he was willing to work seven more years for her hand in marriage. Now if Jacob did all that just to be with somebody's daughter, then why are we so quick to give up on stuff when obstacles arise? Whenever you are trying to take hold of God's promises, understand that Satan will not take it sitting down. There will be all sorts of roadblocks and attacks, and some days it will feel like you are Super Mario. Just as you make it past the lava pits and balls of fire...just as you think you're about to win the game, you discover that the princess ain't even in that castle! Like Mario, you must keep going to fight on a new, more difficult level. Like Jacob, you may have to work for more time than you thought you would. But I just wanted to encourage you today to stay focused on what God promised you. Your struggle won't last always. Jacob's son with Rachel would go on to save entire nations of people from starving to death. When you put it that way, 14 years ain't so bad. If you stay focused on what you're gaining, you can survive the process to getting there.

READ TODAY: GENESIS 29:20

DASSIT.

Dassit. – a slang term literally meaning "that's it."

Example: Ugh. The drive thru line is wrapped around the building.
All I wanted was some fries and dassit!

Have you ever felt like someone was putting you in a box?
Perhaps people got so used to you being one way, that they wanted you
to remain in that place. In Hollywood, they call it being "typecast."
This is when you've done so well playing a certain type of character,
that it becomes difficult to get cast as something different. Think
about how well Jaleel White played Steve Urkel and how well Jasmine
Guy played Whitley Gilbert. After those roles, it became difficult for
people to see them as anything else, and neither of them took on much
more work after those shows ended. Imagine feeling like you're Steve
Urkel, and dassit. It must be difficult. Perhaps you feel like you are
those kids' mom and dassit. Maybe you feel like you are his wife and
dassit. Maybe you feel like you are her husband and dassit. Maybe you
feel like you are a singer and dassit. Maybe you feel like you work to be
the provider and dassit. Well, beloved, God has sent me to encourage
you today. Just because you play one role very well, does not mean
that you have to limit yourself to it. Other people may make you feel
like that's all you are, but don't you dare start believing that about
yourself. You are so much more than meets the eye, and you would be
doing the world a disservice by placing yourself in a box. Break out of
it today. Pray and ask God to show you how.

READ TODAY: PHILIPPIANS 4:13

LOUDER FOR THE PEOPLE IN THE BACK…

Louder for the people in the back! – a phrase used to indicate that a person is saying or doing something that should be repeated boldly for all to hear.

Example: Person A: If you treat servers badly, I will never go anywhere with you again.
Person B: Amen! Say it louder for the people in the back!

What are you afraid of? I continue to harp on this point because I believe there are several of you who have gifts that you are not using due to fear. I want you to close your eyes and…oh wait…if you close your eyes, you can't read the rest. Alright, keep your eyes open, but I want you to think about the gift or gifts that God has blessed you with. What special thing has He placed inside of you? Don't just think about the "gifts" that seem to get the most shine like singing or preaching. Think about yourself and how God made you. What about you seems a little different from those around you? For me, I can say that I specialize in clarity. Sometimes friends will come to me with complex issues that are causing confusion (and disturbing the peace). I listen, try to understand what they are saying, and then offer about 2 to 3ish words. Those 2 to 3 words will make what seemed like a difficult algebraic equation about as clear as $0+0=0$. It's no wonder that I make a living as an optometrist. I am blessed to make the world super clear for people all day, every day. I make no qualms about the fact that it's a gift from God. I haven't always embraced it, but now that I have, I can walk boldly. In the Bible, Paul laid his hands on Timothy to encourage him to "stir up the gift" that was already inside of him. Paul then reminded Timothy to be bold and not to operate in fear. I can't lay hands on you like Paul did, but allow these words to touch your heart today. Let's get it!

READ TODAY: 2 TIMOTHY 1:6-7

THE TOE-POINT

The toe-point – what millions of women do when they pose for full-body photos.

Example: I'm sorry, can we take that picture again? I didn't have the toe-point right on that one.

If you're not on social media, you probably have no idea what "toe-point" I'm talking about. (Actually, if you're not on social media, you probably have no idea what any of this book is talking about. It's okay to gift it to someone who can relate. I promise, I won't take it personally!) If you are on social media though, you know exaaaaactly what "toe-point" means. When women are trying to look cute in full body photos, they will point the toe of one foot at a roughly 45-degree angle to the ground. This helps to accentuate the appearance of a woman's figure by widening the hip area to create more of an hourglass shape. Well today I want to talk to you about the most important "toe-point" of all. When you allow God to order the steps of your life, it means that you will point your toes in whatever direction He sends you in, and then you will begin to follow that path. In life, there are several paths you can take...or perhaps only two. There's God's way and then there is any other way. The Bible tells us that there is a way that may appear to be very right to us, but because we are mere mortals, we have no idea that it only ends in destruction. How many times of trying to do things our own way does it take for us to understand that we do not know how to take care of ourselves better than God? The old saints would say, "He's been better to me than I've been to myself." It took me getting older to truly understand and relate to that, but I get it now. If you are worried and unsure which direction to point your toes, pray today for God's guidance, and don't make a move until you know which way He is sending you.

READ TODAY: PSALM 37:23

IKYFL

IKYFL – an acronym used to express disbelief and sometimes anger. It stands for "I Know You *redacted* Lying." For black people, it is the equivalent of saying, "You gotta be kidding me!"

Example: *Checks Bank Account* Oh IKYFL! Where is my direct deposit? It didn't come through!

Have you ever been lied to or lied on? Let's talk about being lied on. If you've ever been lied on, you know that it is a terrible feeling to have people out there spreading false information about you. When you realize that you are being lied on, what can you really do? I had a person who was lying on me once. The person was angry that I wasn't doing what they wanted me to do, so as a form of "punishment," they went spreading lies to different friends, family members, and even business associates. It was too much, and I didn't have the time nor the energy to figure out who was told what and how to defend myself. Although I was hurting, all I knew to do was to put it in the hands of the Lord. There was only one real friend who heard the lies and said, "Oh IKYFL!" That friend was led by the Holy Spirit and also knew my character well enough to stand up for me. Many others would realize (without me having to say anything) as time went on. Lying is Satan's bread and butter. They call him the "accuser of the brethren." His plan is to lie to God about **you** day and night. The devil is jealous of us, and so He seeks to convince God that we are unworthy of His love. Today, I want us to give praises to God for the ability to rebuke the devil and say, "IKYFL!" Take comfort in knowing that if someone is lying on you, God's got your back. Take more comfort in knowing that even if you can't defend yourself, the truth will eventually come to light. Take eeeeven more comfort in knowing that anyone who listens to, believes, and then spreads a lie about you, was someone who needed to be out of your circle anyway!

READ TODAY: REVELATION 12:10-11

YOU ALREADY KNOW!

You already know! – a phrase used when you know someone can relate to what's going on without the need for further explanation.

Example: Person A: Oh, I see you broke out the card table! Spades?
Person B: You already know!

Hmm…I'm not sure how to start off today's devotion. So confusing is life. Confusing life is so. Life confusing so is. Is life so confusing? Ugh! Life is so confusing! Or is it? Just like I made an unnecessarily jumbled mess of today's devotion intro, it's becoming more apparent that many of us do this same thing with our lives. It's one thing to actually be confused, but it's an entirely different thing to act like you're confused when you're not. Have you ever seen a kid who doesn't want to do their math homework? Some of these kids are so slick and will act confused so that you get frustrated enough to let them quit. I think we are this way with God sometimes. Have you ever prayed about something, gotten God's answer, and then acted confused as if you weren't sure what He said? Perhaps God's answer was very clear, but you tried your best to make it mean something different. Maybe you tricked yourself into thinking that something cut and dry was up for interpretation. No, Rodney…God was not telling you it's okay to keep selling weed to the middle school kids because you are paying your mama's cell phone bill with the money, and the Bible says you're supposed to honor your father and mother. That's not it, beloved! You are not confused. Perhaps you just don't want to listen. God is not the author of confusion, so even if you are confused about something, you have probably been listening to Satan and hoping to fenagle your way out of what you already know. When you have the Holy Spirit living inside of you, it's hard to make the claim that you honestly don't know what you know. Pray today and ask God to help you in the battle to acknowledge what you already know.

READ TODAY: 1 JOHN 2:20

KAREN

Karen – slang for entitled, predatory Caucasian women who use their white privilege and presumed innocence to terrorize others.

Example: I was walking my dog in my neighborhood when this Karen started harassing me. She demanded to know where I lived and threated to call the cops if I didn't answer her questions.

Did y'all know that there was a Karen in the Bible? Yup Joseph was sold into slavery by his brothers. He ended up in the home of an Egyptian leader named Potiphar. Now Joseph was a hard-working man who was successful at whatever he did. He was placed in charge of all of Potiphar's affairs. The Bible also says that Joseph was fine and had a nice bawwdy. I'm pretty sure many women were thirsting after this fine and successful young man. But the crazy part is that Potiphar's own wife wanted to be "ravished" by Joseph. He refused to dishonor God and his master, so he turned her down. But sis was persistent. Day after day, she tried to get Joseph to boink her, and every day he refused. One day she grabbed at his cloak, but he wasn't playing with her. He twisted out of the cloak, left it in her hand, and ran off. Karen got upset, played the victim, and told everyone that Joseph tried to take advantage of her. Joseph got locked up behind Karen's shenanigans, not unlike many people who are victimized by Karens to this day. I know it sounds crazy, but if you continue to read the story about Joseph, you will understand how going to the prison set him up to eventually go to the palace. Even during the time he spent locked up, God was with him, and he had favor. I just want to encourage you today that although it may seem like someone got away with doing something to you unfairly, don't get tied up in trying to take revenge. Maybe God is trying to move you to a different place in order to elevate you even higher than you ever imagined. God can use anything and anyone to bless you...even a Karen.

READ TODAY: GENESIS 39:19-23

#TAGAFRIEND

#TagAFriend – a hashtag used to ask people to "mention" another friend's name under a post which will send them a notification to come and check it out.

Example: If you know anyone looking for a job, we are hiring. Full-time positions start at $18/hour. #TagAFriend

In the Bible, Moses used his rod to part the Red Sea so that the children of Israel could walk across it on dry land to escape Egyptian bondage. You've probably heard of the story. But there was another situation where the Israelites found themselves in a battle with the Amalekites. God told Moses to carry his rod, which was apparently pretty lit. Whenever he held the rod up in the air, the Israelites would prevail in the battle, but whenever he put it down, they would start getting their butts beat. After a while, Moses began struggling to hold up the rod because his arms were tired. That's when he tagged some friends to come over and help. Aaron and Hur found a place for Moses to sit down while they stood beside him and held his arms up. The Israelites were victorious. I think many of us get frustrated because we know that so many people are depending on our stability for their victory. Yes, we are exhausted, but if we were to clock out, other people would be affected. What do we do in that scenario? Don't be too prideful to tag a friend. It's okay to admit that you are about to fall out and that you need help. It's okay to tag someone into the ring and let them know that you are not okay and that you need prayer. It's okay to tag someone in and let them know that you are feeling weak and need someone to intercede on your behalf until you regain strength. Some of us will give up all together before we ask for help. Even more of you are probably thinking that you don't have anyone to tag. Awesome! You have just identified something new to pray about. Ask God to send you a friend who can and will stand in the gap when the need arises.

READ TODAY: EXODUS 17:8-13

BRUH

Bruh – slang for the word "brother." When used alone, it can mean that a person is at a loss for words.

Example: Person A: Did you read today's devotion? God be knowing!
Person B: Bruh!!!

A brother is meant to be a blessing. I know it's not possible for everyone to have a biological brother, but sometimes the "brothers" who aren't related to you can be just as dope. If you are a woman, you want a brother who will love and protect you. A great brother is dependable and will sometimes sacrifice to make sure that you are ok. Brothers are also known to tell you the hard truth about yourself even when everyone else is lying to spare your feelings. If you are a man and have a good brother, you have probably experienced some of those same characteristics from him. A good brother will also be loyal. He will seek to motivate and challenge you to do better. He will be a listening ear, but he will also offer wisdom as well as words of caution. It breaks my heart to see when people let petty issues stand in between a beautiful thing like brotherhood. Brotherhood can be hampered by things like jealously, dishonesty, pride, miscommunication, and differences of opinion. I submit to you that none of these things are worth losing a **good** brother. It's a fact of life that you will sometimes have to part ways with toxic people in order to move forward and maintain peace. I just don't want you throwing away a brother if it's not absolutely necessary. If you must remove a brother from your life, don't do it based on emotions. Pray and ask God to make it clear and send you that confirmation. He will. And if you have lost a brother over something that's not worth it, pray and ask God to restore that. If you do have good brothers, understand that the devil would love nothing more than to break up that powerful bond. Cover those relationships in prayer.

READ TODAY: HEBREWS 13:1

I CAN'T UNSEE IT.

I can't unsee it. – when your attention is called to something that you previously missed, and then it becomes impossible to ignore.

Example: Somebody said Kirk Franklin and Plies might secretly be the same person, and now I can't unsee it.

My older brother, a college professor, introduced me to his Kirk Franklin-Plies Unification Theory (KFPUT) in which he postulates that these two men, who look a lot alike, might be one in the same. "Think about it. No one has ever seen them in the same place at the same time..." he said. And now whenever I look at Plies, I see Kirk Franklin. I can't unsee it. Once your consciousness has been awakened to something, it becomes very difficult to act as if it hasn't. A person who is "woke" is nothing more than a person who has opened their eyes to see something that they can't pretend not to have seen. Some people purposely stay "sleep" because they know that if they know better, they will have to start doing better. Just think about all the people who don't want to know what hot dogs really are so that they can keep eating them in peace. So let's talk about the thing that **you** can't unsee. Did God give you a vision? Do you remember what it was? Did you see yourself creating something great? Were you helping people? Were you transforming your health? Were you starting a business or a school? Were you writing a book or preaching His word? It doesn't matter how many years pass by, when God shows you a vision, you can't unsee it. You can try your best to act like the vision doesn't exist, but even God says, "Aht! Aht! I'll tell you what...since you want to act like you don't remember the vision, how about you write it down and put it somewhere that will stay in your face?" He wants us to write it down and then put it in a place where we can't unsee it. If you haven't already, let's do that today!

READ TODAY: HABAKKUK 2:2-3

#DATENIGHT

#DateNight – a hashtag that usually accompanies a post about a romantic appointment with someone.

Example: Bae took me to dinner and to see a play! #DateNight

You know what I love to see? I love to see married couples who have been together a long time, but still go on dates. I love to see couples who have a day or night of the week that is automatically earmarked for quality time together. It's just dope to see people who don't play 'bout each other. There are couples who are extremely intentional about the fact that no matter what else is going on, and no matter how upset they are with each other…that time slot is for **us**. There's only so long they can go on being mad or cold towards one another before #DateNight comes back around, and they are reminded of their commitment to love and friendship. What I like most is to see people who put strict boundaries up around their quality time. "If you ain't dead or in jail…Thursday nights?? We got plans. And even if you are in jail, I'll come during visiting hours and put some money on your books, baby." It's beautiful. So now let's talk about how important it is to be intentional about our quality time with God. Let me help you…there will **always** be an attack on your time with God. There will **always** be something that "comes up" to steal it away. Once you start skipping it for something/someone else, it's only a matter of time before you forget about it all together. Sundays are awesome. That weekly church service is a good way to get you refocused on God for the week. But if you rely on Sunday only, you will starve. That's why I'm glad you picked up this book. It's a good way to launch you into a routine of spending more One-on-one time strengthening your relationship with the Lord. Maybe you'll have to wake up before everyone else or sit in your car during lunch. But whatever you must do to keep your date with God, it's worth it!

READ TODAY: PSALM 63:1-8

I SEE YOU BOO!

I see you boo! – a compliment letting someone know that you have noticed an impressive thing that they have going on.

Example: Person A: I have been working out and doing my squats every day!
Person B: Okay! I see you boo!

I love it when we compliment each other this way. So often, we work hard to make things happen, but no one notices or acknowledges our efforts. It's easy to get discouraged when you're busting your butt working two jobs to feed people who never stop to thank you. It's easy to get discouraged when you are trying your best at work, but your boss is always picking your projects apart for imperfections. It's really easy to get discouraged when you've worked hard on a term paper but get it back with red markings all over the place. Some kids even get traumatized because no matter how hard they work, it's never enough to gain the approval of their parents. I just want to encourage you today. You're doing a good job. You're doing hard things that you will probably never get recognized for because you are just that kind of a person. There may never come a time when someone yells out, "I see you boo!" but I want you to know that God sees you boo! His eyes are always upon you, and He sees you boo. The Bible tells us that we shouldn't do things looking for the accolades of men anyway. God sees what we do in secret and will reward us openly.

READ TODAY: PSALM 34:15

241

THE UNFOLLOW BUTTON IS RIGHT THERE.

The unfollow button is right there. – what people say when they don't care whether you remain social media acquaintances or not.

Example: I love black people. I celebrate blackness. Everything on my page is going to be black blackity black black black. And if you don't like that, the unfollow button is right there!

I've never understood this weird phenomenon of following people on social media that you don't like. Beloved, it is free to unfollow someone. If someone's online behavior disturbs your spirit, you don't have to keep seeing them on there if you simply unfollow. If seeing someone's posts makes your blood pressure go up, why do you continue to follow their page? You see it all the time with athletes and other celebrities. Random strangers (whose opinions don't matter) go on to their pages to spew hatred or to tell them how they should dress, do their hair, or raise their own kids. Sir and ma'am...why are you even here when the unfollow button is right there? And just like those people are free to unfollow what isn't right for them, so are you. Some of us are continuing to follow certain religious traditions because we were told that we had to. We don't like it or even understand it, but we do it because we feel that we have no choice. That is untrue. If it doesn't follow God's word, you don't have to follow it. The Bible tells us that the overwhelming rules and regulations of the Old Testament were in place for a reason, but that reason has now been accomplished through Christ. In essence, we were freed to unfollow those laws as long as we followed a life of faith in God through Christ instead. Study God's word for yourself. If something you are accustomed to doing isn't lining up with the word, the unfollow button is right there.

READ TODAY: GALATIANS 3:23-29

THIS IS MY PAGE.

This is my page. – what people say when they want to remind you that you are visiting their profile and that they are at liberty to do, say, or post whatever they see fit while on their own turf.

Example: I said what I said, and this is my page! If you don't like it, don't look at it!

One thing that social media has brought to many people is the opportunity for ownership. It gives everyone an opportunity to make a small corner of the world their own. Imagine how liberating that must feel to those people around the world who have never had their own spaces. And while ownership of anything is awesome, it can be either a blessing or a curse. It's a blessing when you understand that it is a privilege and a responsibility. It is a blessing when you do the work and learn how to take care of the thing that you have taken ownership of. Ownership can feel like a curse when you're not ready for it. If you've ever owned a home, you know exactly what I'm talking about. When you're the owner, the buck stops with you. There is no other person who is responsible to maintain something that is yours. It's evident on social media that some people understand how to manage ownership and others do not. "This is my page, and I don't care what anyone else has to say…" sounds cute until you're losing a job over some online controversy. It's cute until you're getting passed over for jobs because potential employers have taken a peek at foolishness on your social media pages. It's cute until you push away your real family and friends for trying to tell you the truth. It's cute until the fake friends who like everything you post and agree with all of your foolery are nowhere to be found when you need someone. We are to be good stewards over everything that God has placed in our hands, and that includes social media. Treat your page as if it really belongs to God…because it does. Everything does.

READ TODAY: PSALM 24:1

WELL SAID.

Well said. – a response used to compliment someone who has done a good job expressing a thought or idea.

Example: Person A: In summary, if you see injustice happening to brown and black people and turn a blind eye to it...don't invite me to your "multicultural church." I'm not coming.
Person B: Well said.

It's not just what you say. It's how you say it. If the point is to communicate, you have to do it on all fronts. If your goal is to get a message across, it's important to think about more than just whether you're right or wrong. If someone comes up to you and nonchalantly whispers, "say my man...your house is on fire," you're less likely to believe that this person is telling the truth. If someone approaches you with a sense of urgency and yells, "YOUR HOUSE IS ON FIYAAH!!" then you are more likely to move swiftly to do what needs to be done. Do you remember that episode of The Cosby Show where Vanessa brought her fiancé, Dabnis Brickey, home? Heathcliff told Dabnis that he didn't have a problem with him per se, but that he had been like a nice meal served to them on a garbage can lid. In other words, it was **how** Vanessa chose to go about it. Dabnis was the truth. He was hard-working, mature, responsible, and actually loved 'Nessa. But they struggled to receive him due to the presentation. Think about that the next time you are attempting to get a message across to someone. The Bible tells us that our words should be seasoned with grace. It also says that a soft answer turns away wrath, but grievous words stir up anger. We are to speak the truth in love. You could be right all day long, but if you say it with a wrong spirit, good luck in being effective. Let's pray today that God will help us to be more intentional about how we say what we say when we say it.

READ TODAY: COLOSSIANS 4:6

#MOTIVATIONMONDAY

#MotivationMonday – a hashtag used to accompany content that will inspire others at the beginning of the work week.

Example: Three years ago this man was living out of his car. Now he is a best-selling author and a millionaire! #MotivationMonday

As a nation, we shell out millions (probably billions) of dollars on things that we think will motivate us. Motivation is powerful and therefore valuable. When you lack motivation, even easy tasks seem grueling. You can have a refrigerator full of groceries, but if there is no motivation to cook, you will end up ordering takeout. You can have a whole room full of workout equipment right at home, but without the motivation to exercise, it will only get dusty. You can have a whole book idea in your head, but without the motivation to write, you will never become a published author. I wish I could put motivation in a bottle and sell it for profit. But since that's not an option, I'll just tell you what the Bible says. Do everything...and I mean everything...as if you were doing it for the Lord. If you are writing a paper, do it as if the Lord Himself is going to grade it. If you are trying to be a good parent, do it as if the Lord Himself gave you His own personal kid to raise. Motivation comes when you tie whatever you are doing back to your purpose in God. I was down in the dumps one day last week, and I got to working on an assignment that God had given me. I started working with the tears still in my eyes, not understanding why I had to keep pushing when I should have been allowed to stop and have a nice little breakdown. By the end of it, my Help had come, and I was clear that focusing on what God told me to do was the very best thing for my broken heart. If you're struggling with motivation, maybe you have become distracted with too many things that have nothing to do with God. You're not doing it for approval from anyone else. Your reward is with Him...not them.

READ TODAY: COLOSSIANS 3:23-24

#TRANSFORMATIONTUESDAY

#TransformationTuesday – a popular hashtag that encourages users to use Tuesdays to post about any kind of transformation that they have made.

Example: *posts before and after pictures of weight-loss journey*
Caption: Hard work pays off! #TransformationTuesday

Let's talk about transformations. Transformations aren't just subtle changes. They are drastic modifications that are usually the result of drastic measures. The social media transformations that I enjoy the most are the ones where someone has taken control of their fitness. I like these because they give you a clear visual representation of a changed mind. You know what's crazy? As drastic as transformations are, the truth is that they are **not** the result of drastic measures. They are honestly the result of one very simple adjustment. The Bible tells us that we are transformed by the renewing of our minds. It makes complete sense. Once your mind changes on a matter, everything else flows from there. Have you ever had a light bulb to go off about something, and it shifted your entire way of life? I have. If you've ever seen a person who finally understands their own worth, then you know it is quite a sight to see! Is there an area in your life where you need a drastic change? It could be a change in your health, finances, relationship, family, career, or even your peace. The only way to make a true transformation is to renew or refresh your mind with God's word. I think of our minds as webpage browsers. Sometimes we must press the refresh button to receive the most up-to-date and accurate information. There is nothing more embarrassing than realizing that you have been making moves based on info that is no longer valid. Refresh the pages of your mind today with God's word that never gets stale.

READ TODAY: ROMANS 12:2

#UNBOTHERED

#Unbothered – a hashtag used to indicate that a person is not being affected by something that was meant to trouble them.

Example: You can lie on me all you want to. The people who matter to me already know the truth. #Unbothered

There have been those people who seem to find enjoyment in frustrating others. Even in kindergarten, I can remember a kid who did menacing stuff to other kids just hoping to get a rise out of someone. Maybe it's some pitiful way for people to seek attention when they aren't getting it elsewhere. Perhaps they lack their own inner peace and seek to disrupt yours out of jealousy. I'm not really sure why some people are this way, but I know we're not about to waste our time and energy trying to figure it out. Don't give negative people the pleasure of seeing you bothered by their shenanigans. Some people do low down stuff and then sit and wait for your response. They wait for you to "come out of character" and retaliate so that they can prove that you aren't any better than they are. The goal is to place your peace on a shelf that is so high, that even your own mama can't reach it! Your mission, if you choose to accept it, is to respond in a way that no one is expecting. When someone is trying to antagonize you, pray for them. Yeah, that'll get 'em! That'll get 'em real good, and they won't even see that coming. They think you're going to lose your cool, and meanwhile you're calmly asking God to help them. You see, God has already told us not to take revenge on people because that job belongs to Him. But think about how scary it would be to have God setting up to take revenge out on you! I shudder at the thought. Whoever is on the other end of that needs your prayers. Ask God to take it easy on them because perhaps they didn't know that you were one of His. The next time you feel yourself getting bothered, simply stop to pray for that person, and watch how quickly you calm down.

READ TODAY: ROMANS 12:19

JESUS DID NOT DIE FOR THIS.

Jesus did not die for this. – a phrase used to react to people who are doing dumb things that seem extremely unnecessary.

Example: I just watched a video of people going "ice swimming" in Antarctica. They literally swim in freezing water that has ice floating in it...for fun. Why?! Jesus did not die for this!

"Jesus did not die for this" has become a running joke online. We have a great laugh at all the crazy things that are not worth Jesus giving up His whole life for us to be out here doing. There is so much irony in this particular joke because...well...Jesus died for all of it. I remember going to the movie theater to see *The Passion of The Christ*. I was a G the whole time and did not cry until the very end when He got up and the tomb was empty. After that, I was a wreck. I recall that I was on a trip with my church's college ministry. I went back to my hotel room and made myself communion with a cap full of coke for the blood and a small piece of pizza crust for the body. I lifted that crust up to heaven and with a face full of tears and a cracking voice recited, "This is My body, which was broken for you..." with my whole heart. I can laugh at that now, but I was dead serious about that "body" and "blood." The reason I was so "toe up" was because I began to realize just how much Jesus sacrificed to take the penalty for the crazy stuff that I would do...me. That being said, I don't know what crazy stuff you have done, but I can guarantee you that Jesus did, in fact, die for that. He absolutely did. Today, let's just take some time to thank God for His grace and for sacrificing His only begotten Son for the completely unnecessary and sinful things that we didn't even have to do!

READ TODAY: ROMANS 5:6-11

STEP AWAY FROM THE PHONE.

Step away from the phone. – used to tell someone that they should put their phone down and take a few minutes to breathe before they do or say something that would be detrimental.

Example: Person A: Ugh! I hate my boss and let me tell you why!
Person B: Step away from the phone friend. Don't forget you have bills to pay and mouths to feed.

Have you ever acted on an impulse and regretted it? Social media is optimized for impulsive behavior. It is a place where people will say and do harmful things under the impression that it doesn't matter because, "it's just social media." Well nowadays, anything you do or say online, even if it appears to be private, can easily become permanent public knowledge. All it takes is a screenshot. That's why it's best not to let your impulses get the best of you. It's not wise online or anywhere else. One of my favorite preachers of all time, Dr. Charles Stanley, often taught about the acronym H.A.L.T., which stands for Hungry, Angry, Lonely, or Tired. Before you make a move, ask yourself if you are either of these things. If so, stop what you are doing until you have addressed these issues first. It can save you a lot of regret. I have put this into practice and have found myself stepping away from something and saying, "You know what? I'm hungry and tired. Let me get some food and a nap before I do or say something crazy." It's simple, but it works. When you are experiencing the symptoms of H.A.L.T., that is the prime time for Satan to attack. This is because your flesh is in an elevated state while your spirit is in a state of suppression. That's the best time to stop (halt), feed your spirit, and starve your flesh.

READ TODAY: PROVERBS 25:28

AIGHT, SO BOOM...

Aight, so boom... – a story telling device used by black people to introduce an exciting narrative.

Example: Aight, so boom...it was me, Rico, the guy from AutoZone, and his wife. We were all just standing there when we heard gunshots like "bow bow bow bow bow!" Five of em...

When you hear a black person say, "Aight so boom," you know that they are setting up to tell you something pretty interesting. You don't use that intro unless you are coming with some heat behind it. Everything said after, "Aight so boom," has to escalate in stepwise fashion until the story reaches its climax. Today's devotion is to encourage you. Yes, you! Life has had its share of ups and downs, and perhaps things haven't always gone as planned. But I want to transform that phrase into a **command** that I speaketh over thee this day. "Aight...so boom." When something booms, it experiences rapid growth, increase, expansion, or elevation. So many of you think that the things that have happened in the past have disqualified you, when in all reality, those experiences (once processed correctly) were the very things that developed and matured you in private. There will come a time when you go from developing quietly underground, to breaking through the soil. To the people around you, it will look like your elevation happened so quickly. They won't even know by looking at you how much time you actually spent in that darkroom that developed your picture and made you ready for the "boom." Don't get caught up in trying to live in the mistakes of the past. Aight...it happened, and it's a part of your story now...so take it and use it to boom and bloom. Do we understand each other? Aight...so boom!

READ TODAY: ISAIAH 54:3-4

MAJOR SIDE-EYE

Major side-eye – a phrase used to express distrust of someone or something.

Example: He wants me to join his multi-level marketing company. He keeps talking about how much money I will make, but I'm giving it major side-eye because he still lives with his mama and rides the bus. It sounds like a pyramid scheme to me.

Side-eying ain't new. It's been going on since the Bible days, and as a matter of fact, the Bible encourages it. When you give someone the side-eye, you continue to face forward, while moving only your eyes to the side to keep an eye on that particular subject. The goal is to watch them without allowing them to realize that you are doing it. See when someone doesn't know that they are being watched, they are going to be their authentic selves. When someone doesn't know that they are being watched, there is no incentive to be fake. Valuable information is gained from a well-timed side eye. The Bible calls it something different. It says that we are to walk "circumspectly." Now I'm no English major, but when I break that word down, it seems like a fancy way of saying side-eye. Circum = circle, and spect = view, look, or spectate. A person who walks circumspectly is viewing everything around them…360 degrees of perspective. It is me, or did the Bible just tell us to keep our heads on a swivel? The Bible even tells us that we must **watch** and pray. That's because we don't need to be naïve. There are wolves out there dressed in sheep's clothing hoping to take advantage of your generous heart. It's all a part of Satan's strategy to defeat you. He wants you to get caught up in some kind of foolish deception because then you'll be distracted from your purpose. Be careful about believing any and everybody. Pray and ask God for discernment. Examine everything with the help of the Holy Spirit, and give major side-eye until you know that it's really coming from God.

READ TODAY: EPHESIANS 5:15-17

I AIN'T THE ONE.

I ain't the one. – what people say when they want others to know that they are the wrong person to be trifled with.

> Example: The lady at the drive-thru wanted to have a stank attitude with me. Tuh! I'll burn this whole place down, cuz I ain't the one!

In the Bible, David was said to be a man after God's own heart. There was no doubt that He was anointed by God and a worshipper. As a matter of fact, some of the song lyrics that he wrote to God are still being used by others to worship God every day. But David wasn't perfect. He had done some pretty jacked up things in his day. I've already told you the story of David and Bathsheba, so you know how he had a woman's innocent husband killed to avoid him finding out that David had gotten his wife pregnant. Yeah, that was trash. There's no way around that being trash. However, God sent a prophet named Nathan to talk to David. He described the incident to King David but changed up the details to throw him off. David got mad and said that the perpetrator should be put to death. Nathan told David like Beyoncé, "Baby it's youuu…" David thought he wasn't the one, but he was. "Thou art the man," Nathan said. King David was the trifling one. King David was the one who deserved the death sentence. He did have to suffer some consequences, but God decided to spare his life. My message to you is never to forget where you came from and how God had mercy on you. Don't point the finger at others who don't have it all together, because you "ain't the one" to be talking if we are quite honest. If it had not been for the Lord who was on your side, where would you even be? Exactly. You are the one that God had mercy on.

READ TODAY: 2 SAMUEL 12:13
(BUT THE WHOLE CHAPTER IS LIT)

IJS

ijs – an acronym that stands for "I'm just sayin'."

Example: I don't have a date for Friday night, ijs.

When someone adds "ijs" to the end of a sentence, it transforms whatever they are saying into a much more passively aggressive statement. People will literally say anything and add ijs to the end of it because they feel it absolves them of having to explain anything further or stand behind a clear opinion. To say, "Oh I'm just saying random stuff for no reason…" is as passive-aggressive as it gets. It has become a social media staple to toss random words around without regard to their gravity. The Bible warns against this. It says that we will eventually have to be held accountable for the "idle" words that we have spoken. When you look up the meaning of the word idle, you come across descriptors such as "lazy," "pointless," and "without purpose." Is social media giving you a platform for words that are lazy and pointless? When you use "ijs" to make an idle statement, it may absolve you of the accountability online, but it still stands with God. Let us repent and ask for forgiveness for any idle or reckless words of our own. Moving forward, let's allow our words to be the opposite of idle. Instead of lazy, let our words be full of life and tied to some action. Instead of pointless, let's use our words to point people in a more positive direction. Instead of having no purpose, let's use our words to make an impact.

READ TODAY: MATTHEW 12:36

GOTEEM!

Goteem! – what you say after you have tricked someone into believing something, usually a prank or practical joke. It literally means, "Got him!" @welvendagreat is credited with this term.

Example: Your Ex: I miss you and want you back.
　　　　You:　　Wow! I feel the same way!
　　　　Your Ex: Really?!
　　　　You.　　Nah, I just forgot to block you. Goteem!

The Bible warns us on multiple occasions not to be deceived. Deception is Satan's main tool in his strategy to defeat us. He has no real power, so all he can do is get you to make your own ignorant moves based on false information. Everything that he accomplishes is done through deception. Have you ever been deceived? Maybe you thought that everything was fine, and it wasn't until much later that you realized you had been operating based on a trick the whole time. Do not be discouraged. It happens to the best of us if we aren't careful. Look at Eve. She was tricked into thinking that whatever she did would be fine, even though God told them not to eat from every tree. Even now, many are living under the deception that it doesn't matter what we say or do. We still think that it doesn't matter what tree we eat from, because God still loves us. And while it's true that God will continue to love us, you have been tricked if you think that our actions don't come with consequences attached. One day it feels like you're living your best life, and the next day it's "Goteem! You have liver failure from drinking too much!" Most times it's a lot more subtle than that. You can literally be deceived into thinking that you aren't as valuable as you are, and before you know it, you have settled for things that should have been beneath you. Goteem!! Listen, don't let the devil get you in this way. Be intentional, strategic, and prayerful. Let the Holy Spirit lead you in all things big and small. Every tree is not good for fruit.

READ TODAY: 1 PETER 5:8-9

SLAY

Slay – to "kill" the figurative competition, usually with fashion.

Example: Yessss!! I love your outfit! You came to slay hunni!

Have y'all ever paid attention to the book of Psalms in the Bible. No, I mean really paid attention to it? There are a whole lot of psalms in there…150 to be exact. Thanks David! Now some of the psalms get more attention than others, especially the more poetic ones and the ones that get put in gospel songs. But to be honest, some of them will leave you scratching your head and thinking somebody needs to go check on ol' Dave to make sure he's okay. Like, "Aye Dave…you good my boy? You need me to call somebody to come get you?" The 59th Psalm is one of those ones. David was going through some thangs because King Saul had started to go a little insane and wanted to kill him. David knew that Saul was plotting to kill him, so he ran away and went into hiding. It made for some pretty wild psalm lyrics. But what stands out in this psalm is verse 11. Although David was asking God to defeat his enemies, he requested for God not to actually slay them. He didn't want them dead or completely eliminated. He simply wanted them scattered and rendered powerless so that anybody who sees them would be reminded of how God had won the victory on his behalf. That being said, sometimes God will slay your giants completely, and sometimes He will simply render them powerless in your life. When you look at the thing that used to oppress you and see that it is now under your feet…you can't help but be reminded of God's goodness and give Him praise. Some of you are waiting on God to slay things and people, when the even bigger flex is for God to simply move them to a new position…under your feet.

READ TODAY: PSALM 59:11

255

THIS LIVES IN MY HEAD RENT FREE.

This lives in my head rent free. – used to describe some kind of enjoyable content (usually a song or viral video) that you think about fairly often.

Example: Oh…Oh…Oh…O'Reillyyy AUTO PARTS!! I'm sorry, but this song lives in my head rent free.

Certain things just stick with you. I'm not 100% sure what the formula is, but there is an entire billion-dollar industry dedicated to getting things to live in **your** head. It's called marketing. Here in Alabama, there is an attorney's office called Goldberg & Associates…I can tell you straight off the dome that their phone number is 800-600-6014. That's because they sang it over and over again on a TV commercial for about 20 years or so. It was a simple jingle, but very catchy. But out of all of the things that live in your head rent-free, make sure you add the important things in there as well. How messed up would it be if I could rap all of Biggie's lyrics, but didn't know any helpful scriptures when I needed them? I'm one of those people who can hear one random word or phrase and then burst out in the corresponding song that it reminded me of.

Them: And I….

Me: *singing* AM TELLING YOU!

I'm not going!

Yeah, that's me. But how messed up would it be if someone was in need of an encouraging word, and I couldn't recall to my mind what any of God's promises were? That's why we must study, memorize, and meditate on good things like the word of God. Let it live in your head and in your heart rent-free forever. Can you find a verse to memorize today?

READ TODAY: PHILIPPIANS 4:8

"HIDE YOUR KIDS, HIDE YOUR WIFE, & HIDE YOUR HUSBAND." -ANTOINE DODSON

Hide your kids, hide your wife, and hide your husband. – a quote from a viral news interview where Antoine Dodson vividly and hilariously describes how a neighborhood predator had been climbing in windows and trying to assault people in the Lincoln Park projects.

Example: (Go watch the video) Google: Antoine Dodson interview.

It's been over 10 years now since this video went viral, but I can still quote it verbatim. The situation itself wasn't funny, but Antoine's lively personality was impossible to ignore. He passionately warned the people that the community was not safe and that they should hide their loved ones to protect them. A similar situation happened in the Old Testament of the Bible when the children of Israel were living in slavery in Egypt. God sent several plagues as a warning to Pharaoh that he should let God's people go free. The final plague was one that couldn't be ignored. Every firstborn person and animal in Egypt would die that night. However, death would pass over any house that followed God's directions. Moses instructed the Hebrew people to smear the blood of a lamb over their door posts. When death passed through, their homes would be hidden, and the people inside would be protected. Do you want/need protection for your household? You can't be with your spouse or your kids everywhere they go. All you can do is hide them under the blood of Jesus, the Lamb who was slain for us. This is the ultimate protection because it means that they will be okay in life or even in death. Evangelism isn't just some big mission trip to a 3rd world country. Have you shared the gospel with your own family? Are you teaching your children what it means to have their own relationship with God? Are you covering them in prayer? The best way to hide your family is to make sure they are covered under the blood of Jesus.

READ TODAY: EXODUS 12:13

DOUBLE RAINBOW ALL THE WAY!

Double rainbow all the way! – a quote from a viral YouTube video posted by user @Yosemitebear in 2010 after seeing a beautiful double rainbow in his front yard.

Example:(Go watch the video) Google: Double Rainbow original video

I suppose we are in a viral video series right now, because this video also lives in my head rent free even after 10 years. Similar to yesterday's video, this one also spun off with t-shirts, hats, cups, and several really great autotune songs. The creator of this video was a man named Paul Vasquez aka Yosemitebear (RIP Paul, he passed away in 2020). If you took time to watch the video, you will see a man who was absolutely amazed by God's creation. He didn't know whether to laugh or cry, and at some points he did both simultaneously. He kept repeating, "What does this mean??!!?" Paul felt it to be no coincidence that this beautiful double rainbow would appear in his front yard. In the Bible, God formed the rainbow as a sign to Noah after the flood. He promised Noah that the earth would never again have to experience a devastating flood of that magnitude. What can we take from this? Storms may come in your life, but God has promised that they will not be strong enough to wipe you out. You may experience some rain, but it's only temporary and it cannot destroy you. You may be in a storm right now, but I just want to encourage you that God has more power than your storm, and He has already fixed it so that the trouble can't last always. Keep believing and get to the other side of it. Next time you see a rainbow, I pray that you will remember what it means: Your storm has a **limit**.

READ TODAY: GENESIS 9:13-15

AMIRITE?

amirite? – a slang way of asking, "Am I right?" It usually assumes agreement.

Example: Hey guys, there's absolutely nothing wrong with eating an entire pizza alone, amirite?!

So apparently "amirite" has been added as a word in the dictionary, and I am weeeeeak about it! I guess it goes to show you the power of social media. But just for a moment today, I want to talk about the actual question, "Am I right?" Kudos to anyone who asketh such a question. People asking themselves or others, "Am I right?" should be the backbone of humanity. My best homegirl (Adrienne, hey girl hey!) is quick to tell me her thought process on something, and then ask me if I think she's right or wrong. Now most of the time she's right, but every so often she is wrong, and I have to be the one to tell her. She doesn't get angry. She takes what I say and considers it seriously, because she trusts me and the fact that I care about her. She does the same for me. In my opinion (just my own opinion here), this is the difference between people who are good and people who are great. People who are great don't assume that every thought process, every feeling, or every idea that comes to their mind is perfect. A great person knows that anyone could be subject to bias. A great person knows that feelings and emotions can sometimes cloud judgement. A great person identifies trustworthy people who will be honest with them, even if they are wrong. Not only does a person seek wise counsel from friends, but they also seek it from God. There is nothing wrong with asking God whether you are right or wrong, and then listening for His answer in an unbiased way. As a matter of fact, that's probably one of the very best things a person can do. Don't assume that you're right simply because you feel it. Ask and you shall receive.

READ TODAY: PSALM 139:23-24

#TAKEMEBACK

#TakeMeBack – a hashtag used to express a desire to return to something, usually a simpler time or a vacation.

Example: This job is working my nerves! This time last week, I was boo'd up on a beautiful beach in Mexico. #TakeMeBack

Have you ever been in a situation where you didn't know how good you had it until it was too late? I think about childhood. We had no bills, free food, clothes, shoes, someone to drive us around, and naps. We had naps and didn't appreciate them! No one called you lazy for going to sleep for long periods of time in the middle of the day, and we didn't understand what blessings we had! I digress. Some days I wish to be taken back to the days where I had naps and someone to take care of me. Some of you may have experienced a breakup and didn't realize what you had in that person until they were gone. Maybe you sit and reminisce on all of the good times and wish you could be taken back to those days or be taken back by that person. While it may be fun to appreciate and reminisce on past experiences, we can't become obsessed with them. We've all seen that person who gets stuck in a decade and can't get out. We've all seen the person who couldn't let the Jheri curl go. Hey, I may or may not be stuck in the 90s myself, but that's my business…y'all just keep me lifted in prayer! The Bible tells us not to look back, but forward. Sometimes I hear people saying that they are "trying to get back to" doing or being certain things. But I'm quick to tell people not to romanticize the past as if all of the golden days are behind them. We are to look and move forward with the understanding that God can do a completely new and better thing with our lives. Those good times and memories had their place, but we must trust God enough to know that better is available. Let's not say #TakeMeBack anymore. Our new prayer should be "Lord, #TakeMeForward."

READ TODAY: ISAIAH 43:18-19

#MELANIN

#Melanin – a hashtag celebrating the pigment that makes dark skin possible.

Example: The same girls who used to make fun of me for being black will run to a tanning bed to look darker. #Melanin

A famous person once said, "They hate us cause they ain't us." There are conflicting resources on who said it first, so we'll just say it's an old African Proverb (it's not). If you weren't already aware, melanin is a miracle and a gift. Not only is it absolutely beautiful, but an abundance of it also offers certain benefits and protections. I read somewhere that the full benefits aren't understood very well because the research on melanin is scarce. Mmm…imagine that. They don't care to know more about melanin…shocking. Actually, it's not shocking even in the least bit. The world has spent so much time trying to oppress darker-skinned individuals, that it only makes sense to keep them in the dark about their own advantages. People will literally make you feel bad about your difference while at the same time trying to figure out how to get what you have. People will literally oppress you and then turn around and make you feel as if it's your fault for being oppressed or that it's just all in your head. Don't fall for this. It's not just skin-tone. It could be any characteristic that you have, down to the way you walk, talk, and dress. If you aren't careful, you will end up with a form of subtle self-hatred. Don't hate yourself because of your differences. Embrace them and understand that God knew exactly what He was doing when He created you. If He sprinkled a little more of this and a little less of that, it was for a purpose. Don't hide your differences. Harness their power to make a difference in the world, big or small. Now…somebody go research melanin! For all we know, there's a cure for cancer in there somewhere! I'm just sayin'.

READ TODAY: JEREMIAH 1:5

MY BIGGEST FLEX

My biggest flex – a way to describe the most impressive thing you've ever done.

Example: My biggest flex was going from growing up with a mother who was in jail, to graduating law school and helping her get exonerated for a crime that she did not commit.

When we think about what it means to flex, we often think about it in terms of muscles. A flex is literally an expansion of something that is already existing. A flex simply allows us to visualize and appreciate it more fully. A guy who works out a lot can seem like the average Joe when he is fully clothed. But have you ever been shocked to discover that someone you thought was average, was lowkey swole? Yeah, that tends to happen when you join the corporate kickball team and James from accounting shows up in gym shorts and a tank top to lead the team to victory over the rival firm. It's not that James has a different body or different muscles than he had in the morning meeting. It's just that nobody knew he had it like that until the opportunity arose to flex them. The time and effort that had been put forth in the gym, when no one was watching, is what prepared James's muscles to flex/expand when his team needed someone strong. Well God wants to bless you with increase and expansion both in the natural and spiritual realms. He knows that there are people who need the strength that you (lowkey) have. To others, you may look like the average Joe, and they are going to be shocked when they discover just how much power you really have. It's just important that you prepare yourself, do the work, and invest the time to grow stronger even when no one is watching you. When the opportunity arises for expansion, you will be strong and prepared for the occasion…both naturally and spiritually. The biggest flex is when you realize that you can do all things through Christ who strengthens you.

READ TODAY: PSALM 115:14-15

AIGHT, BET.

Aight, bet. – what black people say when they are done talking about a thing and are preparing to be about a thing.

Example: Georgia: *cheats Stacy Abrams in governor's race, 2018*
Stacy: Aight, bet.
Georgia: *turns to a blue state in 2020 general election to help Dems win the White House and two senate seats because Stacy helped get so many people to the polls*

If a black person ever stops talking and just says, "aight, bet…" I need you to get to your designated safe place. No seriously, that means that they are no longer arguing, negotiating, or going back and forth with you on anything. Conversations cease, because that black person has made up in their mind that they will do exactly what needs to be done. It may not be today, and it may not be tomorrow, but you can rest assured that you have it coming. If a black woman says, "aight, bet…" you may come home to your car and clothes burning in the front yard *Waiting To Exhale* style. If a black man says, "aight, bet…" and then walks to his trunk, you might want to run away in a zig-zag pattern. Okay, these are some extremely stereotypical examples, but we will allow it for the purposes of illustration. The point is that action **will** be taken. The assurance of action that we have when a black person says aight and bet, should be the same level of assurance we have when God makes us a promise. If God gives you a promise, you can take that to the bank! If God gave you a promise, aight…you can bet on it being true. Whenever we don't see them happening, it's only because we haven't fulfilled our part. Many promises in the Bible were issued with "if" clauses. "**If** you are willing and obedient, you will eat the good of the land," for example. If you aren't eating the good of the land, it's not because God lied to you. All the promises of God are "yes" and "amen." In this devotional we say that the promises of God are "aight" and "bet."

READ TODAY: 2 CORINTHIANS 1:20

SICUUUD!

Sicuuud! – internet slang spelling for "sick of it."

Example: I just paid all these bills and 10 minutes later, I get an email
saying my new bill is ready to view. Sicuuud! Can I live?

Maybe it's a certain age that people get to, or maybe it's just
some invisible threshold that gets reached. But there comes a time in
life when you just get sick of your own foolishness...hopefully. I don't
know if there's a certain number of pizzas, burgers, wings, fries, pants
that no longer fit, or bad doctor reports that you have to get before you
just sit there like...what am I even doing? I don't know if there is a
certain number of drunken weekends, hangovers, or "secks" with
strangers before you just...get sick of it. I don't know if there's a
certain amount of money spent on trivial items, credit card debt, or
random Amazon packages at the door, before you're just...over it. I
don't know what threshold you are currently reaching, but let this be
your reminder that better is available. When we try to do things our
own way, we are placing a burden on ourselves that is too heavy to
bear. We may be able to tote it for a certain period of time, but
eventually we will become overwhelmed and sick of it. God offers us
the opportunity to exchange our foolish ways for His. When you
submit to God's will, you will find that you can drop the heavy weight
and pick up something much lighter. Pray today and tell God how
tired you are. It's okay to let Him know that you are sick of it. Ask
Him to take those foolish desires away and replace them with whatever
would be most pleasing in His sight.

READ TODAY: MATTHEW 11:28-30

REPOST

Repost – the act of taking online content that has already been posted by someone else and posting it again so that more people have a chance to view it.

Example: I had to repost this video of the two mistresses fighting at the funeral! So sad that the poor wife had to jump in and break it up!

When a person reposts a status, picture, or video, it is because they feel it deserves to be repeated and shared with their social media friends who may not have seen the original person's post. Some people will repost just about anything, while others are a little more selective. I feel like I'm some sort of Facebook OG, because I was on it back when only college students were allowed to join. Back then, there was no option to repost. Once reposting became an option, it basically gave birth to what it means to "go viral." A virus is something that replicates or repeats itself. A person could say something once online, yet it gets replicated and seen over and over again because people think it's worth repeating. What comes to mind is a time in the Bible where something God said was repeated. David said that God had spoken this once, yet he had heard it twice…that power belongs to God. Maybe God actually repeated it for Himself, maybe someone else heard it and repeated it back to David, or maybe it just bounced off the wall and echoed. But if we are going to make anything go viral, let it be this same thing that God wanted David to hear more than once. Power belongs to God. Power doesn't belong to your government, to your job, or to your money. All power is in God's hand, and it belongs to Him. He said what He said! So when problems arise in your life, go ahead and repeat, repost, retweet, reuse, and recycle **that**! Say it as much as you need to, and say it to whatever situation needs to hear it. Power belongs to God!

READ TODAY: PSALM 62:10-11

YEEN LION.

Yeen Lion. – an internet slang spelling of "You ain't lying."

Example: Person A: It's hot out here!
Person B: Yeen Lion! I can't do hell cuz dis tew murch!

I think life has taught us to always be on the lookout for lies. But what happens when somebody ain't lying? What happens when a person or thing is the genuine truth? I saw something circulating on IG last week that said, "Learn to recognize the green flags too." That got me bruh. We are always taught not to ignore red flags, but you really don't hear much about what to do with the green ones. I suppose it's because the red flags that we ignore can have such dire consequences. Whew Chile, you can ignore one red flag and end up a single parent with an empty bank account, a jacked-up credit score, and a torn-up transmission! So yeah...red flags are important. But when did life get to be all about avoiding trouble, and not about enjoying abundance? I'm not what the world labels a "prosperity preacher," but come on onnnn. Jesus came that we might have life, and that we might have it more abundantly! Don't get so obsessed with finding the red flags that you completely miss the good/green ones. Don't become so frozen with fear that you can't even take a step in the right direction. That's why you have to get a really good, healthy, working relationship with the Holy Spirit. He will help you to discern what is what and who is who. Without discernment, the devil can deceive you into thinking backwards. He can have you thinking a green flag is a bad thing like, "Hmmm...he's 30 with a PhD and ain't got no kids. Something must be wrong with him." The devil will have you thinking stuff like, "Hmmm...she's beautiful, educated, funny, has a good career, and loves the Lord. She's too intimidating!" See what I'm saying??! See how crazy all that sounds? Yet we do it all the time. Let's pray and ask God to help us to discern good from evil. Yes, Satan does have a strategy to defeat us. But God has a much better strategy to bless us!

READ TODAY: JOHN 10:10

TRENDING

Trending – a term used to describe someone or something that has become a popular topic of conversation online.

Example: Why is Krispy Kreme trending today? Are they giving away free doughnuts?

As the years go by, it becomes more and more apparent that social media helps to enable a herd mentality. The bandwagons are overflowing with passengers, and one of the ways that social media has further cultivated this mentality is by introducing "trending topics." This is a way for users to know what "everyone else" is thinking about and talking about so that they can be a part of it too. If I go on Twitter, for example, and see that the #1 trending topic in America is "BBL," the next thing I'm going to do is try to figure out what BBL stands for. Now that I have determined that BBL stands for Brazilian Butt Lift, the next thing I'll want to do is figure out exactly what that is and why people are talking about it today...and on and on we go. Social media has successfully decided what I'm thinking about and learning about. See if you don't set your own mind on something, the world will set it for you, and there's no telling what that could mean. That's why I'm glad that you're reading this devotional and taking time every day to look at scriptures. It would be nice if you could do it in the mornings because it gives you a chance to set your mind on things above before the world tries to take control of your thoughts with its general foolishness. We should set our mind on things like gratitude, Christ's love for us, better ways to love others, and how to make the world a better place.

READ TODAY: COLOSSIANS 3:1-2 (NIV)

EXPLORE PAGE

Explore Page – a segment of Instagram that allows a user to explore public content from other users who they may not be following. An algorithm allows each user's explore page to be specifically tailored to their own interests.

Example: My explore page is nothing but pictures of tacos, natural hair care, handsome men, sandy beaches, black love, praise breaks, and dream homes.

Explore pages be knowin'. If you want to get to know somebody, tell them to let you see their explore page. Actually, don't do that. You will probably scare them away. Explore pages are quite personal because they are often a reflection of you and the things that you pay attention to. My own explore page is what is referenced in the example sentence above. But some people can't share what's on their explore page, because they don't want you to know their secret indulgences. Do you log on and see a bunch of big booty women bent over in the camera with no clothes on? It's because they know that's what you like to see. Do you see bitter relationship/breakup memes? Do you see racist or misogynistic posts? What does your explore page say about you? Could you show your explore page, without shame, to anyone who asked to see it? Hopefully you will never have to do that, but I just want you to think about it hypothetically. Have you gotten comfortable viewing things that sow seeds of lust, greed, bitterness, or even hatred? Are you okay with it simply because no one knows? Let this be your reminder that God sees, knows, and cares about everything concerning you. Pray and ask God to help you examine your own ways. It's not about appearing to be holy for the benefit of others. It's about loving and honoring God with your whole heart.

READ TODAY: PROVERBS 5:21

RUSSIAN BOT

Russian bots – internet trolls sponsored by the Russian government used to collect information and sway social and political interests in favor of Russia.

Example: I just got a DM from some gorgeous man asking if he could be my sugar daddy. He's either a scammer or a Russian bot!

I think we all know that Russia has been wild for a long time. It seems like they are always trying to do some sneaky ish. They stay trying to spy on folks. Russia even sought to interfere in the past two presidential elections here in the United States. And for all the foul things that we know Russia is doing, there are many, many more things that we have no idea about. But one thing is for sure, we know not to trust Russia. So if Russia has people acting as bots to carry out deceptive plots, don't you think Satan does the same thing and worse? You see, Satan is even more deceptive than Russia. He will use the very people that are supposed to be trustworthy to lead you astray. That's right, I'm talking about religious people. Some of them are false prophet bots. If you don't have a sense of discernment, you can barely tell the difference between someone who is preaching God's word and someone who is using **sprinkles** of God's word to lead you astray. The Bible calls them "wolves in sheep's clothing," and tells us that we will know them by their fruit. In other words, they may look like these meek, mild, and righteous characters, but what are they producing? Is it rotten fruit? Are they causing you more confusion? Are you losing sleep or being tormented in your dreams ever since connecting with that person? I know it sounds crazy, but if the Russians are out here doing it on the internet, you better believe that Satan is trying to do it in your life. Let the Holy Spirit guide you, and also examine the associated fruit. Let's pray today and ask God to open our eyes to anyone who is trying to deceive us.

READ TODAY: MATTHEW 7:15-18

JUST HERE FOR THE COMMENTS

Just here for the comments – what people say when they are following a post, not to actively participate in the conversation, but to see what others have to say about it.

Example: Post: Men, do you think a woman should have to work and pay half the bills?
Person A & Person B: *arguing*
Person C: I'm just here for the comments!

If there's one thing that I don't like about social media, it's the fact that it has confused so many people into thinking that their opinions matter more than they do. And I mean no disrespect to anyone's opinion, but don't let social media fool you into thinking that you must form and voice an opinion on any and everything. I'm not going to lie, I used to be that way too. I would comment on every social issue, scandal, or current event that would come across my timeline. Sometimes FB will bring up a memory of an opinion that I had posted, and I will look at it and wonder what was wrong with me and why I thought all of that was necessary to say. You will see people all over the internet wasting precious time and energy all up in Kool-Aids that they don't even know the flavors to. (If you didn't grow up in the 90s, that means they were all up in other people's business and didn't even have factual information.) I've literally seen people in comment sections discussing how a happily married couple had too many children because they are expensive. Like...huh? How do you know what their finances are? It's okay to be quiet sometimes and mind your own business. We are living in a society where people who still live with their mama will get online and try to tell a millionaire how to run their business. It's okay to use that time and energy to mind your own business so that you can even have something that people could form an opinion about. Even the Bible says so. Look!

READ TODAY: 1 THESSALONIANS 4:11

CUFFING SEASON

Cuffing Season – a time of year when temperatures begin to drop, major Holidays are coming up, people are tired of running the summer streets, and are realizing that they want to be boo'd up.

Example: Person A: I got like 3 different DM slides today, what is happening?
Person B: Look at the calendar. It's cuffing season.

Cuffing season is when single people start getting paired up in preparation for the colder months. When it's warm outside, people feel comfortable running the streets and gaining attention from multiple romantic interests. But if you want a Thanksgiving dinner date, a Christmas gift, someone to kiss on New Year's, and a Valentine's Day gift, you need to get somebody locked down in a more serious relationship. That's called cuffing. It typically starts in October and runs through Valentine's Day. After Valentine's Day, the necessity starts to fade, and the breakups happen. The term "cuffing" makes reference to being handcuffed to someone or to being on lockdown with them. In the Bible, the Apostle Paul had to issue a warning to some believers who were cuffing. It had nothing to do with romantic interests though. These people were trying to handcuff themselves to the old religious laws that called for people to prove their righteousness by how well they could adhere to the rules. When Jesus came, He set us free from that kind of religious system, and it became more about our faith in God and our relationship with Him. So why were people trying to handcuff themselves back to the old way which was impossible to follow perfectly? The truth is that they had just gotten comfortable. Paul told them not to get tangled up in the bondage of the old way. So if you find yourself thinking that you have to follow some set of holy rules in order to be perfect, yet you ignore the Holy Spirit...you too, are cuffed and confused. Be free today!

READ TODAY: GALATIANS 5:1

I'M HOLLERING!

I'm hollering! – a common phrase used to indicate that something is funny, and that the person is "hollering" with laughter. About 8 times out of 10, the person saying this is somewhere not actually making any noise.

Example: Person A: ...and then I said, "I ain't Effie, and you ain't Curtis! Because I am going!"
Person B: I'm hollering! You so crazy!

Let's see...hollering is great for a sporting event. It's good to holler for help in the event of an emergency. It's even nice to be able to let out a good holler when something is hilarious. But there's something annoying about hollering when you shouldn't have to holler. If you have children, you know exactly what I'm talking about. Our parents did it to us, and now it's our turn. If I was downstairs and my mom called my name from upstairs, the next step was to respond with, "Yes ma'am!" while simultaneously dropping whatever the heck I was doing and heading upstairs to see what she wanted. What was **not** going to happen was my mom hollering back and forth with me all across the house. My mom felt that she deserved enough respect to not have to scream and holler a whole conversation with her children. And honestly, that's how it is with God. When He speaks to us, He doesn't holler back and forth. Sometimes we look for God in the things that make the most noise, but so often, that's not Him. The prophet Elijah referred to it as a "still small voice." Everything won't be a Damascus Road experience where God knocks you off your horse, blinds you for a while, and then speaks to you in a loud voice like He did to Saul/Apostle Paul. Sometimes it's as gentle as an "Aye...chill." Trust me, you don't want to get to that point where He has to get your attention with a "holler." So settle yourself, and listen for His gentle voice. It's not any less serious than His holler.

READ TODAY: 1 KINGS 19:11-13

SORRY, NOT SORRY.

Sorry, not sorry. – a popular phrase used to apologize for something that you do not actually regret.

Example: I went to the state fair three nights in a row just for the funnel cake. I didn't ride a single ride. Sorry, not sorry.

If you get out in society doing things that are deemed "socially unacceptable," the consequences range in severity. There are mild penalties like crazy stares or awkward silences. More moderate penalties include losing friends or being ostracized by certain people. The most severe penalties can land you in jail or even on death row. Sadly, yet not surprisingly, having faith in God is becoming more and more socially unacceptable. And don't even get me started on Jesus! Listen, they **might** let you get away with talking about God, but at the name of Jesus?? They mad. People will now give you flack for mentioning Jesus, but don't mind electing a presidential candidate who brags about sexually assaulting women. Yeah, the math ain't mathing. You see, being a true follower of Christ (and not just a cultural Christian) will never be the socially acceptable thing to do. One of Satan's trickiest tricks is to get people to submerge themselves in the culture of Christianity, while not actually following Christ. These people may go to church every Sunday, which gives them a false sense of security simply because they are in close proximity to the faith, but they don't truly buy it. It's like people who go and sit in Starbucks because it's popular and they like the atmosphere...but they never actually buy any coffee. So since it's never going to be socially acceptable, it's best that we settle it within ourselves that we do not care. If having a real relationship with Jesus gets us crazy stares or noses turned up, so be it. Sorry, not sorry. Since the Bible days, people have been locked up and received the death penalty just for claiming Christ...and here we are in a free society, ashamed of the gospel. Nope, that's not okay.

READ TODAY: ROMANS 1:16

READY TO RISK IT ALL

Ready to risk it all – when someone is preparing to take an action wherein the reward *seems* to be greater than the potential losses that may come as a consequence.

Example: He's eating dinner with his wife and kids, but the way he's staring at the waitress suggests that he's ready to risk it all.

Today we will talk about a man in the Bible who was ready to risk it all. Jesus needed time to pray, so he told the disciples to go ahead and get in the ship and head to the other side without Him. The wind and waves started tossing the boat all around. Jesus walks up (on the water), and the disciples freaked out thinking He was a ghost. Jesus told them to chill out and that it was only Him. Peter said, "Okay, if it's really you Jesus, let me walk to you on the water." Jesus told Him to come on. Peter must have recognized the voice, because he decided to risk it all and step out of the boat. He got out there and was doing well until he got distracted by the wind and waves. He started to freak out and sink. Jesus rescued him and said, "smh, you gotta stop doubting. You woulda been straight." Here are the lessons. The only reason they were on the boat to start off with, was because they were being obedient to what Jesus told them to do. We see here that obedience to God doesn't mean that you are exempt from experiencing storms or harsh conditions. We also see that Peter was familiar enough with the voice of Jesus to risk stepping out of the boat. It's important to spend time with the Lord and to know His voice. You'll never be able to step out on faith if you don't know it's Him. Also, Peter was fine when his focus was on Jesus. The distractions are what cause you to sink. Lastly, even when Peter's doubt made him sink, Jesus was there to rescue him. So as scary as it may feel, your obedience to God and your faith in Him is not the risk. The risk is in doubting Him. Get to know God's voice so you can hear, obey, and step out on faith without sinking.

READ TODAY: MATTHEW 14:26-32

I'M ABOUT TO GO LIVE.

I'm about to go live. – what people post to let others know that they are getting ready to begin a live online broadcast that allows users to see events taking place in real time.

Example: I'm at the grocery store, and these two elderly ladies are in here fighting over the last roll of tissue! I'm about to go live!

Do you remember when FB and the other platforms gave people the ability to start broadcasting live? It has become an extremely powerful tool. During the pandemic/quarantine, live broadcasts of church, concerts, weddings, and funerals, kept us feeling connected. Racist behavior gets exposed on live videos. They can even save lives because certain out of control cops know to "reel it in" when there is a live audience. When I was working on my website, there was a button at the top that said, "Go Live." Once the site was complete, I could click on that button and make my work visible to the world. Some of you have gifts, talents, abilities, and projects that God has given you to do. Yet, you continue to delay in releasing it to the world. For some of you the delay is from God. You're still building your "site," and that's okay. But an overwhelming majority of you know exactly what God told you to do, yet you refuse to put in the work for it to be released. The world needs what you have. Has God spoken a word over your life or given you a vision? Are you procrastinating and lying to yourself that it's because of God's timing? After I wrote my first book, dozens of people told me that they had a book that they were supposed to be writing too. Some hadn't started, and others started and then stopped. Listen! I don't know where you are in the process of being obedient to God's assignment over your life, but at some point, you have to stop acting like you don't know what you're supposed to be doing. At some point, you have to give that gift back to the world. Even if it's just to reach one person...get ready to go live.

READ TODAY: MATTHEW 5:16

THANKS FOR COMING TO MY TED TALK.

Thanks for coming to my Ted Talk. – a comical way of thanking people for listening to your thoughts on a matter.

Example: Dear black people: I know our parents taught us to order the steak medium-well, but if you want to know what steak is supposed to taste like, you should order medium. Thanks for coming to my TED Talk!

If you've never heard of TED, it is a nonprofit organization committed to spreading ideas that could potentially make a difference in the world. These ideas are spread by people who are making or have already made an impact in their field. These people make short speeches, of 18 minutes or less, to a live and diverse audience. Many of the speeches are made available for free online to make the ideas available even more widely. I've had a couple of real-life friends who have been asked to give TED talks, and it's a huge deal. Long before TED talks were a thing, Jesus was basically giving them. He was committed to spreading ideas that would change the world. He did this by giving short talks known as parables. Each parable was a simple story/narrative that He used to help people understand certain concepts more easily. Using parables also made His lessons relatable and easy to remember. I think we can learn a lot from Jesus and His style of communication. We have to remember that everyone is on a different level, and that's okay. If you're trying to reach someone, you don't have to come at them with some deep and complicated dissertation to make yourself sound impressive. We know you're smart. We know you went to cOlleGE little buddy. Cool, but try to put yourself in the same shoes as the person you are trying to reach, and then go from there. Let's pray and ask God to help us become more effective and relatable communicators in all facets of life. Thanks for coming to my TED Talk!

READ TODAY: MATTHEW 13:34-35

WEEKEND ME PLEASE.

Weekend Me Please. – an abbreviated way to say, "I'm tired of working, and I need the weekend to hurry up and get here."

Example: If I have to answer one more unnecessary question, I am going to scream! Weekend Me Please!

I'm probably the only person here who watched the show *Downton Abbey*, but it was lowkey bomb. In it, the Dowager Countess of Grantham, Lady Violet Crawley, hears someone refer to the weekend and is genuinely confused as to what that is. "WeekEND? What is a WeekEND?" She had been born into so much money that she didn't even understand the concept of a "work week" or it ending. If you're anything like Lady Crawley, you can skip this one. For the rest of us, we need to understand the importance of having time off to rest. In today's society, people will try to make you feel bad about resting, but that's a trick of the enemy. God designed our bodies to require rest. I understand that some of you feel the need to have two and three different jobs with no days off, but I pray that it's only temporary. Going without proper rest is risky. Your immune system can't fight off diseases as well without rest, and your mind can't fight off attacks from the devil as well either. When you are exhausted, you are much more vulnerable to a satanic attack. Things aren't as clear. Your mind and body are so worn out, that you can't make good decisions or exercise the right restraint. I encourage you to use your weekends wisely. Most of us do too much on the weekends and jam-pack as much as we can into it before Monday morning. I do it all the time…God is still working on me! But I know I need to do better at saying "no" to weekend tasks, obligations, or events that will put me in a place of too much fatigue…or…or God, just hear me out. Make me rich so I don't have to work so much anyway. Well until then, I suppose I will have to learn discipline and rest.

READ TODAY: MARK 6:30-31

ONE THING ABOUT ME…

One thing about me… – a phrase used to describe a characteristic about yourself that remains consistent.

Example: One thing about me…I'm gonna finish my whole plate
          if the food is good. I don't care about trying to be cute!

Between church and social media, there are a lot of people who want to paint their lives as this picture of perfection. It used to be the church more than anybody, but I think it's safe to say that social media has taken first place. We are overrun with images of people who want us to see their perfect engagement, perfect wedding, perfect car, perfect home, perfect pregnancy, perfect baby, perfect relationship, perfect career, perfect body, and perfect family. This is what we see, and yet it is very common knowledge that nobody is perfect. There is at least one "thing" about every human that disqualifies us for angelhood. Even the great Apostle Paul, who wrote almost two-thirds of the New Testament, will tell you that he was missing the mark for perfection. We don't know exactly what He was referring to, but he called it a "thorn" in his flesh. He asked God several times to remove it, but the answer was no. Imagine that. God said no. He told Paul that he had to keep it because that was what kept him from "feeling himself" too much and becoming conceited. I mean think about it, some people start a church in their living room with their cats and start acting high siddity. Paul was given revelation after revelation, and God knew he wouldn't know how to act without his thorn. You may have one thorn or several. Maybe God will take it from you, and maybe He won't. I pray that He does, but either way, your thorn doesn't have to define you. Just because your thorn is still present, doesn't mean you have to bow down to it or let it control you. God told Paul that even with the thorn, His grace was enough to carry him through his lack of perfection. That same grace is available to us for ours.

READ TODAY: 2 CORINTHIANS 12:7-10

WHYYYY ARE YOU LIKE THIS?!

Whyyyy are you like this?! – a question that gets asked to people who do silly things on the internet.

Example: Person A: *posts picture with new boyfriend who is actually just a stick figure drawn in next to her*
Person B: Whyyyy are you like this?!

Yeah, so I get asked this question all the time by my internet peers. Apparently I say and post things that beg the question. I guess my foolish antics have them wondering why I am the way that I am. I usually reply with, "When I find out, I'll let you know!" The truth is, I've already found out. I didn't always know, but as it turns out, God made me the way that I am for His glory. He did the same thing with you. Everything about you was intentional. Think about yourself for a moment. I'm not talking about the crazy mindsets that you've adopted as a result of trauma. I'm not talking about the guarded, bitter, fearful, prideful, materialistic, or sinful you. I'm talking about the real you. The one that is loving, giving, kind, caring, smart, cool, funny, awkward, nerdy, or silly. I'm talking about the way God made you. The exact set of characteristics that you have are not going to be identical to anybody else's in the world. Amongst other things, I am smart and have a very umm…different…sense of humor. I didn't always know why it mattered for me to be this way, but just look. God is using it. You're reading this book, ain't ya? Well your mission, if you choose to accept it, is to figure out why you are the way that you are and then leverage that to be a blessing to others and to bring God glory. We must stop being so ashamed about the traits that make us different. All that means is that you have something different to offer. If you already know, that is awesome. Pray and ask God to reveal a strategy on how to pull it all together to make an impact.

READ TODAY: REVELATION 4:11

#LATEPOST

#LatePost – a hashtag used to indicate that the events referenced in a post occurred sometime in the past.

Example: We were busy celebrating, but I just want to wish a happy belated birthday to my son, Roscoe Jr! #LatePost

I went to a Jill Scott concert once, and there were several people up front holding up their phones to record. Jill asked them to put the phones down and just be present in the moment. They could worry about making a post later. It was all about prioritizing. What sense does it make to have one of the greatest musicians of all time right in front of you with your face buried in a cell phone? Well there was a time in the Bible where a few women also prioritized the wrong thing. Jesus told a parable about 10 virgins. Five were wise and five were foolish. They had all been invited to a wedding. They weren't sure exactly when it would start, but they knew the groom would eventually come get them for it. Well the groom took longer than expected. The wise virgins had brought enough extra oil to keep their lamps going despite the additional wait time. The foolish virgins had come with their lamps but no extra oil. They had to run out, but by the time they got back, the groom had already come and taken those who were ready into the wedding. They tried to get in, but the door was already locked. I'm sure they spent their time getting all dressed up for the wedding, but didn't take into account the most important thing…being able to get in. This is a roundabout way of saying check on your priorities. Are you present on social media, but absent with the people at your own home? Are you on time for work, but late accepting the call that God put on your life? Newsflash! You have no idea when your last day will be. We all have to stand and be accountable for what we did and didn't do. But if you stay present and ready, like the wise virgins, you won't have to scramble. Don't be late getting to your purpose. Your tardiness may cause you to miss out.

READ TODAY: MATTHEW 25:10-13

#FIXITJESUS

#FixItJesus – a hashtag that became popular after reality star Phaedra Parks used the well-known phrase when battling it out with one of her castmates.

Example: How come every time I go to McDonald's the ice cream machine is broken? #FixItJesus

Do you have a relationship that is broken like the McDonald's ice cream machine? Perhaps you fell out with your own mother years ago and have since become estranged. Maybe you became roommates with a friend, and long story short, it wasn't a good idea. Now you don't speak. Perhaps you loaned a family member some money, but when you asked to be paid back, they started acting funny and making you out to be the bad guy. It put a strain on your relationship, and you are no longer close. You really hate to see good relationships going to the wayside because of things that aren't so important in the grand scheme. Sadly, our conflict resolution skills aren't always the best. Instead of fixing what is broken, many of us just throw the whole thing away. But no one is perfect, so what if it was a misunderstanding or a mistake that led to the rift? What if the whole thing wasn't supposed to get thrown away? Jesus gave us a formula for conflict resolution. He said if someone did something wrong to you, first try to go to them one-on-one with no one else around to let them know. Y'all might be able to squash it then and there. If that doesn't work, take two or three folks with you who may be able to help make peace. If that doesn't work, seek help from trusted spiritual leaders who may be able to give solid advice from that standpoint. Now if that doesn't work, it is what it is, and if I see you in the street, I'm crossing to the other side! See some of y'all are just skipping to that last part, but Jesus has given us guidelines on how to try to fix it first. I say let's go with that! Pray today and ask God to open your heart and theirs to forgiveness and restoration.

READ TODAY: MATTHEW 18:15-17

THAT AWKWARD MOMENT WHEN...

That Awkward Moment When... – used to describe an uncomfortable situation.

Example: That awkward moment when you really don't feel like picking up your pace, but you see someone holding the door open for you and waiting, and you wish they wouldn't...

Have you ever heard the Holy Spirit telling you to do something that you knew would be uncomfortable? I'm getting a touch of anxiety just thinking about it. Has God ever told you to go pray with somebody?! Whew! There is always that awkward moment where you have to decide whether to look crazy and obey or be cool and disobedient. When you obey, it's awkward because it usually catches people off guard when you ask to pray with them. And then it's awkward again because you have to hope that you can pray on the spot without sounding like a complete idiot. It's awkward one more time, because that person may do anything from having a breakdown to standing there awkwardly in silence the whole time. All I can tell you though, is that it is better to suck it up and obey. Whether they "respond" in the moment or not, you are sowing a seed into their life, and reminding them that God has not forgotten about them. You never know what a person is on the verge of doing, so don't take it lightly if God is telling **you** to pray **with** that person. I've been the person who was too embarrassed to be obedient. I figured I could just go and pray **for** that person even though I clearly heard God say to pray **with** them. It's a terrible feeling, and your disobedience kind of haunts you. You begin to regret not getting over yourself to be obedient and help someone who needed it. All I can tell you is that it may seem scary to obey God's voice, but the more you do it, the less awkward it gets over time. It just takes practice. Resolve in your head that obeying God is more important than that person's opinion of your coolness in that moment.

READ TODAY: EPHESIANS 6:18-20

CATCH FLIGHTS, NOT FEELINGS.

Catch flights, not feelings. – a phrase used by people who would rather travel the world and be at peace than waste time being troubled over a relationship.

Example: She left my message on read, but that's okay. I catch flights, not feelings. Off to Mexico!

Feelings man…what are they really? When we say a person has "caught" feelings, it means that they have unexpectedly and perhaps unintentionally started to fall for someone romantically. Maybe they were just looking for casual companionship or someone that they could pass the time with. Before they knew it, however, they started really caring for the person. This person "caught" feelings. I think it's hilarious that we say "caught" as if the person has contracted a disease. Perhaps that's because having feelings and emotions can be brutal. But feelings, in their proper context, don't have to be so terrible. They can be great as long as you don't let them control you in a negative way. You see, unchecked feelings can make you do stupid things. One of the dumbest things that feelings can make you do is not listen to God. Feelings can make you jump ahead of Him to do things just because they "feel" right. This is problematic, and a person who allows their feelings to take precedence over God will always struggle to move forward in life. It's like a plane that is unable to take off because the emotional baggage is too heavy. God is preparing you for takeoff, but a part of that process is letting go of anything that could hold you down or disrupt your flight pattern. Again, feelings are great in their proper place. You don't want to become some guarded, bitter, cold, and non-feeling robot. The key is learning to identify feelings that are healthy and ones that are meant to distract you from your purpose. Let's pray today and ask God to help you separate your feelings from His voice so that you can catch your flight and control your feelings.

READ TODAY: ISAIAH 40:31

BIG THINGS POPPIN'

Big Things Poppin' – a phrase that was once used to signify that great things were starting to happen for someone's life.

Example: I just opened my own clothing boutique, and my boyfriend proposed at the grand opening! Big Things poppin'!

To take it a step further, some people will expand this phrase to say, "Big things poppin'...little things stoppin'." That is a profound statement that is definitely worth exploring today. If you see someone who is truly successful (I'm not talking about stunting for the 'gram but miserable in real life successful), I want you to understand that there is more to it than meets the eye. They would have you to think that it came easy, when in reality, the struggle was real. There are things that you will get wrong and need to correct. Most people will give up during this time period when all that's really needed are adjustments. Some practices will have to be stopped, while others will have to be started. The big takeaway here, is that in order for big things to pop and to continue popping, little things need to be stopping. The Bible teaches us that a person who cannot be faithful over small things, will not be trusted to handle big things. The key is to treat the little things with the same excellence that you would give to a big thing. Stop assuming that because a thing is small, that your stewardship over it isn't important. Those little things that you ignore or fail to do properly when a thing is small, can prevent it from growing big and being sustainable. Let's pray today and ask God to help us to see the importance of our faithfulness even in the little things.

READ TODAY: LUKE 16:10-11

DRINKING WATER AND MINDING MY BUSINESS

Drinking water and minding my business – a formula for peace of mind and clear skin.

Example: Person A: I haven't seen you in a while. You look amazing! What have you been doing?
Person B: Just drinking water and minding my business!

If there's one thing that nosey folks love, it's social media. Can you blame them? Back in the day, nosey folks had to do a lot more legwork. They had to call around town to get the gossip. They had to pretend to care if somebody was okay while really just fishing for info. They had to join a whole street committee! Some would literally have to sit on their porch or in a window all day like Pearl from *227*. Now, social media makes it easy to be nosey because people voluntarily post their personal business for the world to see. But just because it's easy, doesn't mean we have to take part. I used to be much more active on Facebook than I am now. There was an instance where someone posted a picture congratulating two people who had gotten married. Before I knew it, I had gone down a rabbit hole. I found out where these people were from, how they met, what they did for a living, how many kids they had, and what the groom's ex-wife looked like. These were strangers, and I was all up in their business! I think I was just about to click on the ex-wife's boyfriend's page when I said to myself, "Alright now Lori, THAT IS ENOUGH!" It was something about being three layers deep into the lives of strangers that made me realize that I could be using that time to do something that was going to propel me forward in life, even if that thing was to simply take a nap and rejuvenate myself. If you aren't careful, you'll spend so much time in other people's business that you don't take care of your own. I know social media makes it seem acceptable, but when you find yourself going too far, stop and think about what better thing this could be distracting you from.

READ TODAY: 1 THESSALONIANS 4:11

BEARD GAME STRONG

Beard Game Strong – a phrase used to compliment a man on how luxurious and well-groomed his facial hair is.

Example: He doesn't have any hair up top, but that beard game strong!

Most (but not all) women of a certain age, truly appreciate a man with a nice beard. We particularly enjoy beards that are well-groomed. The thing about beards though, is that a nice one can cover up a good bit of a man's face. It is **very** possible to meet, fall in love with, and marry a man whose full face you have never actually seen. I once heard it said that beards, hats, and glasses on men are like makeup and wigs on women. That's because they are all things that can make someone look more attractive while obscuring their true, natural appearance. There is nothing wrong with any of these things, but I just want us to understand that everything is not always as it appears on the surface. This applies to everything. If you only look at things with your natural eyes, you are asking to be deceived. We must use our spiritual discernment to judge stuff properly. Don't assume that you can trust someone just because they "look" honest and innocent. Scammers are everywhere. By the same token, you cannot assume that someone who looks rough around the edges is evil. The word "beard" has become so synonymous with a false appearance that it is now used to refer to a woman who is being used by a gay man wishing to appear straight in the eyes of the public. Y'all, they literally call the woman a beard. I just want to caution everyone today to stop relying on those physical eyes, because there are some strong and deceptive beard games going on out here. It's not just men, either. Women, children, politicians, corporations, religious leaders, media outlets...can all have beards obscuring their true nature. I don't want you to be afraid. I simply want you to be aware. This is why we must pray about everything...no more assuming.

READ TODAY: PHILIPPIANS 1:9-10

I CAN'T!

I can't! – a popular expression meaning that a person is unable to deal with something. It may be used either comically or seriously.

Example: Person A: I just found out that there is no A/C in my dorm, and I have to bring my own box fan. I can't!

Are you, or is someone you know, a control freak? You may be entitled to compensation. "New research" shows that being obsessed with control can lead to serious side effects such as stress, anxiety, depression, heart attack, or stroke. If you have experienced difficulty letting go of control, there is a class-action lawsuit in your favor due to the manufacturer's failure to disclose the addictive nature of needing to be in control. Okay, there's no settlement. But the incessant need to be in control of everything around you is something that you simply **can't** do. I mean...technically you can do it, but it won't end well. The settlement may not be real, but the symptoms I named are very real and tied to people's inability to relax, which causes stress. There is a condition we see in the eye known as CSR (Central Serous Retinopathy) that causes mild to severe vision loss. I mentioned CSR because it is heavily associated with patients who have "Type A" personalities. These are people who constantly feel the need to be perfect and in control. Anyone who feels that way will be under a lot of stress which can affect health, and even vision. I want you to understand that **God** is in control. You **can't** be in control, because you are not perfect. You can't do what God does, so please stop trying. You can't even control if it rains today or not. And stop trying to control other people too, because you will drive them away. Please just submit to God's control and yield to Him. You're making yourself and the people around you sick. At the end of the day, if God doesn't do it, it's not going to get done.

READ TODAY: PSALM 37:23

A WORD!

A word! – an expression used to note that someone is telling the truth.

Example: Person A: All business ain't good business. You don't have to accept every deal that comes across the table if it will cost you your peace!
Person B: Yesss! A word!

I'm not sure how long you have been reading this devotional, but if you've been reading it for a while, my prayer is that you are gaining a clearer picture of just how powerful God's word is. The Bible is jam-packed with so much wisdom and knowledge that truly stands the test of time. I got some negative reviews on my last book because the pages give you a scripture reference instead of just printing the verse in the book. And guess what?! I did it again! The audacity of me wanting people to go to their Bible and actually search it! You may open your Bible (or the app) to look for one scripture and end up reading the whole chapter! While I understand that it may not be the most convenient thing for some people, my prayer is that we all begin to see God's word, not as a burden, but as a blessing and a secret weapon. It is such a powerful tool in our arsenal. There are so many answers right there just waiting for us to read and take heed. I'm going to let y'all in on a little secret that my pastor told me. See back in the day, if you wanted to find information on a specific topic in the Bible, you had to go and search something called a concordance. Nowadays, all you have to do is go to Google and type "what does the Bible say about _____," and boom! A whole list of related scriptures will pop up in 0.03 seconds! Try it the next time you are going through something. You will never get so spiritually mature that you don't need the word. Writing these books has truly been a blessing to me simply because it forces me to be all up in my word, and chile I love it there. God's word...Get in there! Yeah, yeah! Get in there!

READ TODAY: PSALM 119:105

#MESSAGE

#Message – a hashtag used to indicate that the related content contains an underlying life lesson.

Example: *Post* Parents, play with your kids sometimes! #Message

Messages are often used to replace direct, face to face communication. We can't always go and find an individual to speak with them in person. This might be due to distance, other obligations, or even just due to our own non-confrontational nature. Instead, we send messages. Messages can come in the form of a letter, a text message, or an e-mail. They can also come via a messenger, wherein we employ someone else to deliver the communication on our behalf. Messages may also come from our actions. Some people don't know how to verbally say, "Hey...I'm mad at you," and so they take actions to get their point across. If someone gives you the silent treatment, for example, they do it to send a message that they are upset. Maybe they don't think words are enough to make you understand. Well God also sends us messages. He doesn't usually come down from heaven and talk to us face to face, but He uses other methods to communicate. One of the main ways He likes to communicate to us is through our life experiences. It's a good idea to pay attention to everything that goes on in your life and seek to find the message. There is always some type of lesson or wisdom that can be gained from everything you encounter. Ask a preacher. They see lessons everywhere, and I do mean everywhere. They are always talking about, "See as I was watching the football game last night, I saw the kicker come out with limp, and I said, 'Lord...what are You trying to show me?'" This is hilarious, but I am not exaggerating at alllllll. We should be like this with our lives. God, what are you trying to show me? What was I supposed to learn from this? Let's pray and ask God to clearly reveal His messages to us so that we may learn and move on to our next lesson.

READ TODAY: PROVERBS 4:7

GET YOUR LIFE!

Get Your Life! – a phrase that is a shortened version of "Get your life together!" Usually used when someone is displaying behavior that is unwise.

Example: Your parents are paying $30,000 a year for you to attend college, and you're skipping classes and failing them?! You need to get your life, sir!

The saying, "get your life," implies that your life has actually gone somewhere on its own and that you need to go retrieve it. The truth is, that can actually happen. I think that's why people have those mid-life crises. It's as if they fell asleep behind the wheel of their own life for 20 years and are just now realizing that they haven't done any of the things that they set out to do. If you are experiencing a mid or quarter-life crisis, it's an awful feeling. The good news is that you're not stuck. The first thing you need to do is calm down. Don't start freaking out and doing crazy outlandish things trying to fill the void that you feel. Don't go finding a side piece, breaking up your family, or tricking your retirement fund away on a Ferrari like they do on TV. Instead, remember that we have a God of restoration. Don't focus on the past or the years that you felt you wasted, except to figure out what the lesson was in all of it and how to charter a better path. Pray and ask God to restore your joy and peace, and to show you what the next steps of your life should be. Ask Him to help revitalize relationships that may have become stagnant over the years. Finally… and this is the key…focus on your God-given assignment. That is the only thing that will fill the void. No new relationship or material possession will be able to help you get your life. The devil will try to trick you into thinking that the crisis is about being unhappy, but the truth is, it's about a call that has gone unanswered. You will never feel like you are where you're supposed to be if you are ignoring or running away from God's will, purpose, and assignment for your life.

READ TODAY: JOEL 2:25-26

LIFE WAS GIVEN.

Life Was Given. – a phrase used to mean that seeing or hearing something has inspired you.

Example: I just listened to India Arie's *Voyage To India* album again after almost 20 years, and it is still amazing! Life was given!

Sometimes we say stuff not realizing how profound it really is. When we say that life has been given, it is the perfect way to speak of inspiration. The word inspiration literally means to breathe air/oxygen into your body, which we all know is how we survive. When you inspire, life is quite literally being given. It's the opposite of what happens when a person expires (aka dies). When Jesus came and did the work at Calvary, everyone thought that His life had been taken from Him. The truth is, they couldn't kill Jesus. He only died because He **gave** His own life. The Bible says He "laid down" His life for us, His friends. His life was not taken, but literally given for our sins. But the dope thing about Jesus laying down His life was that He also had the power to pick it back up again, which is exactly what He did on the third day. What everyone thought was expired, was resurrected and again able to inspire. That same resurrection continues to inspire us to this day. All I want you to do now is to meditate on the fact that the same power that raised Jesus from the dead and gave Him life again, is the exact same power that is available to raise you up from a life of sin and free you from the shackles of death. Jesus literally gave His life so that an abundant life could be given unto us. That is such a blessing. It means that sin and death have no more power over us. That's all the inspiration we need. Life was given!

READ TODAY: JOHN 15:13

TIME SLOW DOWN!

Time Slow Down! – what parents say when they realize that their children are growing up fast.

Example: It seems like she was just starting kindergarten the other day, and now she's 16 with her driver's license. Time slow down!

Let me just meet you at the front door on this one. Y'all can just stop saying this one because time is not about to slow down. Time, by definition, cannot and will not ever slow down or speed up until the Lord returns. So yeah...we can quit talking to time and telling it to stop being time. All we can do is stop wasting it. We all need to do a better job of enjoying every single day and making the most of it. Tomorrow isn't promised to us, and to be quite honest, neither is the rest of today. I got a call the other day that my favorite first cousin passed away suddenly and unexpectedly. It was so extremely hard to process, but all I could really do was remind myself to live. There's no time for things like unforgiveness, bitterness, laziness, and fear. Time isn't slowing down, but the Bible tells us that we need to learn how to "number" our days. This basically means that we need to stop taking them for granted as if there is an unlimited supply. We must apply wisdom to each day. This might mean stopping to smell the roses instead of letting time pass you by and then begging it to slow down. No, you slow down. Enjoy your kids, spend quality time with them, and be wise enough to know that they will grow up. Work hard to build a foundation for wealth in your youth, knowing that your body won't always have so much energy. Take the vision that God gave you and work the strategy while the windows of opportunity are open. We rush around all day and barely take time to appreciate life and the people we love. This must change. Let's pray today and ask God to show us how to eliminate the things that are stealing our time so that we can make the most out of the moments that we are blessed with.

READ TODAY: PSALM 90:12

YOU WOKE UP AND CHOSE VIOLENCE.

You woke up and chose violence. – when a person decides to do or say something to make people mad early in the day.

Example: Person A: Beyoncé is just okay.
Person B: Oh you woke up and chose violence, I see.

I'm not sure you are human if you've never felt angry. There is a high chance that you will get angry again at some point, and there is a small chance that you might be angry right now. The most important thing to understand about your anger is that you can't let it make you do stuff. It's okay to *feel* anger, but it's not okay to *do* anger. Once you allow anger to be an action verb, you have chosen violence. Violence is more than just throwing hands or throwing plates at the wall. It can be verbal. Anger can cause you to speak to someone in a violent way. Violence can be emotional wherein you manipulate or abuse someone's emotions out of anger. Violence is when you do **anything** to harm another individual **on purpose**. I don't consider myself to be a violent person. I'm no perfect saint, so there have definitely been times when I have hurt people. But I can honestly say that I don't do things with the intent to make another person feel pain. So it baffles me whenever I see people who purposely choose violence. Sometimes I will see it and wonder to myself, "…dang how did it even get to that point? Out of all the options, why did they choose violence?" The Bible gives us the answer. It says that anger "rests" in the bosom of a fool. That means that although we all experience anger, only a fool let's it sit there for long. As soon as you feel yourself getting tight up in the chest, you must act quickly to get that anger off of you. If you let it rest there, you will soon become violent. Sometimes it's just practical things like removing yourself from a volatile situation. Other times you may have to get spiritual and fast/pray it off of you. Feeling angry isn't the sin. You just can't let it sit with you and make you a violent fool.

READ TODAY: ECCLESIASTES 7:9

OKAY, BYE!

Okay Bye! – what you say after you make a strong statement, but don't want to stick around to discuss it further.

Example: I'm just concerned that y'all are posting up these men that you'll have to go back and delete after your tax money dries up...okay bye!

Have you ever had to sit and watch someone heading down the wrong path because you didn't know how to intervene? It's really hard when it's someone that you care about. There are people who literally knew the groom (or bride) was cheating, but kept their mouth shut and watched their friend walk down the aisle anyway. There are people who knew that their friend was overweight and unhealthy but kept their mouth shut and watched them die early of a heart attack. The problem is that people want to avoid conversations that may feel uncomfortable but don't realize that their own comfort is not more important than someone's life. Many of us pre-assume (I know it's presume) that the person will not be receptive. Maybe they will, and maybe they won't, but don't let that be your easy cop out. Don't absolve yourself from the responsibility of being a true friend to someone you love by convincing yourself that they won't listen to you. So what is the best approach? First of all, understand that yes, you are taking a risk because you can't control how a person will react. You must mentally prepare to be okay with that. Second, the Bible tells us that we must speak the truth in love. That means that it definitely matters **how** you say a thing. Pray and ask God to give you the right words to say. Lastly, know what to do if they don't receive it. Don't get offended or mad. Don't try to force them to do something. That's when you say, "Okay, bye..." and just lift them up in prayer. Move on and be satisfied with the fact that you planted a seed. It may just come up for them later. Okay, bye!

READ TODAY: MATTHEW 10:14

BOY BYE!/GIRL BYE!

Boy Bye!/Girl Bye! – a phrase used to dismiss someone who has just said or done something that was so utterly absurd.

Example: ...and then he asked me if he could use my car. Boy bye! I just met you a week ago.

Okay, so I'm really not the "cut you off" as a first resort kinda gal. I really think people should try to repair broken things before tossing them away. Now I admit that I don't keep that same energy with household items, but I think people are a little more valuable than an air fryer. HOWEVER COMMA, there are times in life where people do need to be dismissed. We've all seen the pro-athlete who had the entire world at their fingertips but threw it all away messing around with the shady entourage from back home. I do understand the high value that we place on loyalty, but sometimes we have to ask ourselves exactly what we are being loyal to and why? Just because that person helped you sneak out the house one time 15 years ago, doesn't mean you need to carry them into every season of your life when they no longer fit. You have to ask yourself if being connected to that person is hurting you or slowing your forward progress. Does being around that person help to bring out the sinful nature that you are working hard to overcome? Do you find yourself making poor decisions when you're around them? It's okay to say goodbye to people who have no desire to do better with their lives along with you. It's like standing next to an elevator on the ground floor. You have all the ability in the world to go up to the penthouse, but the people around you don't like heights. It's okay to step on the elevator alone. And when you get up there, don't let anybody who **chose** to stay at ground level make you feel guilty about it. There is a time for everything, and we have to stop believing that everyone is supposed to be a permanent fixture in our lives. Pray and ask God to reveal any acquaintances that it might be time to step away from.

READ TODAY: ECCLESIASTES 3:1

ROTFL

ROTFL - an acronym for "Rolling On The Floor Laughing."

Example: Person A: ....and then I told her that's not a gold tooth! It's a piece of corn that I'm saving for later!
Person B: ROTFL!! You are so funny!

If you don't have a sense of humor, I need you to pray and ask God to bless you with one. One thing that social media will teach you is that there are a lot of sour pusses running around here. What is wrong with y'all? If you can't laugh at jokes, there may be a diagnosis code and a treatment for that. If you're not going to laugh, hey, I can't make you. But why go around raining on everybody else's parade with your always-serious self? Social media is like 75% jokes (I made that percentage up, so please don't reference me in your term papers). If you don't like to laugh, maybe social media isn't the place for you. Saints…we have some of the funniest people in the world amongst our ranks. I love that social media gives them a place to flourish. By the same token (or wait, this seems like it should be a different token), some of the saints can be so deep and spiritual that nobody likes them. That's not even Biblical. There's a time and place for everything. The word tells us that a merry heart helps like medicine. I think this is where they came up with the idea that "laughter is the best medicine." But it also says that a broken spirit can dry you out. Some of the deep saints are drying us out. They can't smile, they can't laugh, they can't crack jokes, and it seems like they can't enjoy life. It seems like all they can do is talk about how angry God is at everybody for everything and how we are all going to hell except them. Bruh! Is this you? I'm going to pray that God will restore unto you the joy of your salvation. Everybody lay your hands on your head and say, Lord, bless me with a good laugh today. Give me something that makes me roll on the floor with laughter. Help me to remember that this is a part of my abundant life package.

READ TODAY: PROVERBS 17:22

NGL

ngl – acronym that stands for "not gonna lie."

Example: ngl, Barney actually had hits lowkey. We clowned him back in the day, but that purple dinosaur had a few bangers.

Lying is whack. I mean think about what lying really is and where it really comes from. Lying is literally the opposite of Jesus. Oh y'all think I'm exaggerating? Jesus defined Himself by saying, "I am the Way, the **Truth**, and the Life, right? QED, Ipso facto, case-in-point, if Jesus is the truth, then He is the exact opposite of a lie. Think about where lies come from. The Bible says that Satan is the father of lies. This tells us that **every lie** was conceived by him. So if Satan is the father, who is the mother? Bingo. When you lie, **you** give birth to an evil seed that the devil deposited inside of you. Hopefully lying is becoming less and less attractive by the minute. See when a person lies, they are quite literally telling God that they don't trust Him. That's right....you feel as if the outcome isn't going to work out favorably for you unless you "help" God out a bit by lying. All the while, Satan is somewhere watching you give birth to his child and glad about it. Lies, like children, have a tendency to grow and take on a life of their own. That's why they are so dangerous. After a while, a lie isn't going to lay on the bed in one spot like a newborn baby. It's going to start wiggling around on the bed until one day it falls off. Before you know it, that lie has a driver's license and a new car that it will use to cause all kinds of mayhem in your life. Meanwhile, if you had simply trusted God with your outcomes, you could have told the truth. If the truth makes you lose something or someone, trust God anyhow. He can restore you with the same person/thing that you lost...or with better. When you lie, you are trusting the devil with your outcome more than you are trusting God. I strongly advise against that, because the devil's goal is always to steal, kill, and destroy the abundant life that was made available to you through Christ.

READ TODAY: JOHN 14:6

297

I WANT ALL THE SMOKE.

I want all the smoke. – a phrase used to invite people to battle you over something that you strongly believe and will fight for.

Example: ...if you think blaming underage children for the behavior of
a grown man is okay, you are a part of the problem. If you
want to fight with me on that, come on! I want all the smoke!

There was a situation in the Bible where smoke was requested. There were three Hebrew boys named of Shadrach, Meshach, and Abednego. They worshipped God but found themselves living and working in Babylon, which was like sin city. One day, King Nebuchadnezzar made a golden statue and made it the law that everyone had to bow down and worship it. Anyone who refused would be cast into a fiery furnace to die. Well these Hebrew boys wanted all the smoke. They said, "Listen King, the bowing down thing? It ain't gon' happen. So put us in the fire if you want, but our God is able to get us out of it. If He does, cool. And even if He does not, He could if He wanted to. But we won't bow, respectfully." So the king got even more upset. They tied them up and the fire was so hot that the men got killed just trying to put them in! They walked into the fire but didn't get burned. They walked into the smoke and didn't suffocate. I guess the fire burned up the ropes that were used to bind them, because they were in there walking around loose. And they were in there chilling with guess who? They say a 4th man was in there with them looking like the Son of God. Jesus, is that you? They came out of the fire looking completely unbothered. Folks say they didn't even smell like smoke! The King was so thrown off that he didn't know what to do BUT praise God, give them a promotion, and tell everybody to put some respeck on God's name. Listen, serving the Lord pays off, okay?! Don't fear the smoke you will get for serving Him. Jesus is right there with you, and He won't let you be burned. He won't even let you smell like smoke!

READ TODAY: DANIEL 3:23-25

WEEERK!

Weeerk! – an updated way of saying "work it girl!"

Example: My girl is walking across that stage getting her doctorate in some stilletos! *hollers* Weeerk boo! Weeeerk!!

I think "weeerk" is such an appropriate term because when a person is doing something on a high level of excellence, it is because they have put in the work to be able to do so. Today I will talk directly to you. To an onlooker, it may seem that what you're doing is easy. But you and I both know that it's not. Only you and God know how much work truly goes into it. You have faced many challenges, but you have found a way to work through each one. You've had to cry sometimes. Maybe God is the only One who saw you when you were just a ball of pain, tears, and anxiety. But look at you! You pulled it together, you embraced the work, and you did what had to be done. You may not have it all together yet, but you have made progress, and I am proud of you. The Bible says that if a person doesn't work, they shouldn't eat. Look at you working **and** eating! You're even helping to feed others at this point. I love that for you. You have chosen to employ the greatest one-two punch that God has given us…faith **and** works. My prayer for you today is that you don't get discouraged. Sometimes it seems like you work so hard, but things aren't progressing as you had planned. I've been there myself. Tuh! I *am* there. But what will get you through is your ability to trust God with everything…even His timing. The harvest is coming. Just keep working and serving. Whatever is right, God said He would pay. Your assignment today is to go listen to a song called "I Will Serve Him" by Chester D.T. Baldwin. Now go forth, weeerk, and win!

READ TODAY: MATTHEW 20:4 (NIV)

PULL UP!

Pull Up! – an expression used to invite someone to travel to your current location.

Example: It's half-off on all drinks until 11! Pull up!

When someone invites you to pull up, it could be a good thing or a bad thing. It could be a casual party invitation like, "We're getting ready to throw some meat on the grill, pull up!" Or it could be an invitation to a fight like, "Oh you wanna be big and bad on FB, huh? If you got something to say to me, pull up and say it to my face. Pull Up!" The thing I love about God is that He not only invites us to pull up, but He actually offers to **pull us up** as well. A pull up in gym class was used to test the strength of your upper body and particularly your arms. Well sometimes we find ourselves in difficult situations that we don't have the strength to pull ourselves out of. Sin is that difficult situation. Our sin causes us separation from God and lands us in a horrible pit that seems to be made of quicksand. We find ourselves sinking ever so deeply in our sin and headed towards death. But God, who is kind, gracious, and full of mercy, extends His hand to us. While we may not have the arm strength to lift ourselves, God's arm is neither too weak nor too short to pull us up and out of any sinful situation that tries to take us down. He doesn't just have upper body strength, He is **The Upper Body**, period. Yes, you may have knowingly jumped headfirst into the very pit that you now find yourself in, but it doesn't matter how you got there. At this point, all that matters is that you grab hold to God's outstretched hand, and allow His love to lift you up to safety. You may feel stuck, but you really don't have to stay there. Stop flailing around trying to fight the quicksand on your own. All you're doing is making matters worse. Calm down and reach up. Cry out to God today. He will hear your cry and pull you up from that low place.

READ TODAY: PSALM 40:1-3

#ADULTING

#Adulting - the act of doing things that must be done by people aged 18 and older in order to not be considered a lazy bum.

Example: It's my off day, and I'm renewing my car tag. #Adulting

Adulting feels childish to me. No, yes, hear me out! There is **so much** to be done. All we want to do is enjoy life and be happy, but so much seems to be required to make that happen. Take the example above, for example. Say I don't renew my car tag. The next thing I know, I'm being given a ticket that I may forget to pay. Now I'm getting arrested, and my car is impounded. Now I am missing my poor child's birthday party because I'm in jail. Now I'm a bad parent, and I just got fired because I didn't show up to work or call because my phone was confiscated. Now I can't make rent, my car is still in the impound, and boom...out on the street just that easy! It's funny because it sounds like an exaggeration, but it's not funny when you realize that it's not. Refusing to "adult" in the natural realm has real consequences, and it is no different spiritually. How we approach things when we are babes in Christ, might be appropriate for one stage of our journey. But as time goes on, we should be evolving as believers. So much of life is about the way you respond when things go down. How you respond to an attack when you've just been enlisted, should not be the way you respond when you've been "on the battlefield" for a while. You might start out throwing hands, but that should evolve to laying hands. As a babe, you may be cussing people out, but that should evolve to casting demons out. If you're not experiencing spiritual growth, that is cause for major concern. You see, adulting in the Holy Spirit causes you to grow fruit...the real, tangible, and noticeable byproducts of time spent with God. That fruit is love, joy, peace, patience, kindness, generosity, faithfulness, and self-control. If you don't see these things beginning to grow in your life over time, you might not be "adulting" in your relationship with Him.

READ TODAY: 1 CORINTHIANS 13:11

CHIIILLLEEEEE

Chiiillleeeee – a modern-day way of saying "ooh child." It is a very versatile word and may be used to start off either gossip or a dramatic story. It can also be used as a response to the drama.

Example: Chiiiillllleeeee! Me and Rodney are done for good now! I'll have to tell you about it later because it's too much to tell in the middle of this AutoZone.

How do y'all think people gossiped about Mary? I imagine it went something like, "Chiiiiilllllleeeee, not Mary pregnant and trying to claim she's still a virgin! Not Joe going along with the story because he got that girl pregnant! Not them telling everybody the baby is the Son of God! Folks do anything for clout these days...smh." Okay, maybe they didn't say it just like that, but it was probably somewhere along those lines. Have you ever been the subject of inaccurate gossip? Your response makes all the difference. When I had people talking about me behind my back, making assumptions, and flat out lying, I honestly didn't know what to do. I didn't have the time nor energy to try to figure out who was told what, much less to show my receipts and set the record straight with all those people. So I did what Mary did. I decided to let Jesus speak for me. That, my friends, requires patience. It may be years down the line, but instead of running around trying to defend yourself to people who probably don't matter, stay focused on moving forward in your own purpose and destiny. It wasn't until Jesus was much older that He performed His first miracle turning water into wine at a wedding. If I was Mary, I would have stood on a table at that reception like, "Booyah!! Told y'all! #FreeJesus!" But I'm sure Mary had a little more class than that. The point is, focus on your assignment and it will only be a matter of time before God sets the record straight on your behalf.

READ TODAY: PSALM 35:24

UNPOPULAR OPINION

Unpopular Opinion - used when someone posts an idea that most people won't agree with.

Example: Unpopular Opinion: Circus Peanuts are actually pretty good.

Don't you dare judge me! Circus Peanuts are good when they are not expired and hard. I know it's an unpopular opinion because no one I know will admit to eating or liking Circus Peanuts, yet according to my research they have been around since the 19th century. Tell me how I'm the only one eating Circus Peanuts, but they have been around since the 1800s. Oh, okay...I'll wait. Somebody else eatin' em too!!! Ahem, I'm sorry for yelling. I just needed to get that off my chesss. See, when you have an unpopular opinion, people will make you feel ashamed for having it. There are even some situations where an unpopular opinion can put you in harm's way. People literally kill each other or start wars over differences of opinion. Some are even delusional enough to think that they are fighting others on behalf of God. What sense does that make when the Bible already told us that our fight is not against flesh and blood? We are dealing with spiritual wickedness, and therefore the warfare is supposed to be done in the spiritual realm. One of my Sunday School Teachers, Ms. Bessie Corley, once told me that we don't argue with people about God. Yet I see it all the time, especially on social media. Our faith can be an extremely unpopular opinion, but you can't force it on anyone. If someone asks an honest question attempting to understand your beliefs, that's one thing. But if you see that someone is there to be argumentative, leave that person alone. If they don't have an ear to hear or a heart to receive, all you will do is stir up strife by continuing to engage. You don't even have to have the last word. If you find yourself getting angry and argumentative, that is not of God nor is it for God. It may not be popular, but if it's on God's behalf, it should still be peaceable, gentle, and productive.

READ TODAY: JAMES 3:17

303

PLEASE DON'T DELETE ME

Please don't delete me! – a phrase used to ask for mercy following a corny joke that is so bad that people consider deleting you from their friends list all together.

Example: Q: What does a nosey pepper do?
A: It gets jalapeño business! Please don't delete me!

Okay, so do y'all remember that time when a pandemic hit, and the churches had to shut down? Many of us regular churchgoers didn't step foot inside of a sanctuary for a year or more. Yeah, it was wild. My mom just kept saying, "Well...I believe God is making the church sit down so we can learn something." She wasn't saying that God sent the pandemic, but that He was using it to help us in this way. Perhaps we as the church had forgotten what it's all about. Perhaps we had taken our focus off of the gospel of Jesus Christ and placed it on ourselves. Maybe we had made it about the programs, performances, and personalities. Maybe we had become Christians culturally but not spiritually. Something similar happened with the church at Ephesus. Paul delivered the message that although they started out well, they had lost sight of their "first love." They needed to repent and get back to their foundation before God was to "remove His candlestick" from that place. Basically, God was going to cut the lights out on them if they didn't get it together. Some might say He was going to have to delete that church. You see, God is serious about His representation. We can't be out here making Him look like He's the problem. It's not fair to the people who really need Him...which is everybody...if we show Him in a bad light. Church, we don't want Him having to cut our lights off. As I write this, many sanctuary lights are still off. Perhaps it is encouraging us to focus on the basics. No more lights, camera, action. No more fashion shows. No more sitting in the pews like spectators. It's time for those of us who worship Him to get back to the basics and do it in spirit and in truth.

READ TODAY: REVELATION 2:4-5

SWIPE LEFT

Swipe Left – the way you reject potential romantic match ups on a dating app called Tinder.

Example: He looked old enough to be my daddy! I had to swipe left!

Have you ever experienced rejection? For some reason, feelings of rejection seem to linger longer than the other emotions. Some folks deal with one rejection for **years**. We've all seen that guy who is always talking about how he doesn't date black women because "all black women are x,y, and z." Some of those guys are in their 40s still dealing with the pain of rejection from one girl in 7th grade. If you feel rejected, you must first understand that it is a part of life. Even Jesus had to experience it...heavily. Him being crucified on the cross was nothing more than the result of people rejecting Him and what He taught. Next, understand that God can use anything, even rejection, to bless you. Sometimes we think we know what we want but have no idea what we need. There are things that seem so desirable in the moment, but we are nearsighted. But God can see down the street and around the corner. He knows what will make us miserable and what will make us happy in the long run. The initial sting of rejection will hurt because you are human. But as a believer, if you find yourself struggling with rejection for long periods of time, perhaps you don't trust God as much as you thought you did. The best thing to do is to take your eyes off of the past events, and tell God thank you. Sometimes your healing is in your gratitude. Can you have faith enough to believe that if God wanted that for you, it couldn't be stopped? Perhaps He won't bring better into your life until you overcome that bitter spirit of rejection. Bitterness about who or what didn't work for you in the past, can blind you to the people and places that are waiting on you with open arms. Today, we say thank you to Jesus for winning the victory over His own rejection, so that we may have the power to overcome it ourselves.

READ TODAY: ROMANS 8:28

KEEP SCROLLING.

Keep scrolling. – a way to instruct people not to stop to engage with certain content on their social media timeline.

Example: If you haven't seen this week's episode of *Baby Mama Island*, keep scrolling! This post contains spoilers!

Most social media platforms have a home page that contains a collection of the most recent posts and activities from the people that you follow. On Facebook, for instance, it's called a "newsfeed." On Twitter it is a "timeline," and on Instagram it is simply called the "feed." If you were to stop and take a long, hard, look at every post, you would be completely overwhelmed. For that reason, most of these home pages are set up for you to be able to simply skim/scroll through and browse. You will stop scrolling when something interesting catches your eye, but you will keep scrolling past things that don't seem noteworthy at first glance. And that's what I want you to know for your life today. The home page of your life may not seem like much now, but keep scrolling! Far too often, we take a look at our current station in life and feel as if that's all there is to see. No ma'am/sir! I need you to keep scrolling, because God isn't done with you. You see, He has already started working on too many good things inside of you for you to give up now. He has plans to prosper you and to finish everything He started with you. Your story isn't over. There may be a lot of junk on the "timeline" of your life right now, but please don't stop there. Keep scrolling down your personal "feed' until you see the noteworthy things that God has up ahead for you. The older saints used to say, "I believe I'll run on and see what the end is gonna be!" Don't give up. I believe Evangelist Dory's word to us was to just keep swimming. Today's word is to just keep scrolling.

READ TODAY: PHILIPPIANS 1:6

STOP SCROLLING.

Stop scrolling. – a way to instruct people to stop and pay attention to certain content.

Example: This family needs help locating a missing teen! Stop scrolling and read the missing person's report!

When something makes you slow your roll and stop your scroll, it is something that catches your eye and seems worth your time in that moment. Some people scroll really fast, and unless it's something that seems worth their time at first glance, they will keep it moving. We do this in life sometimes with people who need help. We will see them, deem them not worthy of our attention or time, and keep on scrolling past them. Sure, it could be the homeless person on the street. But it could also be your own friends, family, co-workers, or church members that you are ignoring. People make subtle and not so subtle cries for help all the time. Is your life too busy to stop and help someone who needs it? Are you too busy chasing after your own blessings to be a blessing to someone else? If your plate is too full to be able to care about others, then maybe some things need to be removed. That's not even God's way. He wants us to see about others. Think about the time when you wished someone would have stopped their busy life to check on you. Think about the time you lost a close loved one, but everyone else seemed to carry on with business as usual. Sometimes we are so worried about being taken advantage of that we don't realize that, yes, God might want someone to use us to help someone else advance. This is where the Holy Spirit comes in. It's not up to you to save everybody and let everybody run you low. Everybody's problem is not your assignment. There are times when you do need to keep scrolling, but the only way you will know the difference is by the Holy Spirit. Let's pray and ask God to show us when to stop scrolling and help someone.

READ TODAY: 1 JOHN 3:17

WHO SENT YOU?

Who Sent You? – a phrase used to express skepticism of someone's motives for being present.

Example: It seems like every time I decide to take a break from men to focus on my goals, some tall, dark, and handsome man falls out of the sky. Who Sent You sir?!

There may come a time, for one reason or another, when you have to block somebody from the privilege of viewing your personal social media pages. Some of those people get the point, accept the block, and keep it moving. There are those, however, who can't accept the boundaries and find ways to get around them. One of those ways is to send someone else to do their dirty work. I've been there before. Shoot, I'm there now! It's not just online. It happens in real life too. It's hard because sometimes you don't know who is present as a friend and who is there only as a puppet for someone who lost their privileges of direct access. You begin to wonder who the snakes are, and which blocked person sent them. It's shameful. First, if someone has you blocked, just respect it and move on man. There are bigger fish to fry than to have someone snooping on your behalf. We are grown! Secondly, the devil operates the same way. He has no real power or control over us. God blocked him a long time ago. Therefore, all he can do is send people to do his dirty work for him. I hate to see when someone is allowing themselves to be used by Satan, but you have to remember that they are just the pawn, and your true battle is never against anyone who is made of flesh and blood. It's against the one who sent them. The true battle is in the spiritual realm with Satan and his demonic forces that can't get direct access to you. Thankfully, we already have the victory there too. But let this be a reminder that when you face someone who is trying to pull you into a fight, take your focus off of that person and instead rebuke the one who **sent** them.

READ TODAY: EPHESIANS 6:11-12

READ FOR FILTH

Read for filth – to insult someone in an extremely harsh manner by calling attention to bad things about them that are true.

Example: Listen, they know better than to try that with me because they know I like to read for filth.

Confession: I used to read people for filth. Yes, in some of my earlier social media days, I would do this any time someone was disrespectful towards me. "See that's why you didn't finish the 10th grade, failed your GED, and got daddy issues because yours left for cigarettes 25 years ago." I was never *that* bad y'all, my goodness...but some people are. That's because it really lives up to its name of being filthy. It's dirty, nasty, and messy. And worst of all...it's true. What we now call "reading for filth" was once known as cutting someone down to the white meat. It's not just a surface wound that they can recover from quickly. It literally goes deep enough to "strike a nerve," and it is a severe laceration that can prove difficult to heal from. It is the verbal equivalent of the Mortal Kombat "Finish Him" move. Why am I saying all of this? It didn't matter how those people came at me. It didn't matter that I knew I could take a few words and shut down the argument for good. What mattered is that it was filthy, and as a follower of Christ I was supposed to have clean hands and a clean heart. Sure, I showed them that they bit off more than they could chew by coming at me sideways. But they were hurt by me, and that wasn't okay. The Bible tells us that if we can't control our own tongues (in this case fingertips), then our religion is in vain. So I shut that down. I don't take it there anymore even though I can. How would you feel if someone took your deepest insecurities and used them as material in an argument? If you are in the business of reading for filth, understand that it's a maturity issue and it doesn't represent God well at all. Are we clear? Are we clean? Are we clean and clear? God bless ya, amen!

READ TODAY: PSALM 51:10

GATHER

Gather – the act of shutting down an individual who has attempted to approach you in a negative way. A person may be gathered either verbally or physically.

Example: My daughter copped an attitude with me, and I had to gather her ungrateful behind. I took back MY cell phone and the keys to MY car that I pay for.

If you think about what it means to gather things or people, you will realize that it is an extremely powerful action to take. When people get "out of line" with us, we have to gather them back together and remind them where they stand. The teen in the example above had clearly lost her mind. She was scatter-brained, if you will. She thought she could get away with being disrespectful to the mother who was providing her with the luxuries that she so freely enjoyed. Try again, boo boo. Her mama had to take that brain of hers and unscatter it for her. When people get out of line, sometimes you have to get them lined back up. Whenever you gather something that was all over the place, you have just made it much more powerful/effective. That's exactly why Jesus told us that when two or three believers gather in His name, that He would be right there in the midst of them. Nothing is more powerful than Jesus being in the midst. If you can find enough people who will come together in agreement and unity, it becomes much easier to accomplish things even in the natural realm. Now think how much more powerful it is when people can gather together **with Jesus** in the spiritual realm. You never know when you will need a mountain moved, so my advice to you is to keep a few like-minded people around who know how to gather with you and pray. If you can't put your finger on who those people are, don't panic. That is your new prayer! Ask God to send some people into your life who won't mind being gathered when the need arises.

READ TODAY: MATTHEW 18:19-20

…RUNS ME LOW

…runs me low – a way of saying that something takes away your energy.

Example: Going to the DMV really runs me low every time.

We all have them…people, places, and things that wear us out and run us low. There are certain people who you hate to see coming, because you know that every encounter takes your energy from a 10 to a 2. We live in human bodies and have human minds, so there is only so much energy that we are allowed before exhaustion starts to set in. We can easily become exhausted physically, mentally, emotionally, and sometimes even spiritually. We require rest and recuperation to re-energize. Without the proper rest, we start shutting down. No matter how much you want to keep going, your body says "nope." If you are mentally exhausted, even your own brain starts having trouble thinking clearly. You can't make heads or tails of simple things, and everything seems cloudy. Our need for rest is one of the major things that differentiate us from God. We can't keep going and going non-stop, but He can. That's a huge part of what makes Him God. Nothing can run Him low. Nothing can steal His energy, and nothing can make Him shut down. God is mighty. Mighty even sounds like an understatement, but He is literally the definition of the word because His energy doesn't vary. Think about how the individuals who exert the most strength can't sustain it for very long. Take track stars, for example. Sprinters exert the most strength and power but can only do so over short distances. Long-distance runners don't travel as fast because they must preserve their energy to finish. Think of God as a track star who can run an endless marathon but with the speed of a 100-yard dash. He's got the strength and the endurance to be there for you whenever you call. He won't be resting, He won't be asleep, and you won't run Him low. Let's take a moment to thank God for His strength and consistency.

READ TODAY: ISAIAH 40:28

DOWN THROUGH THERE

Down through there – a bad place that people get taken to emotionally by other people or situations.

Example: That break up really took him down through there. He's in therapy for it now.

If you hear that someone went "down through there," just know that they went somewhere very unpleasant that no one would ever desire to go. Toxic relationships have taken people down through there. Grief has taken a whole lot of folks down **and** through there. I've even seen grad school load folks up on a train for a long ride down through there on the scenic route! "There" is a very scary, lonely, and dangerous place. There is filled with darkness, heartbreak, fear and torment. You feel all alone even if people are in your face. Sadly, some people never make it out of "there." Some struggle so much that they don't even want to live anymore. You may lose or gain a bunch of weight. You don't care about much, and you don't take care of yourself very well. Some overeat while others turn to substance abuse or other detrimental habits. You struggle to recognize yourself in the mirror. Even the most loving friends and family members don't know how to get you to snap back. Here's what I want you to know if you are "there" right now. God is with you. That's it. That's the devotion. God is still with you. Understand that you aren't going down "to" there. You are going down "through" there. That means you aren't going down there to stay. I'm not psychic, so I can't tell you why you had to go where you went. All I can tell you is that God is with you, it's only temporary, and He can use it for your good in the end. Yes, God can use that place/time in His strategy to **bless** you. Do your best to get through it as well as you can and as quickly as you can. Don't linger any longer than you must, and don't give up while you're down there. My prayer is that you will come out on the other side better than when you went in!

READ TODAY: PSALM 23:4

YOU ON ONE TODAY!

You on one today – what you say on a day when someone's behavior seems to be a bit more erratic than its norm.

Example: You just quit your job, broke up with Rodney, booked a flight to Dubai, and drank Pepsi instead of Coke…and it's just 9am! You on one today!

Some would say being "on one" means that you have stopped caring about things that you normally care about. You may fly off the handle to tell someone off when you are usually a patient person. You may make an impulse purchase when you are usually conservative with your money. Being on one may even cause you to end long-term relationships or hey…cuss out your mama about that thing she did in 1998. I think the thing that you are "on" is called a tangent. You are varying from your normal script, but why? The answer is simple… emotions. Emotions can cause you to do or say things that you would not normally say or do. So when you're "on one," maybe the thing that you are on is an emotional rollercoaster. We all have emotions, so there is nothing wrong with that. But when you let your emotions get in the driver's seat, it won't be long before they get the best of you. (Ladies, pay attention to that menstrual cycle too, because hormonal fluctuations can definitely have a huge effect on your emotions.) Have you ever done anything under the influence of your emotions that you wish you could take back? It's all a part of Satan's strategy to defeat us, but we are aware of it, so we can win. Run everything through the filter of prayer, and don't be so anxious to move quickly. If you feel your emotions taking a turn, just stop whatever you're thinking about doing, talk to God, and give the emotions some time to pass. That's why it's important to be praying on a regular, daily basis anyway. Sometimes you will start the boarding process to get on one and your prayer time will make you step right back off that plane, before it departs.

READ TODAY: PHILIPIANS 4:6-7

IN A WORLD FULL OF…

In a world full of… – a way to compare yourself to others in a superlative way.

Example: In a world full of soggy hotdog buns, I am brioche warmed to perfection.

Do you have trouble fitting in? It's difficult at first, but eventually you get the hang of being a weirdo. Do you know what has made me more of a weirdo than my awkward sense of humor and my refusal to do things that didn't make sense to me? It was my faith. All along, it was my faith that made me stick out like a sore thumb. Maybe you are a spiritual person who has experienced the same thing. Do you ever listen to people telling you their life drama? Sometimes it's wild to hear people trying to make sense of a situation that is **clearly** a spiritual matter. This is not the time to look down or judge that person for not being spiritual. This is your time to make God shine. You see, when they talked to all of their other friends and family members, they left just as confused as when they came…if not more so. But in a world full of carnal-minded people, you have the advantage of operating in both the natural and spiritual realms. Your job is to take what your friend is dealing with in the natural realm and translate it back to them in a spiritual way that they can understand. If you can do this, you can rest easy knowing that your difference has made a difference. This is what happened with Joseph in the Bible. He was different everywhere He went. In a world of single-color coats, he was rocking the coat of many colors. When Joseph got locked up, it was his differences that eventually set him free. And what ended up happening? The people who didn't know God came to Joseph for help interpreting their dreams. See how that works? Stay different. The world may have made fun of your differences in the past, but the truth is, your differences could be their breakthrough…and yours too!

READ TODAY: ROMANS 12:1-2

3 HOURS LATER…

3 Hours Later… – a reference to the timecards used in the TV show *SpongeBob SquarePants*. These were used for scene transitions in which time had elapsed. They are now used heavily on social media.

Example: *3 hours Later* I finally got thorough the drive-thru line!

The songwriter, Jennie Wilson, gives Biggie a run for his money when it comes to having the best opening line of a song. She starts with "Time is filled with swift transitions…" to begin the hymn "Hold To God's Unchanging Hand." Jen was right. Time really is filled with swift transitions. But the thing we rarely talk about is the slow transition. What happens when change is slow to come? I'll just tell you like I told **myself**…the slow cooked meats taste the best. You see, some of us want God to hurry up and give us every desire of our heart, but we resent the fact that He is taking us on a route that takes more time. We just want Him to pop us in the microwave and be done. I know it's frustrating, but let's be clear. What you **don't** want is for God to take short cuts with you. You don't want to miss out on the important lessons that will sustain you when your elevation comes. So you're worried because you don't have that career, job, or spouse that you wanted yet? Look, I know people with high-paying jobs, spouses, and nice homes, who are miserable and realizing that they rushed into something that God didn't say. Bruh! How depressing must it be to get all the stuff you wanted, but with no joy or peace to go along with it? Hear me out: be patient. Wait for the meat to be tender, juicy, and falling from the bone. It doesn't matter if it is 3 hours, 3 days, or 3 years later…your true victory is worth the wait. Oh, and don't just wait any kind of way either. As hard as it may seem, wait **patiently** and with gratitude that you have ox tails slow-cooking and not SPAM straight out the can. No shade to SPAM if you like SPAM…okay, but watch your cholesterol though!

READ TODAY: HABAKKUK 2:3

#PROTIP

#ProTip – advice from people who either are or consider themselves to be professionals in a particular field.

Example: #ProTip If you never define the relationship to start off with, she can't get mad that she's not your only one!

I know y'all probably think writing is my thing, but I'm not some fancy writer. The truth is, I'm just an obedient optometrist lady from Birmingham, AL. God just uses me because He knows I be sayin' yes. I spend the majority of my days giving out #ProTips about eye care. So I'm no spiritual professional, but I do have a tip for you: if you stay ready, you don't have to get ready. That's it! That's the tip. Ha! I told y'all I wasn't a pro! You've probably heard that tip a million times before. It's that thing where they tell you to have your "elevator pitch" always prepared in case you get 30 seconds with a billionaire. It's that thing where you constantly keep updating your resume, even when you aren't looking for a job. When the dream job pops up out of nowhere, your resume is already locked, loaded and rettt ta go. If you stay ready, you won't have to get ready! Did you know that this is in the Bible too? No? If you look at Ephesians Chapter 6, starting around verse 10, you will see what I'm talking about. The passage repeatedly tells us to go ahead and put on the whole armor of God and be ready so that we don't have to get ready when the devil starts trying to wild out. See, when the enemy tries to come at you with his foolishness, that is not the time to be figuring out what to do. When your family is under attack, that's not the time to be trying to figure out how to get a prayer through. When it's a life and death situation and you need to speak a word over it, that's not the time to have no clue what God's promises are. Your assignment is to study over the spiritual armor that is mentioned in Ephesians 6 and ask God to show you practical ways to put it on and keep it on.

READ TODAY: EPHESIANS 6:10-18

BRAND AMBASSADOR

Brand Ambassador – a person who is paid to represent a company in a way that will gain attention, attract new people, and potentially increase sales.

Example: Zendaya is now a brand Ambassador for BVLGARI!

When a person on social media acquires a sizeable number of followers, they are often approached with an opportunity to become a "brand ambassador" for companies hoping to expand their audience. So what does that have to do with you? As a follower of Christ, you are a brand ambassador. If your personal relationship with Christ has been a blessing to you, shouldn't you want others to experience His love as well? They aren't customers in the literal sense, but we do want people to buy into the fact that Jesus is real and God loves us. So how can we be the most effective? We can use our own lives as the "product" that we are hoping to promote. For the longest time, people have believed that this meant pretending to be perfect. If we just make it seem like we are so "blessed" and never have problems, then people will want to buy in to what we are selling. We try to make people think that we never mess up, never get frustrated, and have all the answers. That should make us the perfect ambassadors for the Jesus brand, right? Well that backfires when it comes to Jesus. With all the fake stuff going on in the world, people just want something real at this point. Jesus is the realest of the real, so He doesn't need you faking the funk on His behalf. It's okay to admit that you aren't perfect and that you don't always get things right. It's even okay to admit that you have to cry sometimes. But make sure to let them know that God's grace is sufficient to cover all of that and more. Being a follower of Christ doesn't give you a perfect life. It simply gives you a perfect **way** to manage an imperfect life. Give them truth and let them see you walking it out by faith! The gospel is powerful enough without you having to put on an act.

READ TODAY: EPHESIANS 6:19-20

INTERNET STALKING

Internet Stalking – when a person spends a significant amount of time looking through someone's Facebook page as a means to acquire information about them.

Example: I always do a gentle internet stalking before agreeing to go on a first date with someone.

Some of y'all have internet stalkers and don't even know it. An internet stalker takes full advantage of the info that is posted about you online. You may think that you're introducing yourself to someone for the first time, and they already know your name, age, where you live, what you do for a living, who your ex is, and your arrest record if there be any. Unlike real life stalking, internet stalking isn't illegal because almost all of the info they find is made available...by you. Many people have been taken advantage of this way. It's no coincidence that a con artist comes into your life and just so happens to cheer for the same team and work out at the same gym as you. Satan uses the same tactics. He is neither all-knowing, nor all-powerful. A lot of the info that he uses to attack you, was made available...by you. Are you saying things like... "ugh, I'm so tired of being single," and scrolling Tinder all night? Don't be surprised if Satan takes the info, sees the desperation, and uses it to deceive you with someone who seems to be the perfect match. Sometimes things will look good on the surface, but you still have to watch, pray, and listen to the Holy Spirit to determine whether the things/people entering your life are sent by God. There is a lot of information about you floating around out here, and sneaky people will use it to get close to you. You don't have to be scared though, because there is a prayer that God answers quickly for His children. When you ask God to show you the truth about someone or their intentions, just be ready. Those prayers (in my experience) typically have a 24 to72-hour turnaround. The key is not to ignore the answer if it's not what you wanted to hear.

READ TODAY: 2 TIMOTHY 3:13

MUTUAL FRIENDS

Mutual Friends – a listing of how many social media acquaintances you have in common with another user.

Example: I don't know this lady, but I just accepted her friend request because we have 128 mutual friends.

There is no fancy publishing company helping me to get the word out about this devotional. When I was promoting my last book, one of my friends asked me who I have doing my marketing for me. Pffft!! Who I haaaave??? Chile I have myself and whichever friends and family members think enough of it to share with others. That's how most of you got here, and so I thank God for whichever mutual friend of ours has you reading this book. You and I have another mutual friend as well, and I think you already know that His name is Jesus. Now some of you prefer to be loners, and I get it. I'm an introvert myself, so I know how peaceful and calming it can be to enjoy loads of alone time. But even if you consider yourself to be an introvert or a loner, you still need to be connected to certain people. These are people with whom you share Jesus as a mutual friend. The Bible has several verses that emphasize the importance of fellowship with other believers. It says things like, "Two are better than one..." and "Iron sharpens iron..." It also says, "where two or three are gathered together..." and "forsake not the assembling of yourselves together." Life hits hard at times. Having one or two friends who also know Jesus will come in handy. They will be able to speak life into you when you are ready to give up. They will be able to pray for you when you can't pray for yourself. They will be able to remind you of God's promises when you forget them. If you do not have friends who share that mutual faith bond with you, or if you feel that you do not have enough, pray today for God to send them. Sometimes we don't have things simply because we never asked for them!

READ TODAY: ROMANS 1:12

LOWKEY

Lowkey – subtle or discreet in nature. Slang for the official hyphenated word "low-key."

Example: I bring my flask with me to work. I do well at work, but I
lowkey have a drinking problem.

Think about how many basketball games are so close in the final seconds. Some players love to practice fancy layups and dunks, but the difference between winning and losing often boils down to those missed free throws. The less glamorous stuff always proves to be more crucial in the end. Jesus was more lowkey than people realize. I already know what you're thinking, and yes. He did do some big stuff to grab the people's attention. He did heal people, raise people from the dead, walk on water, and feed thousands of people with a couple fish sammiches. But that's because He knows how we are. We weren't going to follow/believe His power without the demos. But once He got the people's attention, what did He do with it? He used it to teach them lessons about very lowkey things like…their heart. He was always trying to get people to check their motives, their hearts, and their character to make sure that it lined up with love. That's because you can't slide your way into heaven. You can't even work your way in. You can pastor a church of 10,000 members and if your heart isn't right with God, you can forget it at the gate. I suppose getting to know him one-on-One is a little too lowkey for some people because no one actually sees you doing it. Nobody gives you a standing ovation for having a consistent prayer life. No one hands you a trophy for that fast you went on. There are no accolades from your peers for committing to learning the word better. I tell you what, though? God sees the lowkey stuff and is more impressed with that than the person who did all these fancy mission trips just for clout. I just want to encourage you today that God sees what you do in secret but has no problems rewarding you openly.

READ TODAY: MATTHEW 6:1-6

AUTOCORRECT

Autocorrect – the function that people blame whenever they misspell something.

Example: Person A: If you want to be my women, I need to no what
your bringing to the table.
Person A: Sorry! Stupid autocorrect!

When you start typing something on your phone or computer, autocorrect is the function that recognizes when you type a word incorrectly and then automatically changes it for you. It's not a perfect function, however, and will substitute the incorrect word at times. All it can really do is guess which word you meant and try its best. It annoys me sometimes because I'm from the south. Sometimes I want to say "guh!" and it gets changed to "huh!" There will be times when God needs to issue you a correction. The difference is that His corrections are always perfect, but they are not automatic. God allows us freedom to make our own decisions, which means that we can choose whether to accept the corrections or not. He's not going to force anything down your throat, but He will get His point across. He may do it by guiding you to the appropriate scripture of correction. He may do it by speaking to you through a trusted friend or mentor. It may not feel pleasant to receive correction from God, but we know that it is a perfect function. He's not throwing darts at targets in the dark like the autocorrect on my phone. He knows exactly what changes we need. He corrects us now to save us from pain and embarrassment later. Think about a child who gets braces. They may seem painful or embarrassing at the time, but what if that kid grows up and wants to be a news anchor? They will have the teeth for it because correction was given in time. In summary, God corrects you because He knows what you will need down the line. But remember, it's not automatic. There may be some discomfort involved, but let God straighten you up so that you can fly right!

READ TODAY: 2 TIMOTHY 3:16-17

KEEP IT 100

Keep it 100 – a phrase used when an uncomfortable truth needs to be told.

Example: I'm just going to keep it 100. I don't like any of y'all. I'm just here to do my job and get paid. I don't care what your cat did this morning, so please stay away from my desk.

To "keep it 100" literally means to tell 100% of the truth. You may also see it written as "keep it a hundo", "keep it a buck", or "keep it a hunnid." The fact that people have to announce that they're going to be 100% honest, just goes to show you how many people aren't. Have you ever been lied to or deceived by someone? It results in a particularly difficult feeling that you have been violated or made a fool of, especially if it was someone you trusted. I remember when my dad first explained what a "con man" was to me. I had always heard that term but had no idea that con was short for confidence. My mind was blown because it made so much sense. A con man takes advantage of people by first gaining their confidence. This can be done by telling half-truths. When someone mixes lies in with a bit of truth, it is much more believable than someone who tells a 100% lie. Even when the lie is exposed, the fact that truth was mixed in can cause confusion to the victim who will then begin to question if the lie itself was just a mistake. It's really quite evil when people do this. But of course they get it from Satan, the Father of Lies. Remember how he did it to Eve when he lied about the fruit? The serpent wrapped the lie in something that had some truth to it, and she fell for it. God, on the other hand, will always keep it a hundo with you because that's literally who He is. He **is** the truth, so you can always trust what He says. Don't let someone's 50% truth make you question God's 100%. God doesn't lie. He doesn't even make "innocent mistakes." If you are going to have confidence in anyone, let it be Him.

READ TODAY: NUMBERS 23:19

CHEF'S KISS

Chef's Kiss – an expression used to indicate that something was done perfectly or with a high level of excellence.

Example: When the sweet potatoes touch the mac and cheese on my plate? Whew! *chef's kiss*

You know what a chef's kiss is, right? It's when a chef gathers his fingers together at his lips and then releases them into the air as a kiss is blown. This is done when a chef tastes the food and indicates that what they have prepared is delicious and exactly what they were intending for it to be. This has been adapted for social media use to mean much more than just food. People will give a chef's kiss to just about anything that is done very well. So now, let's think about you. God, your creator, is like the chef who prepared you. He knew every ingredient that you would need. He put everything you needed inside of you, and in the perfect proportions. So since you already have been given everything that you need to be excellent, there is no excuse not to be! Far too often, we compare our ingredients to someone else's ingredients while not realizing that we were meant to be a different dish all together. Let this be a reminder that one day you will have to answer for how you spent your time here on earth. Did you take all of your ingredients and walk in your purpose? Were you too busy blaming the chef and thinking that you weren't prepared correctly? It's time for us to be about our Father's business. Whenever I get up there to see the Lord, I really just want to hear Him say, "Well done, My good and faithful servant...*chef's kiss*." All I want is for God to blow me a chef's kiss! Oh, and a hug...I would like a hug if He's doing hugs. Y'all think God gone be doing hugs or nah? Jesus maybe? Actually, a group hug would be dope! My mind is elsewhere now. I really hope you got something out of today's devotion already, because I've moved on to hugs. Have a great day!

READ TODAY: MATTHEW 25:21

THIS!!!

This!!! – what people say when someone has made a really good point about something that others may have missed.

Example: Person A: Why would you invite me on a date, yet expect me to pay?
Person B: This!!!

Today I'm going to tell you a story about how a "this" became a "that." The whole nation of Israel was enslaved in Egypt. A guy named Moses was tending to his father-in-law's flock on the backside of the desert. God appeared to him in the form of a burning bush and started talking to him. He told Moses his assignment and how he was to help the children of Israel get out of Egypt and into a promised land flowing with milk and honey. Moses was a bit concerned, however, that nobody in Egypt would believe that he had been sent by God. So God was like, "Okay fine, what do you have in your hand?" Moses had a rod in his hand that he normally used to tend to the flock. God was like "Ok, you can use that," and proceeded to show Moses how to do a crazy trick with it. He had Moses throw the rod on the ground, and it turned into a snake. Moses ran off like I would have. But God told him to pick it back up, and when he did, it went back to being a regular rod. Further along in the story of Moses, you will see several occasions where he used that same rod to make big stuff happen. So what is the lesson here? Sometimes we feel like we aren't equipped to handle the assignments that are set before us. None of that even matters with God. He can use whatever you already have in your possession like He did with Moses. "Even this?!" you might ask. Yes, God can take your "this" and turn it into a "that." If He has given you something to do, He isn't worried in the least bit about whether or not you are capable. He will either use what you already have or provide you with something new. Now it's just up to you to take your "this" and be obedient with it!

IMMA GO AHEAD AND STOP YOU RIGHT THERE.

Imma go ahead and stop you right there. – a phrase used to interrupt people who are saying (or getting ready to say) foolish things.

Example: Person A: And I don't like the Obamas either because...
Person B: Imma go ahead and stop you right there, because keep their names out ya mouth, okay?

Usually when someone stops you from completing a thought in this manner, it is because they feel that it is either ridiculous or unnecessary, and that continuing it will not end well for you. They feel that you are better off just ending the conversation all together. As much as a person's pride gets hurt, this type of interruption may prove to be helpful more than hurtful. Such was the case with a man named Saul. He spent his days trolling people who claimed to be Christians. He even threw a lot of them in jail. I'm not saying that he murked anybody, but I'm not *not* saying that he murked anybody either. Anyway, your boy was carrying on like this until Jesus was finally like, "Saul, Saul...Imma go ahead and stop you right there." He spoke to Saul on the Damascus Road and interrupted all of his lil' plans. God literally stopped him dead in his tracks by knocking him off of his lil' horse and shining a really bright light that blinded his lil' eyes for three days. After Saul experienced God's interruption, He went on to become the most impactful minister of the gospel even to this day. His name was changed to Paul, and he went on to write almost 2/3 of the New Testament! So yeah...God's interruption is only meant to bless you. Do not let pride or disobedience cause you to keep going when or if God says **stop**. Sometimes His stop sign is literally just there to save your life.

READ TODAY: ACTS 9:1-4

THINK PIECE

Think Piece – an article, blog, or long social media post that seeks to explore a concept in death.

Example: Did you ever read that think piece on why Whitley Gilbert shouldn't have married Dwayne Wayne that day?

Think pieces have remained in abundance online ever since a company named WordPress made it easy for anyone to have their own website/blog. I think it's safe to say, however, that think pieces are nothing new. Back in the day there used to be these things called newspapers. You may have heard of them. They contained articles known as "editorials," which were basically think pieces that had been typed out on paper. A think piece allows the author to explore any topic in depth. Most think pieces are interlaced with the author's opinion, although some are completely objective. The goal is to get people to think more deeply about things that they may have overlooked. Many of Paul's writings in the New Testament are think pieces lowkey. Well let's explore another idea more deeply here. Do you know how to think for yourself? Do you need the thoughts and opinions of others to help you formulate your own? The Bible tells us that we must adopt the same mindset that Christ had. So if you're going to subscribe to any think pieces, they should be the ones that came from Jesus. The Bible documents several. See when you subscribe to any old think piece, you may find yourself confused and conflicted by the end of it. But when you subscribe to a think piece from Jesus, you will find yourself **thinking peace** by the end of it. That's right, He will keep you in perfect peace if you keep your **mind** on him. That's because anything Jesus says is actually not a think piece but a **know** piece! Jesus wasn't giving us opinions and theories. He was giving us nothing but the facts! His words of truth are what allow us to know peace.

READ TODAY: ISAIAH 26:3

ADJACENT

Adjacent – to be next to something but not included in it.

Example: Person A: What part of Atlanta did you say you were from?
Person B: Roswell
Person A: Stop claiming ATL. Anything outside the
perimeter ain't really Atlanta. That's Atlanta-adjacent.

When someone (or something) is said to be "adjacent," it means that although they are in close proximity to something, they are not truly a part of it. One of the biggest examples is real estate. It's so hard to find nice and affordable places to live within the city of Los Angeles, that many people are having to settle for property that is LA-adjacent. Take my mom and dad for instance. Neither of them attended an HBCU for college, but they had four kids who did. They became more acquainted with HBCU life through their children and were therefore HBCU-adjacent. It's ok to be adjacent to some things, just not to this faith. It doesn't matter if you go to church every Sunday or if your grandaddy is the pastor. Your proximity to the faith is no replacement for actual faith. Are you Jesus-adjacent? There are no points received even for singing in the choir if you don't truly believe what you are singing for yourself. You can literally sing songs about worship, and never actually do it. You are worship-adjacent. Jesus broke it down like this. He said that He (Jesus) is in His Father (God) and that we (you and I) are in Him (Jesus) and that He (Jesus) is in us (you and I). Does that sound confusing? Well just know that we ain't adjacent. True believers should be wrapped up, tied up, tangled up, twisted up, and intertwined with the Lord in a way that is everything but "adjacent." Being adjacent doesn't even get you into heaven, so if that has been you, I pray that you will be able to submerge yourself fully into a personal one-on-One relationship with God.

READ TODAY: JOHN 14:20

TRUE STORY

True Story – a phrase used to indicate that what you are saying really did happen in the way that you are describing it.

Example: I love Girl Scout cookies! Jalen Rose threw a box of Samoas at me once, and it hit me in the forehead…true story.

Jalen Rose really did hit me in the forehead with a box of Girl Scout cookies. I was in L.A. for a big optometry convention when my homegirl and I visited Hollywood for a live taping of a game show hosted by Anthony Anderson. Jalen was a guest, and they gave the audience Girl Scout cookies at the end by tossing them into the crowd. Jalen threw one, and it hit my forehead and then landed in my hands… true story. So then let's talk about what happened with Jesus. Before He was crucified on Calvary's cross, He made it pretty clear that He would rise from the dead within three days. It was a true story, but the Romans didn't believe it. They thought that someone would try to steal Jesus's body and just claim that He had risen. So they put a huge stone and guards at the tomb. Imagine their surprise when an earthquake hit to knock the guards down, and an angel rolled the stone away so that Jesus could walk out as scheduled. I'm sure they were even more surprised to see Him walking around town like nothing happened. He was out there showing Himself to people, and letting folks see his wounds! It's all a true story, but many people still don't believe it. They will tell you that His body was stolen or that Jesus didn't exist at all. If you think about all of this from a natural perspective, it can be hard to believe. But if you think about it from a spiritual perspective, knowing that there is so much more going on in this world than what can be seen with our natural eyes, then it makes perfect sense. If you are struggling to believe in any aspect of your faith, pray and ask God to help you with your unbelief. He won't be offended by that, because He knows how to show you better than anyone that what He says is true.

READ TODAY: JOHN 17:17

REAL TALK

Real talk – when somebody speaks candidly in a way that is down to earth, honest, and transparent.

Example: Real talk though, you need to treat your mama right. I didn't get along with mine when she was living, and I regret it.

Here is some real talk for you: marriage is hard. Whoops! Was I not supposed say that? The problem with marriage in the age of social media is that it has largely become glamorized to give people a false perception of ease. Between viral proposal videos, edgy yet enchanting engagement photo shoots, bachelor/bachelorette weekends in Las Vegas or Miami, elegant bridal showers, and six-figure wedding days, it's very easy for the actual marriage to get lost in the shuffle. Nothing is wrong with any of that, but for some people it's just a grab for attention or to make an ex jealous. You would be surprised the lengths that people with broken hearts will go to just to show someone that "I'm better off without you." And to add insult to injury, there are married couples who can't let go of all the attention they were getting now that the wedding is over. Now they have to beef up their social media attention by becoming "influencers." Pictures, videos, and gushy posts make us think that they have the perfect marriage and the perfect spouse when in reality, their home is like walking through a mine field every day. Real talk though? Marriage is hard work, and you need to know that. The devil is afraid of strong marriages and strong families. So not only do you have the practical difficulties of joining lives together, but you also have to fight against Satan's own attempts to divide and conquer. So before you get married, the **least** you must do is make sure that the person you want to marry is the same person God wants you to marry. Don't be afraid to ask Him and find out the truth. Fast, pray, listen, and then obey. This is my real talk, because I have been through a divorce. So I'm not just telling you what I heard...I'm telling you what I know! Make sure it's **God!**

READ TODAY: 2 CORINTHIANS 8:21

CAPTION THIS!

Caption This! – a phrase used when people post a photo, but instead of typing their own description, they ask their social media friends to make something up to describe it.

Example: Person A: *Posts photo of a grizzly bear going through their trash can* Caption This!
Person B: "Bear: Don't judge me! You don't know my story!"

I admire my social media friends who always have clever captions, because I struggle in that area. I got engaged not long ago and, in my head, I was going to make this long beautifully thoughtful caption about our miraculous journey and about how strong our love had grown to be. But by the end of it, all I really said was "I have a fiancé." So I definitely understand when people prefer to ask others to come up with the caption instead. That may be cute on social media, but I need us not to do that in real life. We should never give anyone else the green light to put their description on our picture. In other words, don't let anybody else define you. For some reason, labels make people feel comfortable. They will be quick to label you and put you in whatever box that they see fit. Don't give them that power. God defined you before you were even in your mother's womb. If you're going to give anybody the green light to caption your picture, let it be God. I'll take it a step further and say that perhaps you don't even know what your own caption should be. God has a purpose and a plan for your life, even if you can't see it for yourself just yet. I know people who decided in the 7th grade that they wanted to be doctors, went all the way through college, got accepted into med school, took out student loans, got halfway through, and realized that medicine wasn't for them. If you don't know what plans God has for your life, don't just make up your own or let others define you. Pray and seek God for wisdom, guidance, and direction.

READ TODAY: JEREMIAH 29:11-13

FIND SOMETHING SAFE TO DO.

Find something safe to do. – what people say to let you know that you are barking up the wrong tree.

Example: To the little girl bullying my daughter at school, I suggest you find something safe to do, because I fight kids too.

Do you find yourself worrying all the time? Some of us worry or get anxious about things that we can't control. But some people are so true to the game that they will even sit and worry about things that they *can* control. You see, fear, anxiety, and worry are some of Satan's sneakiest tricks because people don't realize how dangerous they really are. Let me break it down for you. Worry leads to stress. Whenever a person is stressed, adrenaline and a hormone called cortisol get released into the body. Adrenaline increases your heart rate and blood pressure. Cortisol causes the function of your immune and digestive systems to diminish temporarily. So imagine what happens when your body experiences stress on a regular basis. Chronically high blood pressure and increased heart rate can lead to a heart attack or stroke. Immune and digestive systems that do not function properly can lead to all kinds of illnesses, including cancer. In other words, it's dangerous enough to take you out of here. When we are anxious and worried, the root cause is lack of trust in God. We do not believe that He can work **every** sequence of events out in our favor. As bad as something may seem, God can and will use even that for your good. We just have to be patient and walk it out by faith. So the next time you feel yourself going into worry mode, find something safe to do. That is a good time to start praying or start speaking God's word over the situation. You might even have to call a trusted friend to ask for prayer. I was taught a long time ago that if you don't know anything else to do, just call on the name of Jesus out loud. The old saints used to say, "The more I call Him, the better I feel." There is power in that name.

READ TODAY: PHILIPPIANS 4:6-7

CATFISH

Catfish – a person who uses social media to pretend to be someone they are not, usually to pursue deceptive online romances.

Example: How do I explain to my mom that the guy she has fallen in love with on FB is really just a catfish?

There used to be a show called *Catfish* where people who were suspicious of their online romances could go to find help. Apparently it's easy to fall in love with someone just by messaging them, talking on the phone, and exchanging pictures. The problem, however, is that the person on the other end is not who they claim to be. Some catfish are looking for love but feel they can't get it being themselves. It's so disheartening to see people who have opened up their hearts to another person discovering that they were being deceived all along. On the show, the host goes into investigative mode to determine if the person is being catfished, and also tries to locate them for a face-to-face confrontation. At the end of the episodes, you'd be surprised to know that some of the "couples" remain friends or choose to continue the romantic relationship anyway. Some of you are like this. Whoops! You thought you'd be the victim in the story, didn't you? Nope. Some of you are catfishing your way through life because you feel insecure about how God made you. You are showing people a façade. You are hiding behind a mask of what you *think* people would accept, but we both know it's not really you. You're down to earth, so why are you at brunch all the time trying to make bougie people like you? You don't even like accounting, so why are you miserable every day just so you can answer the question, "so...what do you do?" without feeling embarrassed. Don't catfish your way through life, because tomorrow is not promised. God really does want you to live your best life, but that means it has to be **your** life and not someone else's. I'll let you in on a little secret: you're not really fooling anybody...they know.

READ TODAY: PSALM 139:13-17

I'M HERE FOR IT.

I'm here for it. – a phrase used to express that you are in favor of something.

Example: Person A: I think I'm actually starting to like Marcus from marketing. He asked me on a date this weekend.
Person B: Marcus is awesome! I'm here for it!

Have you ever had people in your life that hung around you as long as it was a benefit to them? When they were hungry and knew you were cooking, they had time to come get a plate. When they knew you would be paying the tab, they had no problems going out with you and being best of friends. But would that person keep the same energy if you didn't have so much to offer? If your refrigerator was as empty as theirs, would you still see them? If you weren't paying, would you have to eat alone? Honestly, if you fell on hard times, some of these so-called friends would go ghost quicker than you can say James St. Patrick. I think it's time we all realize that some people are only going to be in our lives for certain seasons. I know you're human, but the attachment you have to people who don't give two farts about you is unhealthy. My message to you is that while friends may come in and out of your life like black kids go in and out of their grandmother's front door, we do have another friend who sticks closer than any brother. And no matter what stage of life you find yourself in, He is here for it. He's here for it right now, and He will be there for it later on. When sin is involved, He may not be in favor of it, but He's not going to leave nor forsake you over it. Rich, poor, right, wrong, up, down...it doesn't matter. God is the only fully consistent being in your life. Nothing has enough power to separate you from God, so if you want to feel tightly attached to someone, I suggest you look at Him. That way, when others come and go, even though you may experience a little disappointment, you can keep it moving on to the next! Today, let's thank and praise God for being here, there, and everywhere for us!

READ TODAY: ROMANS 8:38-39

CHANGE YOUR PASSWORD.

Change Your Password. – what people tell you to do when your account has been hacked and is sending out scam messages.

Example: Hey Pastor, I just got a DM from you asking that I wire funds to you overseas. You need to change your password.

Do you remember when we were kids and we used to ask our parents for things that we weren't sure they'd agree to? I remember I would sometimes practice what I was going to say before I went to talk to them. I tried to figure out the exact combination of words I could say to make them agree to my request. Sometimes I got what I was asking for, and other times I didn't. When I was rejected, I would always feel like maybe I could have been successful if I had asked in a different way. Sometimes we treat God the same way. We feel that perhaps if we ask with a certain combination of words or in a certain way, that we increase our chances of gaining a yes. However, God has already taken the guesswork out of the equation for us. As a matter of fact, He told us exactly what way we should come to Him. He says that we should ask **in faith**. When we ask in faith, we already believe that we will receive the thing that we are asking for. Your faith is the key that unlocks every door. Faith is your password. If you feel like you can manipulate, beg, borrow, steal, or otherwise gain what you want without faith, you are sadly mistaken. Your faith gives you access to much more than your own personal strategies for success do. If you don't believe that, I challenge you to change your password with God. Let me spell it out for you: F-A-I-T-H. That's your access key and your password. He told us to come boldly before His throne of grace to ask for favor. Try it out today! When you pray, go ahead and believe that God can and will grant your request according to His will, and that He is able to do even more than what you prayed for!

READ TODAY: MATTHEW 21:22

IT'S GIVING...

It's giving... – a phrase used to point out that one thing is very similar to another and is giving off similar vibes.

Example: Person A: *Posts photo in canary yellow outfit*
          Person B: It's giving Big Bird at New York Fashion Week.

When you give, it is like planting a seed. When I give to someone, I honestly don't know who deserves to get the thank you... me or them? When you sow a seed, the harvest that you receive in return will be much larger in size than the seeds themselves. It stands to reason that the sower should be more grateful to the ground than the ground should be to the sower. Think about it. In order to reap a harvest, you must be able to sow in **good** ground. Some people won't even allow you to sow into their lives. Some are too prideful to admit that they have a need. Others simply struggle with knowing how to receive goodness (it's me, I'm others). But when you rob people of the opportunity to sow, you are doing them a disservice. I had to learn this. I used to stop people from giving to me not realizing that I would be more of a blessing to them if I simply learned to receive the seed as good ground. The problem with some people is that they eat their seeds instead of sowing them. Think about a person who has some corn kernels. You can plant them, harvest even more corn to eat or sell, and get more corn kernels to plant later. Think of having all those possibilities in your hand and yet choosing to throw those bad boys in the microwave for some popcorn. Now they are gone, and all of those long-term possibilities are canceled for a quick snack. That's exactly what it's like when you aren't giving. You have taken a seed that could have produced an abundant harvest and cut its life-cycle short. Do you have a need that you know is too much for you? That's not the time to wad up with anxiety. That's the time to give and plant whatever seeds you can. How can you be more intentional about giving instead of swallowing all the seeds for yourself?

READ TODAY: ACTS 20:35

WHAT'S ON YOUR MIND?

What's on Your Mind? - the famous "status update" question asked by Facebook to all of its users upon logging in.

Example: Nobody:
             Facebook: What's on your mind?

If you have ever logged into Facebook, you should be very familiar with this question. In order to encourage people to update their status, Facebook asks people to tell us what's on their minds. Well that's a pretty loaded question for some people. It's also a question that some people really shouldn't be answering publicly. We've all seen the person who takes the question quite literally and feels the need to share way too much about what is going on in their mind. We've also seen the people who get Facebook confused with a therapy session. I know that we all have thoughts and feelings that we need to express from time to time, but don't let Facebook fool you. Most of those people reading your posts are just nosey. So what do you do when you need to get your thoughts and feelings out, but realize that social media isn't the best way? This is where therapy and counseling come in to play. I know you've all read a status or two that made you think… "hmm…she really needs to go lay across somebody's couch." I know many people in our community shun the idea of counseling, but if you can find a good therapist, it can be absolutely life changing. If for some reason you can't get access to a professional therapist, at least identify a few wise people who you know will give you advice based on God's word. Most of your FB friends are just there to be friendly and dassit! It doesn't matter what you say or do, even if it's wrong, most of them will applaud, congratulate, and agree with you. Sometimes the things on your mind are toxic and need to be checked, but FB friends don't care enough to rain on anybody's parade. Pray and ask God to provide you with a safe place to share what's on your mind.

READ TODAY: PROVERBS 11:14

HOP ON A ZOOM

Hop on a Zoom – to access a group video meeting/call through an app called Zoom.

Example: I would love to continue this conversation, but I've got to hop on a Zoom real quick.

Have you ever looked back at a situation you were in and wondered why you couldn't see it for what it was at the time? Perhaps you got into a relationship with somebody who really wasn't all that, and you let them take you down through there. Perhaps you got taken advantage of by someone who was only getting close to you for the financial assistance that you could provide for them. Your friends and family were scratching their heads trying to figure out how someone like *you* could be okay with something like *this*. At the time, however, you had no clue. It can be embarrassing after the fact, but don't feel bad. It happens to the best of us. But how can we do better in the future? We need to hop on a Zoom. See the reason why many of us can't see the situation for what it is, is because we are standing too close to make it out. Let's say someone blindfolds me and stands me next to a brick wall with my nose touching a brick. When I am unmasked with my nose to the brick, I have no idea if I am standing at a wall of a castle or the wall of the projects. If I want to know what I'm looking at, what is the first thing I need to do? You guessed it! I need to back up so that I can zoom out. The same thing happens with life. We nosedive deep into situations before we have even identified them. The Bible tells us that exercising wisdom should be our top priority along with gaining an understanding. If you are afraid to back up a little and see the situation for what it really is, what does that say about you? If you are afraid that you won't like what you see and choose to remain willfully ignorant, that's called denial. But that's a whole different conversation for another day.

READ TODAY: PROVERBS 4:7

I GOT HACKED.

I got hacked. – what people say when someone has found a way to breach their electronic security measures and gain access to their personal information.

Example: If you got a weird message from me, please do not click the link. I got hacked.

Hackers be hackin' man, I tell ya. Some hackers are extremely sophisticated and operate as high-level criminal organizations. They will try to hack just about anything with a password. I think hackers know that if they can find a way to dig into your personal information, money can't be too far behind. Social media hackers are a bit of a different breed. They work to gain access to your friend list and your personal messages. This gives them a way to request financial favors from your loved ones while impersonating you. It's wild, but it literally happens all day, every day. And there is another hacker who works around-the-clock trying to gain access to your personal information. Satan is always seeking to hack into your mind. If he can hack into your thoughts, it allows him access to personal information that will allow him to scam you much easier. Have you ever had a thought to come across your mind that you **knew** wasn't coming from God? Satan will attempt to send negative thoughts to your mind in hopes that you will adopt them as your own. His goal is to plant a seed that will grow and create a harvest of more negativity. That's why I urge you to password protect your thoughts with the highest level of encryption, which is God's word. If the thought does not pass through the filter of what God has said, it needs to get locked out of your system. We must challenge every thought before we blindly assume that it's righteous. You have no idea what crazy and unhealthy thoughts Satan may attempt to plant. He might just tell you that you are worth nothing, that no one loves you, and that everyone would be better off if you were dead. Exactly! You need LifeLock aka God's word!

READ TODAY: HEBREWS 4:12

#NOFILTER

#NoFilter – a hashtag people use when posting a photo that has not been altered by an automatic enhancement tool.

Example: I guess my mom just gave me good genes #NoFilter

There's this video on YouTube that I love. It's a clip from a TV show called *Petey Greene's Washington*. If you want, go to YouTube and type 'Petey Greene How To Eat A Watermelon (Subtitled).' Make sure you get the one with the subtitles! I won't spoil it for you, but Petey talks about the importance of being yourself. Far too often, we attempt to alter ourselves to be able to fit with whatever crowd we are in. I know people who change like chameleons to blend in with every environment. I've seen people's accent change and everything! And while it's good to be able to function well in different settings, who told you that you couldn't do that while being yourself? It's called being genuine. When you put on a filter, you are honestly missing the point of your own uniqueness. The world needs us to be genuine. It's critical that we discard the unnecessary filters because, as believers, we are tasked with the big assignment of spreading the gospel. If you are trying to show someone else the light, why are you dimming your own with a filter? People these days are smart. They see right through the fakeness. They are going to wonder what you have to hide, and they won't trust anything that you have to say. Let's just say you're a white person going to do mission work in a black neighborhood. If you go in there like, "Aye bruh lemme holla atcha for a lil' minute playboii..." do you really think anybody is going to hear what you have to say? If you have to run yourself through any filter, let it be through the filter of God's love and of the Holy Spirit. The Holy Spirit can teach you how to speak to others in a way that is both relatable and genuine, while still being the person that He created **you** to be. Go watch that video!

READ TODAY: EPHESIANS 2:10

STRUGGLE PLATE

Struggle Plate – when someone posts a photo of a meal that looks extremely unappetizing.

Example: Please guys, I know it's Thanksgiving, but if it looks like a struggle plate, you don't have to post it.

Let's not act like we've never had a struggle plate before. A struggle plate is when you do your best to make a meal out of very limited resources. All college students are familiar with struggle plates. Sometimes they are a result of not having money. Other times it's because you don't have a car or a ride to go get food. Still other times, struggle plates are simply the result of a person who doesn't know how to cook. Lastly, there are rare incidents where a plate with great food only appears to be a struggle plate because the person doesn't know how to arrange the food properly before snapping the photo. In the culinary world, this important skill is known as "plating." Stay with me. Some of your lives are struggle plates. You are constantly overwhelmed because you feel that you have too much on your plate to handle alone. You look at your struggle plate thinking that maybe if you could just arrange everything better, you'd be okay. But no matter how you try to arrange/plate your dish, you will always have a struggle plate when you have items on there that God never gave you. Did God give you those extra responsibilities, or did you get guilted into it? Did God tell you to do that assignment, or are you just doing it to be seen? Makest thou no mistake about it…you **don't** get extra points for doing stuff you were never instructed to do. I really hope this sets somebody free. Don't you know that a part of Satan's strategy to defeat you is to wear you out? If you are tired, he has a better chance of having his way with you. I think this is a good time to do a plate check. Remove anything that doesn't come from God and keep the things that do. Pray today and ask God to help you see the difference between a God-given task and a distraction.

READ TODAY: MATTHEW 11:28-30

LET'S GET THIS SCHMOOONEY!

Let's get this schmoooney! – what people say when they are feeling ambitious and ready to go work hard for the money.

Example: Rise and shine good people! Let's get this schmoooney!

Are you broke? You might be entitled to compensation. No, seriously, if you are a believer that is constantly broke, you need to know what you are actually entitled to: wealth and prosperity. For some reason, Christians get a bad name for being rich. I wouldn't dare pastor a church. Folks can't stand to see a pastor that's doing well. Sadly, too many crooked pastors have stolen/are stealing money which gives the rest of them a bad name. Imagine working hard for so many years, finally being able to afford your dream car, but settling for something less, just so that no one will question your integrity. Now I don't subscribe to people who only talk about money and blessings all the time, but I'm not gonna lie. We do need to talk about it sometimes just like we need to talk about everything else. It shouldn't be a taboo topic, nor should it be all we care about. As always, the answers are right there in the Bible. In one of his letters, John (the evangelist) expresses his desire to see his acquaintance prosper and be in good health, even as his soul prospers. He was basically telling him that "I see your soul is prospering, and now my desire is for your health and wealth to be on that same wave." The problems come when you are only focused on prosperity naturally, but not spiritually. That is called greed. If you haven't done the work on your heart, mind, and spirit, having money will not end well for you. But the Bible tells us that God is the one who gives us power to get wealth. So if you're broke, I suggest that you start by fixing any brokenness within your heart, mind, or spirit. After that, ask God to provide you with a strategy for wealth creation. Once God has given you the plan, don't be lazy! You have to work the plan and go get this schmooney! Remember, the Bible says that a good man leaves an inheritance to his children's children.

READ TODAY: DEUTERONOMY 8:18

GRABS POPCORN

grabs popscorn– an expression used by an onlooker when they know some drama is about to go down on social media.

Example: Person A: I love my husband! He's so good to me!
Person B: Interesting. You know where he was last night?
Person C: *grabs popcorn*

Have you ever watched drama as it was unfolding on social media? I'll go ahead and admit that I'm guilty. I have literally watched complete strangers going at it. By the time it was all over, I had gone down a rabbit hole wherein I had visited their profile page, the current girlfriend's page, and the baby mama's page. I had learned all kinds of neat facts about these random strangers including where they were from and where they worked. Plenty of time had gone by, and it was at that point that I realized I needed to get a life. What is it about drama and mischief that seems to garner our attention? Does anybody remember *The Jerry Springer Show*? Man, those were some wild times we were living in! No one wanted to admit to watching the show, but we did, and we loved it. I don't want to approach this from a super deep spiritual angle. Let's just be practical for a minute. Find something else to do! I don't care if it's just hugging your children and telling them that you love them...find something else to do! Grabbing popcorn and a front row seat to enjoy somebody else's mess is a waste of time. (I am truly preaching to myself right now, don't judge me.) Do you think that people who are highly successful spend time hoping to catch some juicy scandal in progress? I mean gahlee...even if it's just taking a nap and letting our bodies rest and rejuvenate, there are **plenty** of better things we could be doing. Plus, the Bible says it's not cool...I'm just saying. The next time you are tempted to go down the rabbit hole of someone else's drama, I challenge you to ask God what good thing you could be doing with that time instead.

READ TODAY: PROVERBS 1:22

#FOODPORN

#FoodPorn– a hashtag used to accompany a photo of some good-looking food. It suggests that the food looks so delicious that it will cause you to lust after it.

Example: *posts photo of delicious tacos* Caption: #FoodPorn

During my research for today's devotion, I decided to search #FoodPorn on Instagram, which was a big mistake. But let's talk about gluttony. I know most people don't like to mention this one because they don't like to offend anyone, but since y'all don't know where I stay, I think I'm safe. Gluttony is a sin in which a person goes completely overboard with their eating. A glutton is someone who is greedy for food and eats in excess. I know we cancelled Paula Deen, but if you've ever eaten at any of her restaurants, you may have seen the tip of the gluttony iceberg. I believe her philosophy is simply, "What is the highest amount of butter, sugar, or salt that we can put in each dish before people can't get home safely?" They keep bringing you as much food as you want with no extra charge. You can't take any food home, so you sit and stuff your face. Why is gluttony so acceptable when it is just as much a part of Satan's strategy to defeat you as anything else? Think about how many people get taken out or disabled by strokes and heart attacks each year? If your plan was to steal, kill, and destroy...tuh! Wouldn't cholesterol be a great place to start? Our bodies are the temple of the Holy Spirit. How can the Holy Spirit operate as intended in a body that can barely get around anymore due to excessive weight or some cardiovascular issue? How can we be effective in our assignments if our bodies are shutting down because of our lack of discipline? If you want to do better with your eating habits and health, first start in prayer by rebuking the spirit of gluttony. Next ask God to reveal the strategy that would work best for you. Put the plan into action, and do your best to live a long and healthy life that is pleasing unto God.

READ TODAY: 1 CORINTHIANS 6:19-20

JUST SAY THAT.

Just say that. – a phrase used to encourage people to be honest about their true feelings.

Example: Person A: Crab Legs are nasty, and people who eat them are dumb.
Person B: If you broke, just say that.

Y'all remember when the COVID vaccines came out and a large portion of the country was more afraid of the vaccine than they were of the virus that had literally killed 4.5 million people worldwide in under two years? There was a lot of false information and propaganda being spread. Vaccines became political, and people were fighting back and forth in comment sections about them. People were putting any and everything else in their body, no questions asked, but the thought of getting vaccinated had them down bad. Meanwhile, I'm looking at the whole thing like...aye...if you scared of needles, just say that. I'm sure it doesn't apply to everyone, but no one was addressing the fact that millions of people are too afraid of needles to voluntarily take **any** shot. You see, people will make their problems about everything except what they are actually about. I've seen women pick whole arguments over foolishness when in reality, sis...you just wanted some attention and that was the only way you knew how to get it. Sirs, stop getting online trying to subliminally bash that woman. Clearly you miss her and want her back, so just say that. It doesn't matter what the situation is, your deliverance will be hard to come by if you refuse to acknowledge the reality behind it. If you want to get free from something, start with the truth. Far too many of us are afraid of the very truth that could provide us with the freedom we so desperately desire. I've said this before, but it's worth repeating. When you fear the truth, it is because on some level, you distrust God's ability to take any and every situation and use it for your good. Let's pray today and ask God to increase our faith to believe that the truth is our friend and not our enemy.

READ TODAY: JOHN 8:32-36

NEW PROFILE PIC!

New profile pic! – when you upload a new photo to represent yourself on a social media account.

Example: Wow! After 10 years, you finally have a new profile pic!

On social media, your profile picture is what represents you to the world. It is the first thing people will see when they look at your page. Some people, such as myself, choose a picture that shows how good they looked on that **one** day when they really tried. But if you ran into them (me) on any given day, you may not recognize them (me) at all. Your profile picture is how you represent yourself in the online world, but how do you represent yourself in the real world? And what happens when you want to update that representation? Sadly, when people have gotten used to us being a certain way, they may feel uncomfortable when we start changing. I've known people who wanted to change for the better but were discouraged by those around them who didn't like the updated picture. Take people who try to lose weight, for instance. When they start changing their lifestyle, they can no longer go with you to the all-you-can eat soul food buffet nine days out of the week. So instead of encouraging them in their new journey, you throw shade on it. Take people who make the decision to accept Christ into their lives. It may interrupt some of the ratchet activities they once did with their friends. Instead of congratulating them on their new life in Christ, some will throw shade by constantly trying to remind them of what they used to do. There will always be people who can't stand to see you evolve, but the best thing you can do is stand firm. If you want to update the picture of your life, it doesn't matter what you did yesterday or even this morning. It doesn't matter who gets mad. Once you have a made-up mind, transformation is all yours. Do you realize that you are only one changed mind away from so many beautiful things? Put your best foot forward starting today, and let God handle your past. Your new profile pic is beautiful, by the way. I'm really proud of you.

READ TODAY: 2 CORINTHIANS 5:17

YOUR MEMORIES

Your Memories – a Facebook feature that highlights a user's activity (pictures, videos, posts) from the same day in previous years.

Example: Your Memories: [5 Years Ago Today] *changed your
relationship status from engaged to single*

If you have ever utilized the "Your Memories" feature on FB, then you probably understand the pros and cons of it. On one hand, it's really fun to have a direct view of what was going on in your life a year or ten ago. On the other hand, it can be a bit triggering. Suppose you were mourning the loss of a loved one. Looking at posts and photos about that can have emotional consequences. Suppose you were immature then and saying stuff that you know better than to say now. You may feel embarrassed by reading your own thoughts from 10 years ago. And suppose you were married or dating someone who you are no longer with. Seeing those old photos with your ex can be like ripping the bandage off of a wound that hasn't fully healed. So **if** you are going to look at your memories, you must guard your heart and mind. I'm sure Satan loves the memory feature because he loves to bring up the past. Have you ever just been minding your own business when a thought or visual comes up reminding you of who you used to be and what you used to do? If Satan can remind you of the past mistakes that you have made or things that you aren't proud of, then he has a good chance at hitting you with the guilt and shame, which can both be paralyzing. They can even trick you into thinking that you don't deserve God's blessings. This is nothing but a lie though, because God says that He will "blot out" our wrongdoings. It's like He literally takes white out to redact those parts, so if you are being tormented by a memory...that ain't God. I've seen people's entire day ruined because they looked at their "memories." Instead of worrying about what is behind and beneath you, keep your eyes focused on God, and thank Him for His grace that delivered you from evil.

READ TODAY: ISAIAH 44:22

CHALLENGE

Challenge – what people do online when they get bored.

Example: I'm going to look behind a gas station for some crates to do the Crate Challenge with.

I don't know who first started doing these social media challenges, but they range from annoying to genius. You can pretty much make a challenge out of anything you want. You just turn it into a hashtag and hope that it catches on. Some of the challenges allow people to showcase their talent and creativity, while other challenges are downright ignorant. Some of the most famous challenges include the #IceBucketChallenge, the #CinnamonChallenge, the #MannequinChallenge, and the #RunningManChallenge. In 2021 there arose a new challenge called the #CrateChallenge which is referenced above. Black people all across America started stacking up crates in the shape of a pyramid. The challenge was to run up and back down the other side without falling. A lot of people fell. Most of the people fell. Some of the falls were quite scary. In the midst of a pandemic, when emergency rooms were already completely filled to capacity with COVID patients, my people…my own beloved Nubian kings and queens…decided to put life and limb on the line for…an internet challenge. So here's the thing, life is always going to throw challenges at us. As a nation, we face what seems like a new challenge every day. But look at you! You might be sitting there alone right now experiencing a personal challenge that no one else even knows about. I just wanted to encourage you today that God knows about it. He sees you, and He cares. And not only that, but God has never lost a challenge. He has never lost a battle. There is nothing (and I mean nothing) too hard for God. So instead of tossing and turning all night trying to figure out how you can face your challenge, just give it over to God instead. Newsflash! God is the only One who can do it anyway.

READ TODAY: JEREMIAH 32:27

SEE MORE...

See more... – option to view the full version of a lengthy post that has been shortened to a preview in order to fit on your timeline.

Example: Y'all won't believe what happened to me today! I was in line at the bank, when all of a sudden this...See more...

Some people are a little more long-winded than others. Some people know how to tell a story or express a feeling in a concise, yet effective way. Lord knows I have not learned that skill just yet. Most of my posts on social media have the option to "see more." (As a matter of fact, I have spent **a lot** of time deleting sentences from this book because they would not fit in one page.) Previews give users an opportunity to see what the post is about and decide if they would like to continue viewing it. If a reader's attention is not grabbed with that preview, there is a low chance that they will choose to see more of it. But today I want to talk about your life. Sometimes life hits so hard that we want to simply give up. Sometimes I ask myself why I'm working so hard and what it's all for. Couldn't I just be happy being mediocre? Why do I always feel the need to do more, to be better, and to be the best version of me possible? Sometimes I feel like throwing in the towel. But as the old saints used to say, "I think I'm gonna run on and see what the end's gonna be." What they were saying is that they have seen the preview and are choosing to click "see more." They knew that what God had in store for them was worth seeing but that it would require patience and the will to keep running the race. I want to encourage you today that God has so many great things in store for your life. Now is not the time to give up. Don't let impatience cause you to scroll past the abundant life that you can have in Christ. I know you've been running this marathon for what seems like forever, but I do feel a prophetic unction to let somebody know that you are getting ready to turn a corner, and you will be able to see so much more of why God has you in the race. Now is not the time to faint.

READ TODAY: HEBREWS 12:1

RESPECTFULLY

Respectfully – used as a modifier at the end of a sentence that might be considered disrespectful.

Example: If you barely spoke to me before I won the lottery, don't start talking to me now, respectfully.

God is not impressed with your social status, respectfully. Your social status impresses people, but God is not moved by it. Neither is God depressed by the lack of a silver spoon in your mouth. Anything that God says goes both ways. Anybody can get it. If you are walking uprightly before Him, you can get the blessings that go along with that, whether you are rich or poor. If you live a life that is shady and low down, you can get the consequences that go along with that, whether you are famous or unknown. In the Bible, Paul says that God is no "respecter" of persons, which means that He doesn't respect one person's ranking more than another when it comes to right vs wrong. His word stands and is consistent across the board. So if you have a high social status, that will neither shield nor exempt you from having to do the will of God. This isn't the government where rich people get favored with tax breaks. This isn't the town where the police chief's son gets away with murder. God looks at the heart. Even if you're a prestigious pastor of a prestigious church, that doesn't exempt you from God's heart scan. Aht, aht! No so fast, broke people. He doesn't care about your status either. For one, God gave you the power to get wealth, so if you're a broke believer, you need to figure out where you are currently going wrong. For two, being broke doesn't exempt you from anything either, beloved. You still have an assignment from God over your life, and you still have to walk uprightly before Him. We have to stop using what we have, what we don't have, and where we are in life as an excuse not to obey Him. God has accepted us all as His children regardless of our social standing. So we need to do better, respectfully.

READ TODAY: ACTS 10:34-35

GO LAY DOWN

Go Lay Down – a viral song/prophetic declaration issued by TikTok user @who_she_naje who takes us to church simply by singing about her intentions to "go lay down."

Example: Type "Naje Go Lay Down" in Google to listen to the song for yourself! It'll bless ya spirit!

If you haven't already heard this powerful song…nay…this powerful anthem, today needs to be the day. When I first heard the song, it really resonated deep in my spirit. It was about nothing more than going to lay down, and yet it struck a nerve with millions of people online. See what I realized is that far too many of you don't know how to go lay down. First of all, we need to learn to start turning our devices off and getting our faces out of the screens at a decent time of night. As an optometrist, I can tell you that too much screen time before bed can ruin your sleep cycle. The other reason why many of you cannot go lay down is because you have insomnia. Now some of you really do have insomnia for medical purposes, but some of you cannot get to sleep simply because you are too busy worrying about things that you cannot control. I don't know who this is for, but if God doesn't help you pass that test, it won't be passed. If God does not help you pay that bill, it's not going to get paid. If God does not keep your relationship or your marriage together, it's not going to get kept. If God does not protect that child, he or she just won't be protected. Take the burden off of yourself and put it in God's hands. He is the only One who can do it anyway, whatever it is. Put it in His hands and go lay down. Lay down and rest peacefully knowing that all things really do work together for your good because you really do love the Lord. It's time for you to trust Him for real, for real. God knows exactly what you have need of, and He will perform His word concerning you. So go lay down, beloved.

READ TODAY: PSALM 4:8

…AND IT SHOWS.

…and it shows. – a comical way of judging people who have obviously never had certain life-shaping experiences.

Example: Some of y'all never had to wake up to John P. Kee and Hezekiah Walker blasting on a Saturday morning with your mama telling you to clean the house, and it shows.

The old-school saints used to have the best little sayings and clichés. Half of em weren't accurate or Bible-based or anything, but at least they were cute! I think many of us have evolved beyond churchy catchphrases at this point, but there's one in particular that I really like. They would say, "I've been saved all day, and I'm glad about it." Maybe you've never heard that one, but ask your mama and nem. "I've been with Jesus all day long..." is another one that is similar. In each of these clichés, they were talking about time spent with the Lord. It wasn't just some short-lived moment in the car when that one Kirk Franklin song played on the secular radio station and made you cry and worship for 3 minutes before returning to your favorite hood anthems. It was **all day long**. They used to sing lyrics like, "...and He walks with me, and He talks with me." Listen, when you spend time with God, **it shows.** When you don't spend time with Him, it also shows. You may not be able to appreciate your difference in the moment, but the rest of us can see it on you. Time spent with God helps to keep you in perfect peace. When things don't go your way, but you can still keep your cool…it shows. When someone tries you, but you don't stoop down to their level…it shows. When the devil's attacks come, but your faith isn't shaken…it shows. It shows that you have been with Jesus. In today's scripture, you will see where Peter and John had been with Jesus, and it started showing.

READ TODAY: ACTS 4:13

IMMA STICK BESIDE HIM.

Imma stick beside him. – a quote from a viral video of a woman on the Steve Wilkos show. Her boyfriend was cheating, abusive, and unapologetic, yet she wanted to stay with him.

Example: Steve: This is your man? Look at the screen.
　　　　　Tanya: That's mine, and imma stick beside him.

This quote comes from a viral TikTok sound. I decided to do a little research to find where the audio had come from. It led me to an episode of the Steve Wilkos show. I couldn't believe what I was hearing. This man was treacherous. Tanya brought him to Steve in hopes of getting him to see the light. Make no mistake about it…this man did **not** see the light and did not regret hurting Tanya at all. He busted her lip open while she was holding their 4-week-old son and **did not care**. Yet Tanya refused to leave and said that she would stick beside him, which is crazy. I hope that Tanya realized her value and got out of that abusive situation. But I can't help but wonder how Tanya can stick beside an abusive man, but we can't stick beside a loving God. God has been nothing but good to us. Even when things are hard, He is still being good. But the moment things don't go our way, we start losing faith and trying to go off without Him. Maybe you wanted Big Mama to live forever, and now that she passed, you're mad at God and not sure if He's real anymore. There was a man in the Bible named Job. He suffered loss and pain on an extreme level. The whole time, He kept believing that God would bring him out if it. Job was down so bad that his wife and friends told him to "curse God and die." But Job said, "He's mine, and imma stick beside Him." Job refused, even in so much pain, to turn away from his God or to speak ill of Him. In the end, God restored Job and gave him even more than he had lost. Yes, Job was confused and angry with God at times, but he stuck beside Him. My prayer for you is that you always stick beside God, even in the midst of adversity and confusion. Life is much better with Him than it is without Him.

READ TODAY: JOB 2:9-10

I HATE IT HERE.(2)

I hate it here. – a way to express dissatisfaction with a current situation or location in life.

Example: I'm 43yrs old and so single that my mother is still my emergency contact...I hate it here.

Have you ever found yourself in a place that you did not want to be in? I completely understand that feeling. Perhaps you thought you should be farther along in your career by now. Maybe you are single and not happy about it. Perhaps you thought you would have at least two children already. Maybe you are a single parent wishing that you didn't have to do it all alone. Well there are a couple of things you need to know. The first concept you need to understand is contentment. Contentment doesn't mean settling for less, but it does mean allowing room for **gratitude**. When you are content, you are focused more on your blessings than on the things that you lack. When you are content, you realize that although you aren't living in your dream house, you also aren't living on the street, for example. The second thing you need to understand is that change is possible. Don't get so down about your situation that you lose the will to fight. That is yet another trick of the enemy. As it often does, my mind immediately runs back to *Coming To America*. Does anyone remember the scene where Semmi (played by Arsenio Hall) was down in the dumps because he hated living in the run-down apartment building? He hated it there. Well Prince Akeem told him to "fix up the place," and that was all Semmi needed to hear. By the time Akeem got home, the apartment looked like a luxury high-rise condo. I said all that to say, if you don't like where you are, fix up the place. Pray and ask God for the proper strategy to make the changes that are needed. Jesus made it clear that he wants us to have an abundant life. Learn contentment but understand that transformation is still possible.

READ TODAY: PHILIPPIANS 4:11

IT'S ME. I'M PEOPLE.

It's me. I'm people. – a phrase used to confess something about yourself.

Example: smh...as soon as people get a little stimulus money, they run to the store and buy up all the crab legs. It's me. I'm people.

There's nothing more attractive than a person who is self-aware. I have learned that there's a very thin line between someone being self-aware and being self-absorbed. It can be easy to confuse the two, but for the sake of today's conversation, let's talk about people who are self-aware. People who are self-aware are extremely powerful. Socrates once said (oh wow, I felt smart just then...ayyye! We quotin' Socrates, y'all!) "To know thyself is the beginning of wisdom." My job allows me to meet and spend one-on-one time with new people every day. I've become a keen observer. People who lack self-awareness are much more difficult to treat. They don't know how to help me help them because they honestly don't pay enough attention to themselves to be able to describe their own issues with much detail. Self-aware patients can tell you what's going on, when it started, how it feels, what helps it, and what makes it worse. These patients make it much easier to for me to diagnose their problems and form a treatment plan. That's how life is. When you are self-aware, you know exactly what areas need healing or improvement. You know what people, places, and things need to be avoided for the time being. It's like a woman who is cold and bitter from previous disappointments but wants to get out on the dating scene and find the man of her dreams. Ma'am...sis...you're going to scare him away. The rest of us can see that bitterness on you a mile away! Wisdom and self-awareness say diagnose, treat, and heal first before you get out here giving women a bad name. It's **you**! You're people! When you're self-aware, you can get help. You can go to a trusted friend or wise counsel where you can confess your faults without judgement, gain wisdom concerning the issue, and maybe even get a little prayer.

READ TODAY: JAMES 5:16

WHAT WAS THE END GAME HERE?

What was the end game here? – a way to question someone's rationale by having them explain how they thought things would work out.

Example: You cussed your boss out and walked out of the meeting, but your bills are due, your wife is pregnant, and you can't afford to be unemployed. So what was the end game here?

When people talk about having an end game, my mind always runs to chess. Chess is such a dope game because you have to strategize and think several steps ahead to win. You even have to anticipate whatever moves your opponent might make and visualize what moves you will then make in return. Sometimes I look at how deliberate and intentional good chess players are and wish that we were nearly as intentional with our lives. Far too often, we do things based on impulse and haven't even checked with God first. We make moves that seem smart or good in the moment, yet all we are really doing is leaving our "queen" open and vulnerable to be captured. The first thing you must do is to stop, pray, and seek guidance from the Holy Spirit about what your "end game" needs to be. The next thing we should do is be patient and trust God's process. You may appear to be losing at times like a long-distance runner who strategically hangs back in the crowd of runners all throughout the race. He preserves his energy until the end and then sprints to the finish line when everyone else is too exhausted to catch him. He wins gold although he appeared to be losing the whole time. I suppose what I'm saying is that we should take our cue from God. He always has the end game in mind because He knew the end before there was even a beginning. Heck, He **is** the end and the beginning. If you've ever seen Him work something out in your favor, then you know that you can always look back and see how well He had it planned out the whole time. God be knowin'. He isn't haphazard about our lives, so we shouldn't be either.

READ TODAY: REVELATION 1:8

VIEWS

Views – a number representing how many people have watched the associated social media content.

Example: The video of grandma cussing me out already has 10k views!

If you've been on social media long enough, you will remember when they started counting your views. I'm pretty sure it started with YouTube and then trickled down to the other social platforms. Views are helpful metrics in determining how large of an audience a user has, and it also helps us to understand just how "viral" a video has become. But once viewer counts began to be displayed, I noticed something. I think we all did. There are a lot more people watching you than you realize. There are people who will watch every single thing you post, yet never respond with a "like" or a positive comment. Life is the same way. Some people watch you so that they can imitate you. Some watch you because they are hoping to see you fail. Some just watch because they are nosey and have no business of their own. You have way more spectators than you have fans, and that's actually okay. On social media now, viewership is tied to sponsorship. You can make money simply by providing content that consistently gains high view counts. It has always been this way. Think about TV. The higher the ratings, the more you can charge an advertiser. That's why some people will do just about anything for views. Some are getting paid, some are hoping to get paid, and some just want the attention. But I want you to know that there is only one viewer who truly counts, and that is God. So before you go selling out for attention and high view counts, make sure you aren't doing things that would be displeasing to Him. Remember that God is your true sponsor, and He doesn't need anybody's likes or views to bless you. Also, if you are a person who has a large following and high view counts, think about ways you can use that to bring even more glory to God and not just yourself.

READ TODAY: JOHN 12:43

"YOU'RE NOT THAT CUTE, AND YOUR HAIR IS UNEVEN. YOU LOOK DUSTY." - REGGIE

"You're not that cute, and your hair is uneven. You look dusty." – a viral quote from a show called *Beyond Scared Straight* where teenage offenders are taken to real prisons in hopes of scaring them.

Example: You are such a jerk, and I don't know why I dated you in the first place. You're not that cute, and your hair is uneven. You look dusty...

Sometimes we look at the beautiful images on social media and end up feeling down about ourselves. You see photo after photo of people who are dressed well with beautiful hair and makeup. Don't start comparing yourself to these people. Most social media pages are like highlight reels. That profile pic is from the one time six months ago that they got dolled up and went to their best friend's wedding. No one looks like that all the time, including you. There will be days when you're not that cute, your hair is uneven, and you look dusty. When you are working hard on your assignment, you won't always have time to focus on vanity, and that's okay. You have three kids all under age seven. It's okay if y'all don't all have matching designer outfits, perfect hair, and perfect smiles at all times. Some days you will just be blessed to find matching socks. I want to encourage you to keep your eyes on your purpose and not on the appearance of what I like to call "Pinterest Perfection." Your family photo may not go viral, but is there love in the home? Are you teaching your kids to pray? You may not have the time to spend hours at the salon each week, but are you working towards getting out of debt and leaving an inheritance for your children's children? Sure, you may have a little dust on you, but are you working on your own healing and overcoming the pain of a loss in a healthy way? See what I'm saying? Take the pressure off. It's okay. You're okay. We know you can slay when you get ready.

READ TODAY: PSALM 119:37(KJV)

"I WAS WAITING ON YOU AT THE DO'"
– MS. FOXXY

"I was waiting on you at the do'"– a viral quote from a show called *Beyond Scared Straight* where teenage offenders are taken to real prisons in hopes of scaring them. An inmate known as Ms. Foxxy had been ready and waiting at the prison door to meet one of the teens.

Example: College football season, is that you? I was waiting on you at the do'!

I won't go into a lot of detail, but if you've never seen that video clip...or *Beyond Scared Straight* in general, it's worth looking up. I used to work inside of a prison. Did I ever tell you that? Oh, well yeah...that happened. I've got stories for days. But I think what Ms. Foxxy said to this young man struck a nerve with me because I know that there are people in prison who are literally chomping at the bit for fresh meat. Ms. Foxxy was hoping to help this boy change paths before he ended up in prison with the other inmates who were waiting on him for a different reason all together. Where am I going with this? Jesus is also waiting for you at the door. He waits for you at the door of your heart. He doesn't force or scam His way in, but He will stand there, knock, and wait on you to **let** Him in. By contrast, the devil will try to sneak, slide, and slip stuff into your heart that doesn't belong there. You have to guard your heart carefully for things like anger, bitterness, fear, greed, lust, etc. These are things that do not knock, but simply wait at the door for any crack or opening they can use to violate the boundaries of your heart. Check around the door to your heart. Jesus wants to come in and so does Satan. Who will you decide to let in the door today?

READ TODAY: REVELATION 3:20

RECLAIMING MY TIME!

Reclaiming my time! – a phrase that became popular after Rep. Maxine Waters exercised her right to re-receive her allotted time for discourse in a congressional hearing. One can reclaim their time whenever it becomes obvious that a witness or other party is deliberately wasting said time.

Example: Toxic Ex: How come you never answer my calls or reply to
my messages?
Liberated Individual: Uhh...I'm reclaiming my time!!!

There's just something about wasted time that makes me feel sad. I think about this book. I wanted to get it finished within a certain time period, and I haven't done it. I do have valid reasons, but now that I'm approaching the deadline, I'm having to work my butt off when I could have simply used my time more wisely to avoid all this extra stress on myself chile. So when Rep. Auntie Maxine Waters stood firm to "reclaim her time" during that infamous hearing, so many of us felt it deep down in our souls. Seeing her do this and learning that such a right existed, gave us the permission to exercise it for ourselves. You may feel as if time has been wasted, but God is able to restore unto you all that was lost during that time. The devil tried to steal your joy, your peace, your finances, and your mind. But with God, you can reclaim your time. That's great news! With God, everything that you went through does not have to be for naught. He can use it to mean something. He can use it to teach you something. He can use it to bless you. Never forget that our God is a God of restoration. Reclaim your time by dedicating your past, present, and future back to Him.

READ TODAY: JOEL 2:25-27

KEEP THAT SAME ENERGY

Keep that same energy – used to let people know that you expect them to be consistent in their actions or expectations whenever the tables turn.

Example: To the women saying you don't need a man for anything, keep that same energy when you hear a squirrel in your attic at 3:00am.

Today's devotion won't be long, and you're welcome! You say you love God, right? You say God is good, right? You say you trust Him, right? You say you're blessed of God and highly favored, right? Okay great! Imma need you to keep that same energy when things **aren't** going your way. No, seriously. That's it. That's the devotion. We can't sit here and love God for His wonderful works one minute and then be acting all confused and afraid the moment things don't go according to our own perfect plans. I get it. I understand that the disappointment is real. But folks will literally turn away from God and act like they don't know who He is anymore when the tables seem to be turning. Let me give you a pro-tip. There will be times that your faith is tested. It was happening to people in the Bible days, and it's still happening to us now. Sometimes the tests come to show you that your own "energy" towards God ain't as consistent as you may think it is. Exactly how much does it take for you to forsake God and do things your own way? How much does it take for you to stop trusting Him and turn away in anger? Don't catch a case of "test anxiety" when it comes to the Lord. My prayer is that you will hold on very tightly to the faith that you have in God, so that when the exams come you can keep the same energy you had when you thought class wasn't in session.

READ TODAY: HEBREWS 10:23

SPOILER ALERT

Spoiler Alert– a warning given to notify people that the accompanying post will ruin the viewing experience of a show or movie if they haven't already seen it.

Example: Spoiler Alert! I think that minister was wrong for agreeing to marry Whitley & Dewayne on the spot like that. Obviously some counseling was needed if she was planning to marry a whole other man 5 minutes prior!

I, for one, was glad when people started issuing spoiler alerts. In the early days of social media, people would sit and watch live TV and post about plot twists and things as they were happening. If you just so happened to log in to social media before getting a chance to go and watch your favorite show, some random inconsiderate person would have already spoiled it for everyone. Well…that being said, I have a spoiler alert for you. Stop reading here if you like to be surprised. Skip today's devotion if you want to maintain a little more suspense. If you're still here, brace yourself! Ahem...YOU WON! Nah for real, you won. That's it. That's the devotion. Why are you still here? Go celebrate! God is using everything that you have experienced…the good, the bad, and the ugly…for your good! Spoiler alert! In the end, it all worked out for your good! All of it! Even that hardship made you stronger, faster, wiser, and more grateful. Even that difficult season put you in a position to show others a better way. Spoiler alert! The devil tried it, but it didn't work. You still win! Jesus secured your victory when He beat death, hell, and the grave, so guess what?! Even in death you…you still win! Like bruh! You gonna be dead and still winning. Where they do that at?! It's not a nail-biter. It's not a close race. It's not going into overtime. You won, and it was a blow out! Today, just take a moment and praise God for the victory that is already ours.

READ TODAY: ROMANS 8:37-39

TRIGGERED

Triggered– what people say when something that they have seen or heard reminds them of a past trauma.

Example: I just overheard a boy asking his mom for McDonald's. She asked him if he had McDonald's money. Triggered!

If you've ever experienced any kind of trauma in your life, you already know what it means to be triggered. It could be a word, a place, a song, or even a smell. How do you handle your triggers? In therapy, people who deal with trauma are told to avoid their triggers. That's a good idea, but a smell? How do you avoid a smell? A part of Satan's strategy to defeat you is to gain territory in your mind. These triggers are like the fiery darts he launches at you in hopes of using your own pain to distract you from your purpose. So how do you win? In John chapter 16, when Jesus was on the verge of His own crucifixion, He took some time to mentally prepare His disciples for what was coming. These guys loved Jesus, believed in Him, and looked up to Him. What could be more traumatizing than having Jesus ripped from you in the most violent manner possible? Jesus knew they might be traumatized, lost, and confused if He didn't get ahead of it. Jesus was real with them. He told them that they would indeed experience some trauma, but He also encouraged them with **truth**. The truth was that they could still have peace in knowing that Jesus was exactly who He said He was and that He had already won the victory for them. Triggers aren't nearly as scary when you remember that no weapon formed against you can prosper, that Jesus didn't lie to you, and that your victory has already been secured. This means that no matter how many triggers are pulled, no matter how many fiery darts are aimed, and no matter how many nuclear missiles are launched, they will never have any power to defeat you unless you give it to them. So next time you feel triggered, don't dwell in it. Ask yourself, "What does Satan want to take my attention away from, and why now?" Figure that out, and then keep it moving.

READ TODAY: ISAIAH 54:17

G.O.A.T.

G.O.A.T.– an acronym meaning "greatest of all time."

Example: If you are an *A Different World* fan, then you will agree that Debbie Allen is the G.O.A.T.

Sometimes I wonder about the saints. We go to church, we worship God, and we sing songs about how great He is. But if we believe that God is so great and so powerful, then why do we get in certain situations and act like those situations have God beat? Did you know that there are some Christians who aren't "allowed" to go see a movie? Apparently if they watch a movie, it means that they are living in sin, and it messes with their claim to holiness. Now I'm not here to pick apart anybody's religion, but we have to let the Holy Spirit guide us instead of some list of arbitrary rules. Because when you get to acting as if God is too weak for you to even enjoy the arts, I get confused. The Bible tells us that greater is He that is within me, than he that is in the world. That means that if I have God on the inside of me and put on the full armor of God for protection, then the devil doesn't have any power or authority over my life. I don't care if you put me smack dab in the middle of a crack house...I ain't doing it! And if they aren't careful, the crackheads may get set free by the time I leave. The God in me is **greater**. That's the kind of authority we have access to through Christ. Yet many of us have to isolate ourselves from the world because we aren't walking fully in that authority. That's why we struggle to trust that we will be okay in the midst of adversity of any kind. Let's use Jesus as our example. He wasn't afraid to be around the prostitutes and the drunks, because He was confident in the power of God over evil/demonic influences. Now if your faith and spiritual maturity isn't to that level yet, it's okay! Know thyself and listen to the Holy Spirit concerning what **you** should do. But don't go creating these arbitrary anti-faith laws for other people to follow simply because you're not there yet. Never forget that God is the G.O.A.T. Never elevate a sin or a situation above Him.

READ TODAY: 1 JOHN 4:4

"WE DID IT, JOE!" – V.P. KAMALA HARRIS

"We did it, Joe!"– what then Sen. Kamala Harris said in a phone call to Sen. Joe Biden upon learning that they had won the presidential election. It is now used as a meme.

Example: After a long struggle with infertility, my wife delivered a healthy baby boy at 9:13 this morning! We did it, Joe!

If you've ever seen the W.D.I.J. video, then you know the feeling that it elicits. You see a woman who is both excited, relieved, and in awe of the fact that her hard work had finally paid off. So in the Bible, there was this crazy situation after the death of Jesus, where one of the disciples, Peter, was locked up in prison. Not only was he locked up, but they had plans to kill him. While he was in jail, some of the other believers had gathered to pray for him around the clock. Peter was in the jail sleeping when an angel woke him up and his chains fell off of his hands. The angel guided him out, the gate to the prison opened on its own, and Peter went free. He pulled up to the spot where everybody was praying. The girl who came to the door got so excited when she heard his voice, that she forgot to let him in. She ran to the back where they were praying and exclaimed "We did it, Joe!!" (or some King James Version variation). But the crazy part is that no one believed her. They had prayed so hard and so long that when God actually made it happen, they were caught off guard. So open your eyes! Sometimes the answer to your prayer is already happening and standing right there at the door just waiting for you to recognize it. Sometimes we miss our W.D.I.J. moment because we don't fully believe that all of our planting will eventually lead to a harvest. I remember praying for God to send me some new friends. It wasn't until months after I crossed Delta Sigma Theta...with 85 amazing line sisters that I realized...we did it, Jesus! Take some time today to think about past prayers. How many of them has God subtly answered already? How many might simply be standing at the door waiting on you to recognize and let them in?

READ TODAY: ACTS 12:12-16

THE GHETTO (2)

The Ghetto – how people like to describe dysfunctional things that are operating at levels that are less than acceptable.

Example: My job is the ghetto. My boss is always on vacation and has no idea what's going on, but shows up at random times trying to micromanage everybody.

Again, the woke side of me wants to go into a lengthy discourse on American ghettos and how/why they were created for minorities as a part of an interlocking system of oppression. But alas, this book is a devotional. So let's talk about the earth instead. In December of 2020, a YouTuber named Aliah Sheffield dropped a song called "Earth is Ghetto." In the song, she sings about just how dysfunctional things have gotten here on earth. Well Jesus, over 2,000 years ago, left His beautiful home at the right hand of the Father and came to live in the ghetto…err…I mean earth. Chiiile…it couldn't have been any of us! We would have been down here actin' bougie and not wanting to touch anything nasty or talk to anybody ignorant. We would have turned our noses up at the dysfunctional foolery going on all around us. But Jesus didn't do that. He was born in the most humble way, in a dirty manger not far from where the animals were kept. He was the savior of the whole world, yet the Bible says He "made himself of no reputation" down here in the ghetto. He was the King of kings, and yet He became poor for us. Remember *Coming to America*? Prince Akeem left the comfort of the palace and moved to a rundown apartment in a bad neighborhood because of love. That's what Jesus did in coming here. In the end, He humbled Himself enough to be crucified on the cross for our sins. He came to the "ghetto" and performed the ultimate community service, and not for some marketing photos with us poor folks for clout. He came because He loved us. So Merry Christmas everyone, and thank you Jesus for coming straight to the ghetto!

READ TODAY: 2 CORINTHIANS 8:9

#BIRTHDAYBEHAVIOR

#BirthdayBehavior – a hashtag used to accompany photos or videos of people doing various things to enjoy their birthdays.

Example: *posts video twerking in the club with bottle girls/sparklers*
Caption: #BirthdayBehavior

Research shows that the more birthdays you have, the longer you live. Don't you just love how this book is filled with such deep revelation?! How do you like to spend your birthdays? There are those who dread them and go into a depression because they don't like the thought of growing older. Some see their birthday as just another day that's no different from any other. Still others see their birthday as the one day out of the year that they should be able to do whatever they feel like doing. If you are black, this often includes NOT going to work. Finally, there are those who turn up for the entire month and turn their birth**day** into a whole season. No matter your personal birthday behavior, there are a couple of things that you should always include. First, focus on gratitude. Some people get down on their birthday by thinking about all the things that they *don't* have and all the things that they *haven't* done. Instead of self-pity and regret, focus on what you are grateful for. Focus on the fact that you are still breathing and still have the opportunity to move forward. Second, it's important to focus on your life strategy. Observing birthdays is important because the Bible tells us that we should keep count of our days in order to apply wisdom to them. Although we don't know exactly how many days we have left, we aren't getting any younger. A birthday should give you a heightened sense of urgency for your purpose. In what ways has God called you to change the world? Is it just some vague thing in your head, or have you listened to God for the **strategy**? Birthdays are good days to spend time listening to God and writing down what you hear. Actually, any day is good for all of this. What am I talking about?! If you missed being grateful or strategic on your birthday, just do it today!

READ TODAY: PSALM 90:12

THE MATH AIN'T MATHING.

The math ain't mathing. – what people say when things aren't adding up or making much sense.

Example: She told Robert that she was pregnant with his baby, but the baby is due in June, and Robert was deployed overseas up until January. The math ain't mathing.

A wise person once said, "Men lie, women lie, numbers don't..." But are we sure that numbers don't lie? Well long before social media was a thing, Jesus had followers. I'm not talking about figurative "followers" who view your posts online. I'm talking about actual crowds of people who would walk behind Him from point A to point B in order to be present for whatever impressive or miraculous thing He was going to do or say next. In Matthew 14, the disciples realized that it was getting late and that the people needed food. There were about 5,000 men present, and many of them had women and children with them who were not counted. The disciples were going to send them home to find food, but Jesus wasn't hearing that. The disciples told Jesus that all they had was five loaves of bread and two fishes. Jesus said, "Aight, bet..." He took the fish and loaves, prayed over them, broke them up, fed the entire crowd, and had a bunch of leftovers. Let's see here...that's

$$\frac{(2Fish + 5Loaves) + (1Jesus + 1Prayer)}{(5,000Men + WhoKnowsHowManyWomen)} = FishSammichesForEveryone + 12BasketsofLeftovers$$

The math ain't mathing! You see, when God is involved in your equation, even numbers must bow down in subjection to His supreme authority. I've heard people say things like "The doctor gave me six months to live, and here I am five years later!" I've heard a mother say, "The doctor gave my baby a 10% chance to live, and today he is graduating from high school." Yes, I'll take God's math for 100, Alex.

READ TODAY: MATTHEW 14:13-21

SAY LESS.

Say less. – an expression used to notify someone that no more explanation is needed.

Example: Barber: Okay, what are we doing today?
          Client: Nas 1996…
          Barber: I got you fam, say less.

Have you ever been in a situation where you said way too much? Maybe you had your hopes up about a certain idea and told a friend about it. Perhaps their feedback did nothing but point out negativity, place doubt in your head, and burst your bubble of motivation. You realized that maybe you said too much to the wrong person. Maybe you started crushing on someone new and told a friend about it. The next thing you knew, your friend had followed all their social media pages and was shooting *their* shot with *your* crush. Perhaps you realized that you said too much. Perhaps God had blessed you financially and you shared your testimony with a friend or family member. The next thing you knew, they were either acting jealous of you or asking you to borrow money. Maybe you got into an argument with a family member. Perhaps you took some low blows that you later wanted to take back but couldn't. Today's message is just a reminder that God is fully capable of saying all that needs to be said on your behalf. Don't lose your peace trying to fight every battle on your own. Pay close attention to what you say and who you say it to, and whenever possible, say less with your mouth and say more with your victory. God will fight for you. Let's pray today and ask God for wisdom and discernment on when to speak up and when it's better to say less.

READ TODAY: EXODUS 14:14

THIS YOU?

This you? – a phrase used as a "gotcha" when you unearth evidence (an old photo, tweet, or FB status) that someone is being hypocritical.

Example: Person A: I would never strip for money! It is beneath me!
Person B: *posts pic of Person A swinging naked from a pole while onlookers make it rain with money* This you?

Once upon a time in 2021, a recording was leaked online. In this recording, a gospel artist (who is arguably the greatest gospel artist of all time) was heard cussing out his son. There wasn't any context given as to what had gotten this gospel music giant so heated or what was said to make him go off. The recording was made and leaked by the son who was getting cussed out. He was hoping to "expose" his father as a hypocrite. It was meant to be the ultimate "This you?" gotcha moment. Except it wasn't. In a surprising turn of events, nobody really cared. Most people were just like, "Aww *hugs* praying for your family!" This was an interesting reaction, especially now when people are literally excited to call out and cancel hypocrites. Why did this phenomenon occur? Well, the part that I didn't tell you is that this gospel artist never proclaimed to be "holier than thou." He never attempted to put on the airs of faux perfection that so many Christians do. He had always been about things like grace, mercy, forgiveness, and love. And although his musical gift has impacted the world in grand fashion, he has always shown himself to operate in humility. So when people saw him being "human," they weren't phased. Some "saints" even revealed that they had cussed their own kids clean out a time or two. You see, there's a difference between a hypocrite and someone who is simply human. When you start acting all high, mighty, and judgmental towards others, there will be people chomping at the bit to disprove your subterfuge. But when you show grace, mercy, and love...you are more likely to be shown the same in return.

READ TODAY: JAMES 4:6

#SHAMELESSPLUG

#ShamelessPlug – when someone takes advantage of an opportunity to promote themselves.

Example: If you have enjoyed this devotional, please tell your family, friends, and group chats about it. #ShamelessPlug

This is probably going to sound crazy, but I'm going to share it anyway, because I expect that I'm not the only one. I went for a very long time forgetting to pray for myself. I'm talking about yeeeeearrrrs. I would literally pray for everyone else in the whole entire world and forget to pray for Lori. I didn't pray about the things that I needed, and I shonuff didn't pray for the things I wanted. That's crazy, right?! Well, let me tell you…my life reflected it. I was stressed, depressed, sick, and tired. I was in my 20s and diagnosed with diabetes chile. And it wasn't just diabetes. I had the death trifecta: diabetes, hypertension, and high cholesterol. On top of that, I came down with a random autoimmune disease that messed up my thyroid gland. I was overweight, sad, and very unhealthy. I believe I had adopted this subconscious mindset that praying for myself was selfish, and that my prayers were supposed to be for other people. Well I found out the hard way that this is a trick of the enemy. I "had" not for myself because I "asked" not for myself. We should be shameless in praying for ourselves just like this man named Jabez did in the Bible. He simply asked God to bless him and increase him, and God granted His request. Even **Jesus** had to pray for Himself! Let that sink in. My husband and I (aye! I just got married!) take turns leading the morning prayer, and sometimes he has to come behind my prayer and add stuff on for me because I forgot to mention myself! Some of you struggle with plugging yourself too. Some of you struggle with advocating for yourself not only in prayer, but in life. I'm just here to tell you that there is no shame in asking God to bless, heal, prosper, restore, and increase **you**. There is nothing wrong with being on your own team.

READ TODAY: 1 CHRONICLES 4:10

CONGRATULATIONS!

Congratulations! – what people say repeatedly in your comment section when you have made an accomplishment.

Example: Person A: I finally finished my college degree! Better late than never!
Persons B-Z: Congratulations Person A!

Congratulations! If you are reading this on December 31st, you have made it to the end of another year. It's becoming more and more clear to many of us that this is no small feat. Between a global health crisis, extreme natural disasters, gun violence, terrorism, drunk drivers, and an American diet high in cholesterol, we are blessed to make it out of each year alive. I congratulate you not only for coming out alive, but for coming out better. If you've been keeping up with this book, I expect you to have more wisdom, more knowledge, and more understanding about spiritual matters than you did before you started. I also expect you to know more scripture. Finally, I expect you to have formed a daily routine of spending time with God. This is your secret weapon. I'm not going to lie…the world is looking more and more like a hot mess every day. And while the world is going crazy, you cannot and will not go crazy with it. NOT ON MY WATCH! *slams table like Iyanla* I just want to take this time to thank you for reading the book. We had some good times together. I just want to see you continue your daily routine. Please don't fall off now. Please do me that favor. You can start this book over again or jump on over to my other devotional book (that one is for the people who love the Lord but have ratchet tendencies). There are many other devotionals, so just find one that works for you and keeps you consistent. As I go to my scat, I just want you to remember that only what you do for Christ will last. I want you to remember that the world around you is not stable. It will continue to shift and change. God's word is the **only** thing that will stand forever. – Lori

READ TODAY: ISAIAH 40:8

75828651R00203